# A Fleeting Improvised Man Awakens

## The Art of Losing Control

# Also By DJ

A Fleeting Improvised Man

The Clothes Have No Emperor

# A Fleeting Improvised Man Awakens

DJ

A Fleeting, Improvised Man Awakens
© 2015 by DJ

All rights reserved. Printed in North America.
No part of this book may be used or reproduced in any manner
without written permission except brief quotations
embodied in critical articles or reviews.

This book is a work of non-fiction.
However, certain names, organizations and places
have been altered to maintain anonymity.

For information contact
www.afleetingimprovisedman.com

Book and Cover and interior design by DJ

Canadian Cataloguing in Publication Data
*****************

ISBN:0991995449

First Edition: December 2015

# Dedication

To my teacher Adyashanti as well as my dear brother Jason.

## Content

| | |
|---|---|
| **INTRODUCTION** | 1 |
| **CHAPTER 1** | 5 |
| **CHAPTER 2** | 9 |
| **CHAPTER 3** | 13 |
| **CHAPTER 4** | 17 |
| **CHAPTER 5** | 25 |
| **CHAPTER 6** | 29 |
| **CHAPTER 7** | 37 |
| **CHAPTER 8** | 41 |
| **CHAPTER 9** | 45 |
| **CHAPTER 10** | 49 |
| **CHAPTER 11** | 57 |
| **CHAPTER 12** | 61 |
| **CHAPTER 13** | 65 |

| | |
|---|---|
| **CHAPTER 14** | **69** |
| **CHAPTER 15** | **73** |
| **CHAPTER 16** | **79** |
| **CHAPTER 17** | **85** |
| **CHAPTER 18** | **93** |
| **CHAPTER 19** | **99** |
| **CHAPTER 20** | **107** |
| **CHAPTER 21** | **113** |
| **CHAPTER 22** | **121** |
| **CHAPTER 23** | **125** |
| **CHAPTER 24** | **137** |
| **CHAPTER 25** | **141** |
| **CHAPTER 26** | **149** |
| **CHAPTER 27** | **159** |
| **CHAPTER 28** | **165** |
| **CHAPTER 29** | **169** |

| | |
|---|---|
| **CHAPTER 30** | **175** |
| **CHAPTER 31** | **179** |
| **CHAPTER 32** | **187** |
| **CHAPTER 33** | **191** |
| **CHAPTER 34** | **199** |
| **CHAPTER 35** | **205** |
| **CHAPTER 36** | **209** |
| **CHAPTER 37** | **215** |
| **CHAPTER 38** | **223** |
| **CHAPTER 39** | **227** |
| **CHAPTER 40** | **237** |
| **CHAPTER 41** | **243** |

# Acknowledgements

## Edited by:

Flora Salyers
Michelle Powers
Ida Lawrence

## Illustrated by:

Aisha Mulhall

Additionnal illustrations DJ

# Introduction

*The first rule is to keep an untroubled spirit. The second is to look things in the face and know them for what they are.*
  Marcus Aurelius (Stoic philosopher and Roman emperor)

"Pretty gross," I thought as I inspected the bottom of my backpack. The green, viscous, semi-iridescent blob of mucus that stuck to the bottom of my bag was certainly not indicative of the normal courteous behaviour most Canadian bus passengers displayed. Though off-putting, this thoughtless action was nothing compared to various other forms of repugnant human detritus I had encountered on the floors of assorted Asian mass transit vehicles during my time spent abroad.

  The urine-soaked rear seat of a Thai Tuk Tuk motorcycle cab immediately comes to mind. The *sake* rice wine vomit of a drunken Tokyo *Salaryman* discovered late one evening on the floor of a shiny, sleek, modern subway car is pretty memorable too. Probably worst of all was the pile of human excrement I encountered in China in 1985. Of all the places to be discovered, it appeared smack dab in the middle of the rear aisle of an old rust bucket of a bus which passed for proletarian transportation back in those days. Given the depositor's multi-coloured, vegetable-rich diet and the violent vibrations that emanated from the bus's poorly shock-dampened undercarriage, this display had come to miraculously resemble an abstract art installation piece worthy of the Tate Modern gallery. While Andy Warhol was infamous for his piss paintings, this bit of "poop art," as it were, was likely evacuated from the bottom slit of a toddler's drawers since tradition seemingly dictated that these youngsters could crap virtually anywhere they bloody well pleased!

Those perils of exotic travel once evoked a mixture of incredulity and disdain as well as the occasional giggle or two. These kinds of acts are now recognized to simply be *Maya* (Sanskrit word meaning the play of illusion otherwise known as duality) being Maya or, seen from another perspective, Buddha being Buddha. The transcendent and the immanent, the sacred and the profane, are not different.

> Where there are humans, you'll find flies, and Buddhas.
> Issa Kobayashi (Zen master)

To help you understand my current laissez-faire attitude, you must know where I was headed. You see, I had an appointment with destiny, and I could not afford to be tardy. Spiritual enlightenment was my goal, an ersatz Canadian Tibetan Buddhist hermitage my destination. What occurred there, in that spiritual centre, presently allows me to no longer sweat the small…or large things, in life.

As I sat in that Greyhound bus, wiping the last remnants of the sticky goo off the bottom of my bag, I still had a long, long way to go in my spiritual aspirations, for at that moment I imagined all kinds of horrible invectives I would have liked to hurl at the thoughtless bugger who had messed up my bag.

Once the colour of the bottom of my pack again took on its usual "casually subdued, earthy monochromatic designer tones," or more plainly put, the grimy, mud-stained patina it typically sported due to my adventures throughout Southeast Asian jungles, rice fields, and mountain tops, I considered again what an amazingly intense two-month period of spiritual revelation, elation and transformation I had just experienced. I had the shamanic jungle brew known as *Ayahuasca* to thank for this. I consider this aspect of my spiritual quest my "mystical preamble" to enlightenment. It was chronicled fully in my previous book—*A Fleeting Improvised Man*.

That book outlined the genesis of a spiritual journey that presently found me bound for the shores of a sleepy, little Canadian coastal island. The several thousand strong denizens there were a mixture of retirees, artisans, rural folk and former U.S. draft dodgers. Once upon a time, hippies abounded. Now you were more likely to bump into a retiree or some nouveau riche guy holidaying at his gentrified summer home than you were to meet a counter-culture type.

Of some small fame, and by this I mean pretty miniscule since only the folks from the neighbouring island took any notice, was the island's modest soya sauce works, Japanese-style ceramic ware kiln, meadery, and gourmet coffee roasting company. The island beaches were dotted with shellfish farms. There had once been plans to transform one particularly pristine sandy stretch into a luxury resort, but that idea was eventually quashed by the left-leaning anti-development faction which still wielded a substantial amount of clout. Though idyllic, I was not headed there to experience the surf and local charm. I was about to head ashore chasing but one singular experience: I aimed to become an awakened being posthaste.

At the time, I thought I was on a quest to discover the ultimate nature of reality. Spiritual enlightenment also fit the bill, though I was entirely ignorant of that field. To remedy this situation, my plan was to get accepted into a Buddhist hermitage/retreat centre on the island in hopes that something spiritually significant would transpire. On that count, I would not be disappointed.

Eventually, my seeking terminated in a most fascinating manner. What the Buddha and Indian Hindu luminaries famously spoke of was realized. There was indeed an end to suffering just as the sages of old had promised. My so-called "true nature" was realized, the Absolute was revealed, and the Truth of Being was made manifest. I found out that to realize this stuff of myth and legend and become enlightened was not as difficult as it is sometimes portrayed, although it came at a heavy, heavy cost.

What the quest demanded of me was complete commitment, one hundred percent sincerity and the willingness to no longer cling to anything. That, of course, included giving up my own BS. At journey's end, even the personal sense of "I" was thrown out with the bath water. *Enlightenment turned out to be a whole lot more and less than I ever imagined.*

How I came to discover the ineffable is the story that follows. The tale I am about to tell was certainly not one I could ever have imagined when I first set out. At that point, I was essentially a spiritual ignoramus.

What transpired during my quest shocked me to the core. The subsequent chapters lay out all of the stages leading to my falling out of the dream state, for ultimately that was what my pilgrimage was about, simply coming to perceive things as they really are and having the "dream of me" come to a close in a moment out of time and space which is known in some spiritual circles as *nirvana*. I am not a Buddhist, per se, more like a Truthist or Awakenist, but I find the following story of a chance encounter with the historical Buddha to be particularly illustrative of what I discovered. It succinctly points to my journey's end.

A *Brahman* (high status person) saw the Buddha resting under a tree in meditation. The *Brahman* was impressed with the Buddha's disposition and demeanour.

He asked, "Are you a god?"
"No, *Brahman*, I'm not a god."
"Are you an angel?"
"No," replied the Buddha.
"You must be a spirit then?"
"No, I'm not a spirit," said the Buddha.
"Then what are you?"
"I'm awake."

# Chapter 1

*Again the important point to remember is that you should keep asking yourself questions. Do not make statements…The mind hates that.*

Robert Adams (non-dual teacher)

Before I proceed with the matter at hand—namely describing the sobering effects self-inquiry and meditation can evoke, for those who missed my first book—I would first like to briefly explain what brought me to the terminal stages of the spiritual pilgrimage I am now about to describe.

The gist of the first book is rather straightforward. I set out one day on a spiritual quest hell-bent to discover for myself just what the heck was really going on. I knew that there was a perennial mystery that had long eluded me, and it needed to be resolved. This I aimed to do utilizing direct experience. You see, I had accumulated a huge library of psychological, philosophical and metaphysical writings, but in truth, none of that information made me any the wiser. Further, I had considered the ponderings of innumerable pundits, *literati*, learned fellows and scholars alike and supported, and in return rejected, hundreds of occult theories and philosophical musings. Yet, what did I know for certain through my own direct experience? Not bloody much really.

This state of affairs arose plainly one day when the internal, discerning, intuitive, small quiet voice piped up with, "Why don't you get up off of your duff and find out for yourself just what this spiritual thing is really all about rather than wasting yet more time thinking about it all?"

So in the remaining years afforded me, my intention became to reject the past trend, which had seen me accruing year by year yet more mystical and philosophical material until one day surely a second library would be required to hold it all, and instead discover Truth for myself.

I would endeavour to discern one of the following three possibilities through my own direct experience.

•Attain enlightenment.

•Discover that the whole spiritual milieu was in fact just a big fraudulent put on, populated by narcissistic phonies as fake as those supposed golden lingam or penises and jewels Sathya Sai Baba regularly regurgitated in front of his adoring masses.

•Succumb to old age and fail to reach a resolution on this matter either way.

Any of those outcomes would have been welcome for at least I would come to know something for myself. Taking wisdom on belief or faith alone, substituting one spiritual idea for another, was simply no longer tenable.

Reading those interesting books merely filled my head with endless speculation which appeared to be the musings of minds that knew nothing. I perpetually fiddled while Rome burned, or as my teacher is fond of saying, "I was just rearranging deck chairs on the Titanic." All my fruitless cogitating ever resulted in was yet more of the same. One *belief* was simply substituted for another. But what did I really *know*?

For example, many authors of those books spoke of the soul or reincarnation. Were these things ontologically real? Who is to say? Where is the proof? Was Edgar Cayce really a "sleeping prophet" as reputed, and did I know for certain whether his pronouncements were true? No, I didn't. Likewise, was any channelled material like that found in the Seth books or *A Course in Miracles* actually grounded in wisdom? Again there was uncertainty, for I had no direct experience on the matter myself. I came to realize that believing something never makes it so.

I explained in my first book how I came to adopt the rallying cry of *sapere aude* (Latin for "dare to know for yourself") with the greatest sincerity I could muster. It seemed I no longer had a choice in the matter as my previous book recounted. A "cosmic conspiracy" of sorts seemed to be afoot, and it had me directly in its cross hairs. I set out on Jan. 1, 2008 to attempt to discover the ultimate nature of reality. I described in the first book how the perfect spiritual storm whipped up and forced me to get the hell out of Dodge quickly.

Metaphorically speaking, I was a flatlander who set out to see for myself if the crazy rumours were true. All I had was a vague plan to make it to the coast by train. There I hoped to garner the direct spiritual experience I sought. I had no mentors to draw upon. Once the rails ran out, I intended to settle down for the winter to hopefully utilize entheogens for their intended purpose—revealing the God within. Chief amongst them, at the time, was a little-known South American plant medicine called Ayahuasca.

That brew turned out to be the best medicine I ever consumed, though I can't say it excited my palate much. In fact, it tasted dreadful, but that was a small price to pay for such a tremendously transformative experience. It fostered a wonderfully revelatory foray into the unknown. After some twelve or so sessions, I pretty much got the message and hung up the phone. I still had further to go, deeper to peer, so per my original plan, I next headed out to hook up with a Tibetan Buddhist hermitage run by a Canadian Lama.

That, then, summarizes how I had come to presently be scraping sputum off my backpack. I was island-bound, seeking a hermitage that I had yet to even contact. This was a very long trip to make solely on mere speculation, but it seemed something drove me ahead, and it would not be foiled.

I am an adventurer at heart and quite well-travelled, so I must admit I didn't mind this opportunity to explore a territory quite unknown to me–namely, inner space. In the past, adventure consisted of visiting exotic locales and people. Now my goal was much more refined. Rather than outward bound, I was on the quest to discover "me."

The effects of the recent Ayahuasca therapy, combined with a two-week adventure trek I had just completed through a wilderness coastal rain forest, had invigorated and prepared me for what I was about to face. I was quite upbeat. "Why couldn't the world be my oyster?" I wondered. Still, there was doubt. Would the pearl of inestimable value be denied me? Well, one thing was obvious. I would soon find out one way or another.

Being ever the sensible chap that I am, my plan was to first settle down in the community and then put out tentative feelers regarding the Tibetan Buddhist centre that presently held my interest. After all, I didn't want to be rash and rush into anything too quickly, especially given my relatively low regard for organized religion. Getting embroiled in the flaky, weird machinations of some cult-like organization was something I needed to avoid at all costs. To this end, I secured a volunteer position on a local farm and would scout out the hermitage grounds when the opportune occasion arose.

My greatest concern was not the farm work, for I was intimately familiar with such routine having grown up in the countryside. No, my biggest concern was whether or not there would be a place open for me at the retreat centre given my specific requirements.

Trusting that my initial impression of the hermitage was favourable, I wanted to propose an exchange of sorts. One that would allow me the opportunity to settle down there long term and pursue spirituality relatively undisturbed. In return for being allowed to attend retreats, learn meditation techniques, as well as hopefully receive the "special teachings" from the master/Rinpoche there, I would offer my services.

Specifically, I hoped to secure basic spartan lodging at the centre rent free. Furthermore, I would propose to pay for my own meals and utilities and in return chop wood, haul water or cut the grass when the need arose. Actually, I was open to giving them anything they wanted save one precious commodity—my autonomy. That was not open for discussion. I would never fork over the keys to the family sedan no matter what inducements, or threats, were put forward.

Though I intended to wholeheartedly live in the "spirit" of a monk or true ascetic, I was not at all interested in adopting a new lifestyle. I simply wanted to wake up. Donning the distinct vestments of a particular order, acquiring a foreign language, learning new rituals, chanting, playing exotic instruments or taking up any of the other various and assorted practices a religious person is expected to engage in, held zero appeal for me. Buddha had no issue with not being a Buddhist, so I wouldn't either.

The question then remained how to present myself to a Buddhist organization, tell them I desperately wanted the teachings and would be extremely pleased to meditate in their beautiful surroundings yet largely reject their traditions. This was a peculiar proposition to be sure but not that unusual when one considers the life of Buddha himself.

Buddha, a former prince and East Indian sage, the so-called Awakened One, is purported to have been an inspiration to a coterie of spiritual aspirants some five hundred years before Christ was born. I discovered that this master, himself, came to ultimately adopt the tact I favoured, after exhausting many spiritual cul-de-sacs. He engaged in all manner of unnecessary spiritual practice until he completely exhausted himself. Then he simply sat down under a tree, became entirely still and quiet and his own Buddha-nature then finally caught up with him.

I think it is relevant to remind ourselves that Buddha was never a Buddhist or Christ a Christian. They were just figures that became Truth realized. To be clear, I am not speaking poorly of the Buddhist tradition in particular for all organized religions had seemed pretty worthless to me. To become a member of any religious sect seemed to me to be like aimlessly driving through a fog bank while wearing Vaseline smudged sunglasses. Such a situation was hardly conducive to fostering the clarity I required to easily navigate myself out of that befuddling miasma.

That's not to say that no religious orders are helpful, at times, in some regard. I n fact *Advaita Vedanta*, mystical Christianity, elements of Taoism and Zen Buddhism were inspirational to me, but let's get back to the story immediately at hand shall we?

> Emulsified onto the backdrop of nothing, awareness reveals the cinematography of the essential you.
> J. Hebert (occupation unknown)

# Chapter 2

*Everyone takes the limits of his own vision for the limits of the world.*

Arthur Schopenhauer (German philosopher)

The tiny cable ferry made port, and the industrious Nan recognized me immediately by my clean-shaven pate which I previously described to her in our earlier email correspondence. "Don't mind the clutter," she said as she cleared a space for me amongst the packing boxes in her farm truck. "You don't mind if I make a cider delivery run over to the Bistro on our way home do you...?" Of course, I shook my head no. "Besides," she said, "It'll give you a chance to see downtown...or what there is of it," and off we went as she stomped on the accelerator.

I had arranged to billet with Nan and her family for several weeks. Amongst her varied occupations, I learned that she acted as a part-time crisis counsellor, bookkeeper, parent, as well as held a partnership in the family-run orchard business. I was to provide simple farm labour for this enterprise. Nan and her husband impressed me with their goodwill, positive outlook, and a common sense approach to life which most farm folk embodied. I admired their organic stewardship of the land. I felt warmly welcomed, but admittedly their acreage was not my first choice of places to stay.

Originally I had spied a listing which described another agricultural opportunity on the island. These hosts indicated that they were Buddhist which seemed very apropos to my needs at hand. It would have been the perfect place to get information on the hermitage, I reasoned. Unfortunately, a Canadian Buddhist couple was already lodging there. Undaunted, I accepted the offer to stay at Ocean View Orchard for a few weeks.

Gathered at the table for the first evening dinner with Nan's family and some other farm help, I wondered how I might bring up the subject of the Tibetan Buddhist centre. To nononsense farm folk, such as I presumed the couple before me to be, I reckoned such a topic would be pretty offbeat. The vast majority of farmers I had met were pretty conservative, salt-of-the-earth types. I doubted Buddhism would interest these likely Christian, certainly pragmatic, hardworking apple-cider producers. Would they even be aware of the hermitage's existence, I wondered? When Nan, being ever the charming hostess, inquired as to what in particular had attracted me to their neck of the woods, I found it a convenient entre into bringing up the topic I so yearned to discuss.

"Well," I said, "It's like this. I'm not actually here to sightsee or soak up the local culture, nor look for steady employment. Actually..." and then I paused in slight trepidation, "...well, actually I am here on...well, how do I put this?" I wondered.

Mulling it over in my mind, I wanted to say that I was here on a spiritual pilgrimage of the greatest import. That I had just spent several intense months undergoing one of the most trying periods of my life. In fact I had just plumbed perhaps the greatest spiritual depths natural plant-based, mind altering entheogens could produce and now I had come here to this tiny slice of paradise to finish the job. Instead, I simply asked, "Do you know anything about the local Buddhist hermitage?"

"Oh, you mean The Truth Sangha Centre out on Crofters road...The TSC, right?" She then paused for confirmation.

"Oh, yeah, that's right. The TSC," I replied. I was delighted and a bit surprised that she knew the hermitage by name. "Well," I continued, "I was wondering if you could tell me anything about the TSC?" I explained my desire to live there in exchange for grunt labour. This Tibetan Buddhist venture was a few years old, so I wondered if it had gained any kind of a reputation yet. I asked if she had visited it?

She turned to her husband, and a sly grin began to spread over her face. Her husband returned a similar smile. I wondered what was up. As great and entirely unexpected fortune would have it, it turned out that Nan was none other than the president of the board of directors of the TSC. I couldn't believe my good luck!

I sure didn't see that one coming. Silently, in my head, I let out a protracted and effusive "Yeeesss…" and then thought, "By Jove, there really is a God." I was momentarily stunned and at a loss for words. Seemingly by dumb luck, I had stumbled into the best situation imaginable. How do such things occur?

Dumb luck or grace, who knew, who cared? I simply revelled in my good fortune. As far as securing a place at the hermitage, Nan became an advocate of sorts. She, however, could promise me nothing. My proposal to become the TSC's new resident farm agricultural specialist, as well as live in "yogi," would have to be put in front of the board of directors for a vote. Needless to say, she assured me I had her backing.

All I could do over the ensuing weeks was hope that the vote would eventually fall in my favour. At this point, I really had no fall-back plan. So I crossed my fingers and waited, while in the interim I did my best for the Ocean View Orchard. The hard physical labour was welcomed. I thrived on it as a kid growing up on a beef farm, so it was just like old times again.

> The moment one gives close attention to anything, even a blade of grass, it becomes a mysterious, awesome, indescribably magnificent world in itself.
> Henry Miller (writer)

# Chapter 3

*The trouble with the rat race is that even if you win, you're still a rat.*

Lily Tomlin (actress and comedian)

By now I had been on the farm almost a month. Nan inquired one day if I wanted to help out a local couple. Apparently the husband was in poor health and was presently undergoing the last of his chemotherapy treatment. "Sure", I told Nan, "I'd be happy to lend a hand."

Over lunch, the couple I was stacking firewood for brought up the topic of payment. I said I was happy to do it for no charge. Though they insisted on paying me, I accepted no money. "Who wants to capitalize on someone else's misfortune," I thought.

As the meal progressed, they asked me, just as Nan had done, what was it that had drawn me so far off the beaten track? I explained my interest in Buddhist meditation and The TSC. I then relayed the curious story about my good fortune in winding up at what turned out to be an important board member's residence, all through no effort of my own. I then concluded with:

> But there is no guarantee that I will be accepted into the hermitage as the outcome relies on a vote, and who knows if the decision will be favourable.

To this the affable hostess replied, "Guess what?" I shook my head.

As Nan had done before, the lady of the house gave me a curious grin. Again another huge surprise was in store. "Well, I happen to be on the board of directors too, and you sure got my vote."

"What is going on here?" I wondered. Man, I was batting a thousand. I looked her straight in the eye and asked, "You're not kidding are you?"

"Nope," she said. "I don't think you'll have anything to worry about."

"Well, I'll be damned. Do wonders never cease?" came my final thought on the matter.

As the meal progressed, the couple revealed their long-held association with Buddhism. Their spiritual egos projected the slightly haughty, arrogant and smug attitude many self-satisfied, long-term practitioners engage in when addressing a spiritual neophyte. What did I know of Buddhism they inquired? "Not much," I confessed. "Something about abolishing misery by getting rid of all wants and desires, isn't it?" I asked. They raised their eyebrows disdainfully as if to say, "Man does this fool ever have a lot to learn…," which of course was true.

In fact, I knew nothing at all about the philosophy or practice of waking up to reality. Even fairly common spiritual concepts like Oneness, non-duality, misidentification with the ego, heart openings, the chattering monkey mind, mindfulness or even such basic principles as meditation, were all great mysteries to me. In all candour, I couldn't have been a less well-prepared spiritual aspirant if I had tried—with one exception.

Sure, I knew little about religious concepts, rites and spiritual jargon, but Ayahuasca had authentically opened the doors of perception into realms and ways of perceiving reality afresh that were revolutionary. That was direct experience, which trumped every one of this couple's mental concepts every time.

Though I remained politely silent, I might have told them that, yes it was true; I did not know anything about Buddhist philosophy, but I had not come to this island for that. I was sitting in front of them now for one reason only. I aimed to discover my own innate Buddha nature directly, just as Buddha spent his life encouraging his monks to do. This was, evidently, something this couple had never even considered.

The rather belittling attitude of my hosts offended me not in the least. They were simply ignorant. Our paths were very different. They aimed to impress me with their huge spiritual presence. I aimed simply to awaken.

After a few more weeks of uncertainty, it finally came to pass that the hermitage officially invited me into their ranks. I was very excited and grateful to hear the good news. I learned that I would be permitted to reside in a back room off an agricultural outbuilding, well befitting the simple needs of a monk. A deal was struck whereby I would volunteer at the centre, and in return, I could attend the various scheduled retreats as time and interest permitted.

It would be my responsibility to pay for food and utilities. This arrangement was most agreeable particularly since I would have access to the teachings of a real live "wisdom master." Or so I presumed. The prospect of soon learning to meditate and begin self-inquiry was exciting but also a bit daunting, for after all, I had never sat quietly in my life. I was about to begin to engage in a practice that would occupy the better part of my waking life...perhaps for decades to come. What could this be like, I wondered?

The prospect of silently sitting perched atop a bare cushion in a pose seemingly more suited to a contortionist than a guy with a serious back problem, for hours upon end while endeavouring to control his mind moment by moment, somehow seemed a little daunting to me. I hadn't even begun, and already I was worried. It's quite astonishing what the mind can get up to once it conjures up the fear of the unfamiliar, isn't it? Thomas Merton, Jesuit monk and writer, shares an observation on this theme:

> The man who fears to be alone will never be anything but lonely, no matter how much he may surround himself with people. But the man who learns, in solitude and recollection, to be at peace with his own loneliness, and to prefer its reality to the illusion of merely natural companionship, comes to know the invisible companionship of God.

What was about to unfold at this spiritual centre occurred almost exclusively in the realm of the unknown, so consequently, I experienced varying degrees of fear and angst for most of the time I was there. Thankfully, these feelings were mitigated to some degree by great joy as well. Attraction and repulsion became steadfast companions of mine while I followed the path leading to self-illumination.

Like a moth attracted to the beguiling luminosity of the flame yet also repulsed by the danger the searing heat posed, this kind of push/pull effect is common in authentic spirituality, and I will elaborate on it further much later in the book.

> The moth saw brightness in a woman's chamber—burnt to a crisp.
> Issa Kobayashi (haiku by Zen master)

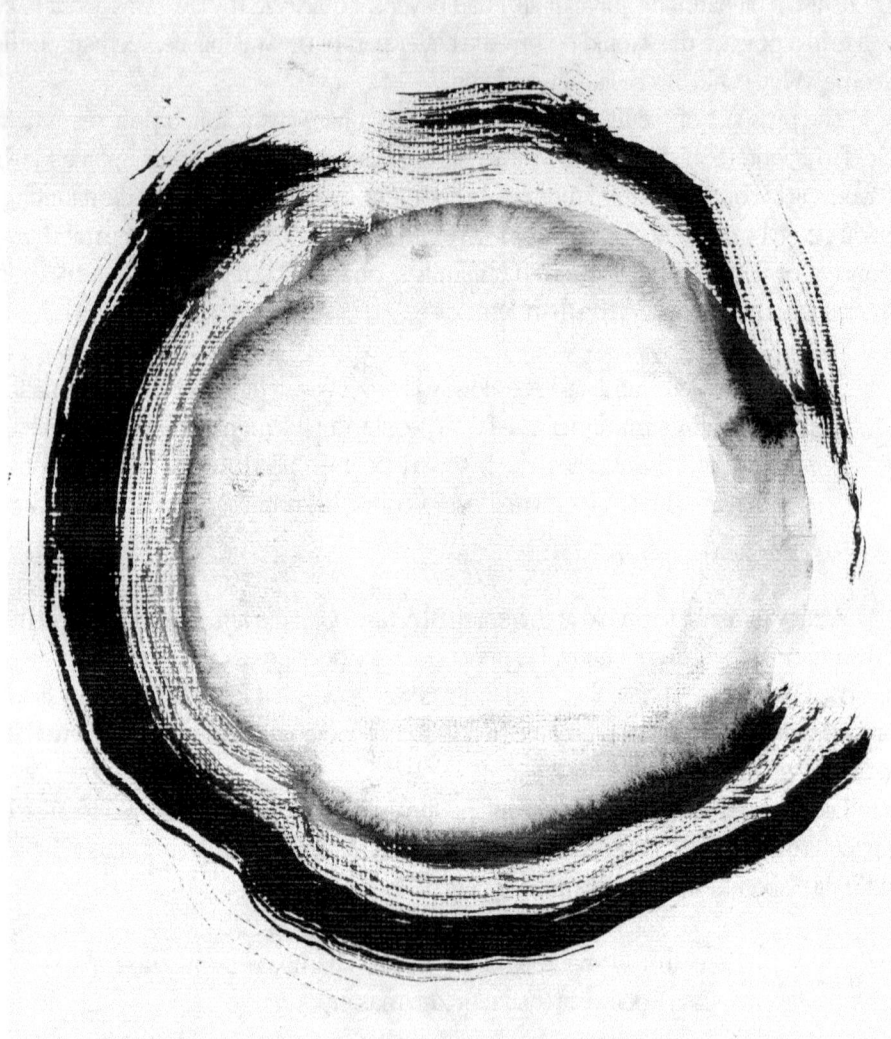

# Chapter 4

*It is impossible for a man to learn what he thinks he already knows.*

Epictetus (Greek philosopher)

"Why has the Rinpoche left for the West?"

"I mean really, in all seriousness can anybody tell me why that dude departed?"

I consider that a damn fine question worthy of careful consideration. I have wondered if it was a purely selfless act (nudge, nudge and a wink), solely carried out for the betterment of all mankind (again nudges and more winks), that the Buddhists headed to Europe and America in number beginning around the middle of the last century, or rather, could other agendas be responsible for this migration.

Given the number of scandals certain Tibetan Lamas and Zen masters have been embroiled in during the last few decades, certainly one must conclude that at least part of the time economic/political drives or the lust for power and wealth, be it organizational or personal, have been at play when it comes to the motives of transplanted wisdom traditions and masters. It is no mystery that, historically, religion has sought fertile, new grounds upon which to "spread the good news" and enrich itself in the process. America is a case in point.

The dawning of the sixties in the American and Canadian West kicked off a radical change in the way people perceived themselves and their role in the greater society at large. While this period was renowned for its peace movement and was a defining decade regarding issues of gender and race equality and relations, it was also a time when new belief systems and spiritual philosophies and practices were being introduced.

Often taking the centre stage of this counterculture movement were the hippies and their controversial use of the newly introduced psychedelic drug, LSD, and to a lesser extent psilocybin mushrooms, as well as more exotic mind-expanding compounds like DMT and mescaline.

But we must not forget that other, less infamous, movements arose then as well like the Transcendental Meditation movement, the Human Potential Movement, the back-to-the-landers drive, the flamboyantly attired and chanting Hare Krishna organization, or the conservatively dressed and regimented Scientology enterprise. There were even less controversial newcomers as well.

The influx of novel Eastern thought to the West included one fairly relaxed and sedate contingent that was pretty much unknown to the American public at that point—the Tibetan Buddhist. Though in short order, one particularly flamboyant and outspoken "crazy wisdom master," Chogyam Trungpa Rinpoche, would rise to the fore and put Tibet's own flavour of Buddhism on the American stage. None of this I knew before setting foot on the hermitage. In fact, I knew nothing about Buddhism at all...well, almost nothing.

Prior to taking up residence at the Buddhist centre, I briefly checked out its website in hopes that it would inspire and educate me. What I encountered proved to have the opposite effect. Instead of presenting an insightful or inspirational spiritual framework to help beginners, like me, get acquainted with Tibetan Buddhism, what I saw mostly smacked of religiosity. Though I had hoped to find information on how Tibetan Buddhism was a useful spiritual philosophy, capable of providing concrete tools to aid me in coming to terms with the ultimate nature of reality, little if anything along these lines was immediately evident. Instead, what I found seemed to be mostly religious proselytizing, dogma and liturgy. With passages like:

> Spiritual grace is a precious human gift passed down throughout the ages.

And,

> The path of Awakening consists of individuals working to make the world a more compassionate, wise place for all sentient beings through acts of hands-on charity, caring and kindness.

And, regarding a recently deceased and influential Western teacher, I read:

> A true knower of the hearts of men, a wise sage, a precious treasure, a living saint to whom is attributed a host of miracles and wonders…

And, (on the bona fides of Rinpoches in general),

> Every lama of the Golden Rosary of the Kagyu has had, and does have, extraordinary experience and realization, uncommon experience and realization, extraordinary learning and extraordinary attainment. And this is true to such an extent that to meet such a lama, to hear his teaching or even his voice, or even to hear the name of one of them has so much blessing, power and benefit, that any person who makes any of these kinds of contact with them will not be reborn in the lower realms for many lifetimes.

And finally,

> The dynasty of lineage holders that make up the precious succession of the Kagyu is known as the Golden Rosary….which descend from the supernal Absolute itself to the blessed yogis such as…(insert famous masters name here)…(insert famous masters name here)…(insert famous maters name here)…etc., etc., etc.

 Holy fuck, talk about the cult of personality! I was shocked to say the least…probably a little appalled too. It is just this kind of nonsense that really puts me off. This from a tradition I had hoped stressed a humble view detached from the materialism of the ego. Even an ignorant spiritual aspirant, such as myself, could see that much of the material featured on this website was simple-minded, chauvinistic, patriarchal, spiritually lightweight fluff. At times it even bordered on dogmatic religious rhetoric, which I found extremely egregious in other popular non-Buddhist traditions. To my sensibilities, this kind of introduction did not bode well.

Sifting through the quaint archaic language that provided reams of biographical information on past masters and their great deeds, interspersed with Tibetan lexicography, the experience felt akin to reading the Bible. Having the opportunity to read biography after biography of each Karmapa (main figurehead) going all the way back to his first incarnation, was entirely irrelevant to satisfying my penchant to gain practical knowledge. Who cared about a bunch of ancient relics?

It seemed to me that what we had here in his Kagyu lineage tradition was just one more religion among a myriad, and that worried me. The website seemed to be yet one more authority telling me how I could improve my lot in life using more moral dictums designed to make me a better human being. "Bah!" I had a whole library full of such nonsense. I wanted the real goods. Instead of thinking about what might make a good Buddha, I endeavoured to become one. How much actual Truth was I going to discern in this tradition, I wondered? This was not a great start, let me tell you.

I will never be an apologist for my iconoclastic viewpoint. To be frank, if any religion, order, lineage or teacher is not prepared to empower me to wake up in my lifetime on my own (authentic) terms, then I am not interested.

Judging from the answer I once got from a question I posed to a Tibetan born Lama staying at the hermitage, I should not have been too surprised at the calibre of material these Tibetan Buddhists had on offer. To this Rinpoche, I directly posed the following question, "How many enlightened beings have you ever bumped into over the course of your lifetime, both in the monasteries you lived at in Tibet during your youth and much later in India and elsewhere?"

He came up with an answer quick and forthright, "Oh…well…let me see…maybe one."

If enlightenment is "a results game" as I contended it must be, then these guys should be asking themselves some long, hard questions. Or maybe just one short, concise one would suffice—"Just what the fuck are we actually accomplishing here, gentleman?"

It seems few seekers are aware that the Dalai Lama (Gelug lineage holder) has stated quite clearly that he is not the best of meditators and admits that he is but a mundane, worldly human being, just like any other shmuck on the face of the planet is. The Maitreya (the anticipated future world Buddha), he ain't.

I have heard it straight from his own mouth that he meditates on *Bodhicitta* in order for the practice to help him reach enlightenment. Taking the man at his word, I think a spiritual tradition has a huge problem when it promotes enlightenment yet its main figurehead remains asleep at the wheel. I was in search of a Buddha, and the best the Tibetan Kagyu tradition could apparently come up with was "maybe one." Many seekers are enamoured by Tibetan exoticism and their "compassion for all sentient beings" shtick. That wouldn't cut it for me. I guess I am having an Emile Zola kind of "J'accuse" moment here. Enough said.

Anyhow, at this point let's consider in some detail the main rival to the Dalai Lama, who just happens to be the primary figurehead of the hermitage I was about to enter. They call this rival his Holiness (this irksome term has no place in true spirituality as no one is elevated above another) the XVII Karmapa.

The first pressing question for me about this Buddhist organization was, strangely enough, which one? Which Karmapa is presently the ultimate figurehead of the Kagyu lineage? Strange question, right? But actually it is quite sensical for in point of fact there were two rival claimants to "the crown." This situation is not unexpected, I guess, for when it comes to matters of power and control, these kinds of messy situations are quite common (a similar scenario has played out in the Karmapa lineage three times already).

Those interested in Western history and the Catholic Church may recall similar shenanigans arising at various times, such as the famous "Great Schism" which was a split in the Catholic Church that resulted in two popes holding office at the same time.

The position of Karmapa is a very powerful one indeed, on par with the Dalai Lama and his Gelug lineage. I soon came to appreciate how important such lineages and lineage holders in general were to the Tibetan Buddhist tradition. In a loose sense, these lineages have historically been analogous to how the monarchy operates.

I was surprised to learn that Tibet was, in essence, governed for centuries by these Buddhist title holders. There was, in fact, no democratic form of government to be had in that country for millennia. Some go so far as to claim its governance was a pretty ruthless and repressive theocracy with few rights afforded to the common folk.

One only has to skip over Michael Parenti's 2007 article entitled "Friendly Feudalism: The Tibet Myth" to get an idea of how repugnant this regime truly was. I'll just include a little snippet to show you what I mean. Here Parenti writes in reference to what he calls the mythology of a pristine spiritual "old Tibet":

> Tibetan Buddhism is cloaked in feudalism…and was not a paradise lost. It was a retrograde repressive theocracy of extreme privilege and poverty, a long way from Shangri-La.

The article points out many atrocities and abuses carried out upon the less advantaged members of society, namely women and serfs. It makes for eye-opening reading, including reports of the sexual abuse of young monastic monks (young boys are still frequently abused in monasteries up to the present day) and the rapes of peasant domestic staff. When one compares the critical account Parenti, as well as others, provides of Tibetan Buddhist repression with the highly idealized official Karmapa foundation literature which extolls their "venerable" tradition, the contrast couldn't be greater:

> The Gyalwang Karmapas rank amongst the most powerful figures of Tibetan Buddhism. The Karmapas were the first lineage of reincarnate Lamas (tulkus) in Tibet to take conscious rebirth in a continuous lineage of reincarnations. The Karmapas are said to be self-recognized, because each Karmapa leaves a letter predicting his next rebirth. Thus, the Gyalwang Karmapas have carried the authentic Buddhist teachings in an uninterrupted lineage of seventeen reincarnations into our modern world.

Evidently, there was a serious problem with the lovely rhetoric above. It seems that the latest directions which indicated future rebirth had gotten a bit "muddled," a bit "misconstrued," and a bit "lost in translation," such that today two claimants exist. Or perhaps more likely it was just a case of politicking. Consider the following online *Asia Times* article dated Dec. 23, 2003 to see what I mean:

> It is not unusual to have two competing candidates for the position of *tulku*. Over the centuries since the 3rd Karmapa started the practice of recognition—subsequently taken up by the Dalai Lamas—competition, intrigue and murder have on occasions beset the different Buddhist lineages. What is fairly unusual is to have two boys separately recognized and brought up to continue a lineage—and for this to be played out in the modern world where competing Karmapa Internet websites struggle to put forward their case.

Furthermore, the *Asia Times* went on to say:

> A bitter legal contest over the assets of Rumtek monastery has resulted in an unfavourable verdict. An Indian court in Sikkim ruled on September 28 that the assets of Rumtek belong to the Karmapa Charitable Trust, set up by the late 16th Karmapa, or head of monastery. The trustees support another claimant to the Karmapa throne, Karmapa Thaye Dorje, whom they say has the right to take over the monastery. Urgyen [sic] Trinley's followers, whose monks currently occupy the premises, made an appeal on December 4 to the Supreme Court.

Long story short, two factions formed, each vying for the former Karmapa's power and assets. His Holiness, Ogyen Trinley Dorje, was being supported by the majority of Karma Kagyu monasteries and Lamas, including the Dalai Lama. He was the figurehead for the hermitage I would join. The Chinese government also gave him their stamp of approval but therein lies part of the problem. The Indian government distrusts China's motives so supports the other Karmapa, Trinley Thaye Dorje. As well, the extremely influential Shamarpa or Shamar Rinpoche, whose official job is to pick the lineage holders successor, also supports this rival Karmapa.

Of historical interest is the fact that a certain Shamarpa of old was judged to be an influence peddler. Apparently, this guy was so incorrigible for so many generations of his incarnation that he was finally banned by the government in the late 1700s from ever reincarnating again. Try going home and having to explain that one to your wife or mother.

His practice then went underground until the ban was officially lifted in 1963 when he was once again free to choose the next Karmapa openly. Is his choice of rival partially due to Indian pressure? Corruption? Who knows, as most of the inner proceedings are carried out in secret. None of this intrigue helped to instil confidence in what was beginning to look ever more like just another religious racket.

Despite the disconcerting information I found on the host website, I still held out hope that at least the Rinpoche holding counsel at the centre could offer me rewarding guidance, wisdom and perhaps even share his "secret" teachings with me. Unfortunately, for a variety of reasons, none of that ever came to pass.

That is not to say that the hermitage was not a conducive setting for spiritual realization to unfold within. In fact, all my expectations were eventually met. It's just a fact that Tibetan Buddhism had little to do with my awakening (or perhaps it had some influence but in a negative way). In the end, things progressed as they would, not as I might have imagined they ought to. And that made all the difference.

> The supreme lesson of human consciousness is to learn how not to know....and not live statically, like machines driven by ideas and principles from the head.
> D.H. Lawrence (writer)

# A Fleeting Improvised Man Awakens

# Chapter 5

*Play your part in the comedy, but don't identify yourself with your role.*
　Wei Wu Wei (writer)

　　The first thing that struck me as I began to enter The TSC's grounds was the swirling interplay of colourful flags fluttering and dancing in the wind. The entrance was adorned by a fifteen-foot tall flag-strewn gateway that straddled a rough gravel laneway. What a cheery sound the Tibetan prayer flags made as they gently flapped in the breeze. Much, much later when I once again gazed up at these pennants, Chan Master Lin-Chi's famous question popped into my head, "Is it the wind that makes these flags rustle and bustle about, or rather is it Mind?" Good question that.

Passing through the welcoming gateway and further on into the spacious grounds proper, the feeling reminded me very much of how I imagined an ancient Greek theatre goer, a *theatrophilos* (literally "lover of the theatre"), must have felt when he gazed up at the great proscenium arch of the newly introduced Greek play house (the *theatron* 700 BC) in anticipation of the show about to commence. Theatre then was a brand new art form, so I imagine there was some excitement and perhaps even a little trepidation involved. That was my feeling exactly, great anticipation for what was about to unfold. Yes, that is it. I was about to engage in some kind of spectacle here; a play of sorts was about to begin. Quite quickly I discovered that what would unfold within these grounds would be a drama of sorts, which is most fitting since tragedy, in particular, was the art form most adored by the ancients.

The bit of performance art about to play out here would be replete with the customary limited contingent of main actors and a small supporting chorus. Surely this unfolding tale would have made good old Aeschylus (524–456 BC) proud for in the style this renowned Greek tragedian pioneered, namely the dominant theme of man and his relationship to God, this production, too, would feature a similar theme. Consider Aeschylus's words:

> And even in our sleep pain that cannot forget falls drop by drop upon the heart, and in our own despair, against our will, comes wisdom to us by the awful grace of God.

My quest, too, would in a sense echo the great playwright's sentiments, for in the end, through a kind of fierce grace not entirely of my own choosing, great wisdom would be imparted. Aeschylus's "awe-full" grace, I suspect, is the same kind that the Gospel of Thomas proclaimed would at first "trouble" and later "astonish" the one who sought, and found, God.

Were Aeschylus still alive, I bet he would have been interested in how the surprising plot twist of this little drama of mine eventually revealed itself. I think the sudden demise of the hero would have caught him quite unawares, as it did me, and thus delight him immensely. No matter the generation, everybody loves a surprise ending.

Looking back to when I first entered the hermitage, I can't stress enough how fantastically ignorant I was of the whole spiritual milieu I was about to become immersed in. I somehow imagined, as I presume many spiritual seekers do in their own way, that all I would need to do is locate the *axis mundi* (axis of the cosmos or Gods navel) which would in turn somehow facilitate my entering "the promised land." The concept of the axis mundi, from the religious or mythological perspective, is thought to be some kind of divine "umbilicus" which connects heaven and earth in the way Jacob's ladder was envisioned to do.

At that time, I did kind of buy into the idea that if I could only locate, or in some way fashion, my own reality bending, DMT-charged "stupa ship", or utilize a meditation-invoked fiery kundalini "flying dragon" of sorts, this kind of cosmic conveyance would then transport me, if not bodily, then at least by way of transcendental consciousness, up to the heavens or hopefully

*Chapter 5*

even beyond. During those first few weeks I spent at the hermitage, I had a certain naïve expectation that one day I would finally be whisked away to merge with God.

In that celestial realm, all my questions would be answered, all wisdom granted, all mysteries revealed. It turned out nothing could have been further from the truth. In fact, there never really was another spiritual realm or plane of existence to ascend to, nor a separate God to discover. In Truth, All is God. How and when and why this realization unfolded will take the remainder of the book to describe.

> This isn't a group project. No one's ever coming. No one's watching. There's literally no one in charge here, this is a psyche ward, the whole island [planet Earth, DJ] is a psyche ward. There's no God. There's no afterlife. Hello…party!
> Benjamin Smythe (spiritual teacher)

*A Fleeting Improvised Man Awakens*

# Chapter 6

*When you come right down to it all you have is yourself. The sun is a thousand rays in your belly. All the rest is nothing.*
    Pablo Picasso (painter)

    Succinctly put "Well, oh well, oh well...what then DJ have you now gotten yourself into this time...?" Or as Henry David Thoreau much more eloquently expressed it, "Go confidently in the direction of your dreams! Live the life you've imagined. As you simplify your life, the laws of the universe will be simpler."
    So, there I found myself, smack dab in the thick of it. No effusive, back-slapping welcome party greeted me. I didn't even get a hello and a curt handshake. Instead, Nan unceremoniously dropped me off on a laneway leading to a barn, and from there I was left to my own devices.

On first impressions, I was pleased enough with my quarters and immediate surroundings. Or at least I saw the potential that lay within them. With a lot of elbow grease and some perspiration, things would turn out just fine.

A more *Waldenesque* setting I doubt there could be. This was familiar ground. Half a year earlier I had left similar surroundings. Then I had been living in a tiny rather ramshackle shack that would have made Henry David Thoreau proud. For four months I lived in total seclusion interacting with not a soul. In fact, I never saw a single person save for one trip to a medical clinic and a single visit from the postman requiring a signature. Simplicity and the bare essentials were second nature to me by now. Here, once again, I could have the peace and quiet I so welcomed. Plus, my new digs came replete with nearby pond, meadow and forest, just as Thoreau's idyllic wilderness home had. I entered the space and looked around. Some TLC would be required to get everything shipshape, but I was game. I removed the pack from my back, took a deep breath and reflected for a moment.

I couldn't help but chuckle a bit upon the realization that "I had made it. Wow, I actually had." A few years earlier, I had hatched a very loose plan to end up precisely where I was now standing. It took exhausting preparation of body and soul, thousands of miles on the road…er tracks, then followed by some on the tarmac once the tracks petered out, temptations of a carnal nature (I met a young woman along the way who quite probably stole my heart in another version of this story) and spiritual revelation born of challenging entheogenic sessions. All that gave way in turn to this ramshackle room, the place of my dreams. It was just as Richard Matheson, writer of *What Dreams May Come*, said, "That which you believe becomes your world."

Regarding my quest, I sure hoped this opportunity would bring closure. The plain, simple fact was that I was here to discover the ultimate nature of reality and would do everything in my power to make the environment and my situation amenable to this singular goal.

To that end, as I described previously, I was not here to wear robes, recite liturgy, chant or do anything else expected of a monk. I was not interested in adopting a new lifestyle. My "job," so to speak, was to "wake-up" not "take-up," so I quite naturally dismissed the Buddhist lifestyle in favour of something else, realizing the Truth directly for myself. U.G. Krishnamurti put my inclination plainly and simply, "Only if you reject all the other paths can you discover your own path."

I suspected at the time that my steadfast stance not to compromise my mission might be problematic and probably would not go down very well with the powers that be. It's strange, but there is often a cost exacted for being truthful, isn't there? I was hoping that my earnest desire to awaken would be noble enough to avoid the full wrath of the teacher. Perhaps he would understand why I wanted to bypass his doctrine in favour of getting down to the heart of the matter. Could I convince the Lama to share his profound teachings with me in exchange for my total dedication to discovering Absolute Reality? Time would tell. Here is some background information on the physical location and my perspective regarding how I hoped to fit in at the hermitage.

## Chapter 6

The rural farm property was a secluded, picturesque, moderate parcel of land. Hay fields and mixed bush comprised the majority of the site, though there was a little marsh area to the rear as well. Its previous owner was renowned for being a founding member of a famous environmental group, so the main house and outbuildings had a funky, rustic, back-to-the-land charm about them.

Several very modest "hobbit hut," domed structures served as living quarters for visiting teachers and retreatants, and a commanding double dome structure functioned as both the dining quarters as well as the recreation area. In addition, strewn around the property were several small trailers or tiny cabins which also served to house retreatants and the occasional visiting monk or two. Approximately twenty people at most could be accommodated in these basic, austere, almost primitive lodgings at any one time.

A yurt served as both meditation hall and a place to receive the *dharma* (spiritual teachings) of the day. This centre, which was still exhibiting signs of growing pangs, would not likely appeal to those seekers who had a hankering for luxury and comfort. Its charm lay in its simplicity and proximity to nature. The main teaching/dining/bath complex was set near the rear of the property, well away from prying eyes. The acreage proper was surrounded by a coniferous rainforest. How sublime!

My "residence" was at the opposite end of the primary complex of buildings, just off of the main highway. My new domicile, though probably unappealing to most, suited my tastes well.

The place I would take over as home was a room in the back of a fairly modern, cement-floored, relatively sound (save for a leaky roof) barn. At the time, the barn seemed to function exclusively as a storage area and was tucked in right beside the forest with a small pond to the rear.

My room was a partitioned off section (once conceived to be some kind of a commercial kitchen though never quite completed) in the rear of the barn. It had proper gypsum walls (though unpainted and fungus stained), a source of water (though unplumbed), electricity and Internet connection as well as a wonderful wood-burning cook stove that would provide winter heat. A great view of the pond was afforded, and immediately adjacent through a side door was a modest greenhouse in need of some upkeep.

This back room had been long neglected and served now as a spot to simply store clutter. By my reckoning, several decades worth of odds and sods had accumulated in it, and it would all have to be chucked out before I could take up residence.

After a day of carting stuff away, the unpainted walls showed themselves. Most would see a disaster. I saw a space befitting a humble mendicant ascetic such as I aspired to be. As far as I was concerned—in consideration of what was really at stake here which had nothing to do with comfort or status—I had the best room in the joint.

One entire corner of my living quarters and a portion of the upper ceiling was inundated with a hideous black mould infestation which resembled a stunning monochromatic Jackson Pollock modern abstract expressionistic piece. After I had been living there for about half a year, someone on the board of directors finally took an interest and offered me some antifungal paint to put down this toxic biohazard, but it was the only artwork that adorned my walls, so I politely declined.

After hours of scrubbing, dusting and sweeping, I deemed my quarters ready for furnishing. I managed to cobble together a kitchen table of sorts, utilizing some saw horses as well as a sheet of plywood that formerly served as a concrete form. I scavenged the makings of a bed from an odd assortment of cast-off mattresses and framing material that people had donated to the hermitage. An elevated, old door served as a makeshift countertop. There were already some shelves and a small cupboard to store the assortment of used pots, pans and serving ware I scavenged from several boxes of donated goods.

Considering the fact that my single room had no running water; musty bedding; a cold, soiled, unpainted cement floor; bug speckled walls; no indoor bathroom nor shower; no washing machine; nor even drapes to cover up the drafty expanse of windows, everything seemed eminently in order. I felt like a kid finishing off his tree fort. Whoopee!

I believed that the living space I had managed to throw together was functional enough to support life yet was spartan enough to please Henry David Thoreau or even dear old Buddha himself. I feel such austere surroundings help to keep the mind on the matter at hand. If I needed a comforting distraction or a momentary break, all I had to do was peer out of the large bank of south-facing glazing and set my eyes upon a conifer-strewn forest which lay to one side of the barn, or shift my gaze to the other side and behold the meadows of hay, or further afield, enjoy an orchard replete with plum and apple trees.

And then there was the wonderful serenity the reflecting pool of the pond offered my weary mind during times of meditation fatigue. Diminutive wild deer were numerous in the field, and huge black ravens, much revered by the original first nation's people who summered on this island, sang out a cacophony of greetings to me from their perches high in the adjacent woods.

Buddhist tradition promoted contemplation surrounded by nature, and today the monastic forest dwelling tradition is still alive and strong in places like Thailand and Burma.

> In village or wilds, valley, plateau:
> that place is delightful where arahants dwell.
> Delightful wilds where the crowds don't delight,
> those free from passion delight, for they're not searching
> for sensual pleasures.
> Arannika Sutta, ""The Wilderness Dweller",
> translated by Thanissaro Bhikkhu.

Though my accommodation and the immediate surroundings were not included in the official consecrated grounds which had been especially blessed by a high Lama, I still chose to adhere to the standard rules, also called precepts, all lay practitioners were expected to follow during their stay at the hermitage. Buddha referred to these moral rules of conduct and ways to live an ascetic lifestyle as *gifts*. I found these duly noted on framed parchment stuck prominently near the dining hall entrance for all to see. They read as follows:

> Refrain from killing living things.
> Refrain from stealing.
> Refrain from un-chastity [sensuality, lust],
> Refrain from lying.
> Refrain from taking intoxicants [To be clearer I might add refrain from taking them to the point of heedlessness or mindlessness as the Buddha originally indicated—DJ].
> Refrain from taking food at inappropriate times [after the noon hour—DJ].
> Refrain from singing, dancing, playing music, gambling or attending entertainment programs [performances].
> Refrain from wearing perfume, cosmetics and garlands [decorative accessories].

I also voluntarily followed two more precepts that ordained novice monks and nuns had the extra pleasure of adhering to:

> Refrain from sitting on high chairs and sleeping on luxurious, soft elevated beds.
> Refrain from accepting money.

All of those precepts came naturally to me except the killing of living things. I am a carnivore, and so, too, I discovered are some Tibetan Buddhists. Almost everyone in Tibet, ordained or otherwise, consumes blood products. I was very surprised to learn this fact as I had always assumed Buddhism was a vegetarian lifestyle. Apparently, this is not the case with Tibetans.

Regarding the Buddha, the Theravada Pali Canon records instances of him consuming animal flesh that was specifically purchased for him. So I figured that by Tibetan Buddhist rules, as well as my own moral compass, all was well regarding my penchant for an occasional Saturday morning BLT and the odd tuna melt here and there. On the other hand, all of the meals served at the retreat were strictly vegetarian. Of course, this is what I ate while on retreat as did any full-time contemplatives lodging there.

Another important tradition was the requirement to *seek refuge*.

Hermitage literature informed me that:

> To *go for Refuge* is to turn decisively away from seeking fulfillment in timebound worldly drives and instead aim for spiritual awakening. Going for Refuge initiates a process of turning towards peace, wisdom, goodness and enlightenment, founded on the heartfelt desire to profoundly connect with Buddha nature.

One takes refuge in the *Three Jewels*, which are known collectively as *the Buddha, the Dharma,* and *the Sangha.*

*The Buddha,* which means the *awakened one,* was the preeminent teacher and guide.

*The Dharma* is the *teaching that illuminates the Path to self-realization.* Dharma also means the *natural law or way of life.* If one lives in harmony with Dharma, it is said, then, that one lives in harmony with the Universe.

*The Sangha* is the *Buddhist spiritual community* of those that practice the Dharma.

All retreat centre participants were encouraged to take refuge by vowing the following:

> Buddham saranam gacchami.
> "To the Buddha for refuge do I go."
> Dharmam saranam gacchami.
> "To the Dharma for refuge do I go."
> Sangham saranam gacchami.
> "To the Sangha for refuge do I go."

By repeating this recitation three times, a participant declared him- or herself to be an adherent of Buddhism. Refuge and the precepts are the basis upon which all other Buddhist practice is built.

It seemed odd to take up residence at a hermitage which for all intents and purposes operated in name only. Does a single contemplative constitute a hermitage? Of course, I realized the centre was still a work in progress. The previous ascetic who lived there for a year had recently left to pursue more sensual pleasures. In fact, he had taken up residence with a local woman. He was replaced with another monk and nun who had been there for a few months prior to my arrival.

The lone monk or *bhikhu* now residing at the centre had apparently begun wearing robes a decade and a half or so earlier, though he was still a relatively young man, barely into his thirties. Just prior to my arrival, the nun residing at the centre had been asked to leave. It turns out that she was a "none nun," a bogus imposter. Apparently, she bought her Tibetan garb locally, convinced everyone that she was a legitimate long-term contemplative and took up residence. This didn't last too long due to her mental health issues. Rumour had it that she had been kicked out of pretty much all of the finer American dharma centres and was now working her way down to places such as ours.

The centre was now occupied full-time by me and the sole bhikhu in residence. We lived at opposite ends of the half-kilometre property.

This Canadian contemplative had a sacred Vietnamese Buddhist monkly moniker conferred upon him while he lived at Plum Village, which is a famous Vietnamese Zen dharma centre located in France. His Vietnamese dharma name sounded to me somewhat like "Fatty," though he was anything but rotund.

In fact, he was a tall, lanky and willowy kind of guy with very little meat on his bones. He mindfully swished around with all the elegance and poise a classically trained dancer carried. The simple, low-calorie vegetarian fare he had subsisted on for decades must have in large part accounted for his lean body mass.

Perhaps stress was another culprit. He usually seemed quite mentally agitated and was rarely at ease in my presence nor, did it seem, anyone else's. Perhaps his disease was the result of trying, and mostly failing, to control his mind for so many years. I imagine that pursuit was not a lot of fun. In fact, I would come to learn that it was quite impossible to control the "chattering monkey mind" for anything more than a brief respite through the practices this monk was taught. I suppose sexual frustration could have been an issue as well.

Perhaps of no great surprise, within several short months monk Fatty would fall in love with a retreatant and soon, thereafter, cast off his robes in favour of marital bliss. A rather intelligent decision I thought.

Bhikhu Fatty occupied a very, very small, simple meditation hut far out into the surrounding fields. His tiny 8 x 10 ft. plain, wooden shack was sparsely furnished with a requisite "low bed." I noted few material possessions of any consequence in his room.

Several other similarly tiny dwellings, as well as the odd trailer or two, lay scattered about the meadow fields to lodge the meditators. Socializing was not encouraged as all retreats were, in theory, silent.

The visiting lama or dharma teacher temporarily resided in a modern addition tacked onto the dining dome. This small room was the most lavishly furnished place in the whole complex, but that is a relative term. To be clear, the centre was a terribly underfunded venture which barely had a shoestring to its name. Any monk or nun living there had to pay for his or her own upkeep. This situation was largely unattractive for potential hermits of low means. It seemed that few contemplatives were able to afford to live there full time.

In fact, the founding head of the centre and main dharma teacher did not even call the place home. This Canadian Rinpoche, who typically went by his given name of Wally, lived well away from the place with his wife in a secluded acreage featuring a rather grand, smartly furnished house with a pool and new SUV proudly parked out front. Wally was also sometimes more formally addressed as "Lama." He also had a remarkably unmemorable, long Tibetan title so full of consonants that to hear it repeated several times in a row reminded me of a Holy Roller speaking in tongues.

The Tibetan honorific *lama* carries a similar meaning to the Sanskrit *guru*. Historically, it was reserved for venerated masters or heads of monasteries though these days it seemed far easier to acquire. Wally was a case in point for he was a *Tulku*. Apparently, this honorific, which implies Rinpocheship (similar to Lama), was quite easy to get conferred on you if you had the right connections. How convenient. His title seemed to me to be as relevant as an honorary degree was. In the mafia, they have this thing about becoming a "made man," but at least in that outfit you actually have to qualify for it.

In Wally's case, a high lama back in Tibet "recognized" him as the reincarnation of a previous mid-level Tibetan monk and *et voila*—instant status, title, power, respect and recognition. I get the distinct impression that's how the "old boys club" (and this Tibetan Buddhism organization is indeed primarily a men's only affair) rewards one of their own. Watch the documentary *Tulku* (written/directed by an actual Western tulku, in fact Chogyam Trungpa's son, who demythologizes the whole affair) to learn how truly suspect this practice is.

I learned much later that Wally was held in low regard in certain important Tibetan Buddhist centres of the USA, very low regard indeed. One aspiring young monk in the making, but yet to be formally given his dharma name, was sent down from our hermitage to a large, well-respected US Buddhist organization to have his Tibetan title officially conferred on him. Wally was prohibited to act in this capacity. Well, this young guy returned from the States quite traumatized and reported that he no longer wished to be a monk at all. He told me that Wally was regarded by those in the know to be an "incompetent pretender" of sorts...or worse, a "buffoon." I could not fault the man for giving up on his desire to join the hermitage. His disenchantment with Tibetan Buddhism was apparently quite complete. Over time, my disdain for the Kagyu lineage pretty much did me in as well, but fortunately this had little bearing on my overall awakening for in the end you have to awaken from all traditions anyhow.

> If you cannot find the truth right where you are,
> where else do you expect to find it?
> Dogen (Zen Master)

# Chapter 7

*Only words and conventions can isolate us from the entirely undefinable something which is everything.*
Alan Watts (scholar and writer)

    This morning I was about to receive my first lesson on meditation. The feeling upon arising was one of trepidation mixed in with a little relief. The air was awash with the excitement a kid feels on his way to summer camp for the first time. I had prepped myself well for the imminent silence I longed to experience.

    My room was sparsely furnished, but it did contain a radio and computer. I was accustomed, or more accurately addicted, to listening to several daily alternative Internet chat shows as well as the CBC radio. It was a difficult decision to make, but these distractions had to go, so I stopped cold turkey. All of my attention had to be focused on the matter at hand. The retreat was billed as "silent," and I aimed to keep it that way. This attitude ended up paying huge dividends. Another inclination of mine also proved similarly rewarding.

My success regarding truth realization can in part be attributed to my inclination to remain sceptical. Here I mean to draw a distinction between close-minded cynicism (don't bother me with the facts, sir, my mind is already made up) and simply having the wherewithal never to leave my common sense at the door. The naïve, easily duped, "Kool-Aid" drinking kind of folks that cults favour, I certainly was not.

Simply put, if you tell me that a thing is so, demonstrate how that may be, or better yet, show me by what means I may ascertain this truth for myself. If you can't, then I don't want to hear from you. The power of discernment cannot be overemphasized in the awakening process. *Sapere aude* comes to mind once more: "Use your own power of wise judgement to discern for yourself the truth of the matter." Thus, the first time I laid eyes upon Lama in the meditation hall, a modicum of suspicion arose.

I knew a thing or two about mass manipulation and mind control and so had long before come to recognize that size indeed does matter. Lama's was magnificently erect and festooned with a patchwork of rainbow hues. Perhaps the only more "well endowed" example I had beheld sat perched high upon the pope's head. Man did this dude ever have a big one—hat, that is.

Laying eyes upon Wally, I saw the stereotypical pastiche of religio-exotica on display. He looked like a flamboyantly attired caricature of the archetypal spiritual guru, seemingly straight out of Central Casting. Wally knelt in full lotus position, regal in his countenance. He sat on a raised dais in the middle of the twenty-four-foot yurt wearing a flowing, garish, neon-lit Tibetan Buddhist costume that would have given *Joseph's Amazing Technicolor Dream Coat* a run for its money. This kind of exotic garb impressed some Western eyes to no end. It was the sort of attire clowns or shamans favoured. Give 'em the old razzle dazzle.

I was equally unimpressed with the tawdry, almost otherworldly, Tibetan religious artefacts and curios that lay strewn about Lama and the yurt's interior. Not wishing to get into too much detail here about such furnishings, I will simply relate what an ex-Catholic friend of mine said upon entering the space for the first time. "What a most uncomfortable and depressing atmosphere," she said. Then my friend added, "These iconographic artworks and religious statuary remind me of the bad old days." Suffice it to say, she never entered the meditation hall again.

I agreed with her that the mouldering contents of the yurt's interior smacked of religiosity. Once, within the Lama's presence, I carelessly referred to something in the yurt as being an *icon*, and he had a hissy fit. Many Buddhists claim that the tradition they practice is not a religion per se. With more exposure I came to feel that The Truth Sangha Centre was merely a small part of a large organization which had its own specific beliefs, cultural systems and world views that relate humanity to an order of existence. That pretty much describes religion in a nutshell, doesn't it? In Wally's case, I think the "lady doth protest too much." For example, Wally would deny that his organization worked in the same manner that any old religion did, just as he would maintain that lipstick on a pig didn't look ridiculous...but...just sayin.

Anyhow, Wally struck quite a vision as he sat there in full lotus position wearing his most impressive regalia. It was just this kind of impression most paying customers demanded. The assembled retreatants seemed to respond well to the Allan Watts like visage (the more mature TV personality persona, replete with customary Machiavellian like goatee) that sat before them. I, on the other hand, was struck by the way the Rinpoche's actions reminded me of those historical Catholic priests who used to enrich themselves by handing out costly indulgences. For in a manner, the rites Wally began to engage in seemed much in this vein though, of course, in the Catholic tradition, the faithful performed the indulgence themselves.

We were required to kneel at his feet while he performed some kind of ritual purification and blessing. What this had to do with realizing the ultimate nature of reality I knew not. As an iconoclast, I found this kind of behaviour quite distasteful.

After the elaborate welcome, Wally then got down to business with a brief introduction regarding the centre, what would be expected of us, and then launched into the importance of maintaining silence during the entirety of the retreat. Next came the part that I was anticipating most. He began to explain the basics of meditation. This practice is regarded as one of the fundamentals of Buddhist practice, yet I knew nothing at all about it.

Years earlier, I had once sat down to try to quell my mind. Just like a turbulent whirlpool, I found there was no way to subdue it. With no technique at my disposal, I attempted to utilize force of will alone. This turned out to be an utter failure. I never attempted this pointless experiment again.

I found Wally's explanation about how the unruly nature of the mind was analogous to the wild spirit of an unbroken horse to be quite fascinating. He then explained that there were several techniques one could employ to pacify the "stallion" enough to put it to bridle.

The primary technique he taught utilized some kind of object for the mind to focus on. This could be the popular *watching the breath*, but first Wally taught us to simply *count our breath*. He instructed us to inhale/exhale and count one. Repeat this again with a two count, and so on, until you forgot the count. Once lost in fantasy, you had to start the count all over again. Apparently, some could barely make it to twenty before they could not recollect their count.

In practice I found this a fairly easy exercise to master. Pretty soon I was easily doing it for forty-five minutes without losing myself. Wally explained that forty-five minutes was the length of time considered to be an "hour of sitting meditation," and that length of time was the mark of an experienced meditator. Being goal driven, I set this as my first test. I wanted to see how an "hour" of sitting really felt as quickly as possible. In a day or so, I got to this mark using the counting method, and then I replaced it with the more advanced method of *following the breath*.

Following the breath is a very powerful method employed by various traditions and paths of contemplation. The breath is always present, so it naturally lends itself to be a convenient object of concentration.

Wally wrapped up the introductory lesson by explaining by what means the *dharma*, which I explained earlier is spiritual knowledge or teachings, was best received. He presented a four-tier continuum from the best to the least efficacious method. At the top was direct dharma transmission from teacher to student. Wally stressed how important transmission was, beyond compare he assured us.

Sadly, it was reserved for the few "special" students deemed worthy enough to have earned the right to receive it. This emphasis on transmission is sometimes called the "Whispering Lineage," because its highest, most secret teachings are still passed on in an unbroken line from teacher to student. These Rinpoches would have us believe that this has been going on since the days of the Buddha himself.

Next, he stressed the importance of kneeling in front of a sage guru. This was the second best route for receiving "the goodies" required to become a master yourself. The third one I can't quite recollect, but perhaps it was direct experience garnered through meditation and insight. The fourth method was the least valuable Wally assured us, as it involved conceptual book learning. Wally really stressed how counterproductive and irrelevant this avenue was and forbade anyone from cracking open a book during the entirety of his retreat.

I considered this last piece of advice carefully but soon started to consult the Internet on certain matters because, unlike most retreatants, I had no prior conceptual framework upon which to draw. My analytical mind demanded a little background information, some kind of conceptual outline to orient myself with. Fortunately, I had a well-stocked library to consult on the premises, but more importantly, I had access to a high speed Internet connection from which to surf the digital infobahn.

> The object of life is not to be on the side of the majority, but to escape finding oneself in the ranks of the insane.
> Marcus Aurelius (Stoic philosopher and Roman emperor)

# Chapter 8

*Don't waste time polishing the turd. It doesn't hold truth and it won't take a shine. If a burning desire for enlightenment is not present, no amount of meditation and practices will help.*

Richard Rose (spiritual teacher)

    *Zen*, a Japanese Buddhist tradition transplanted from China, resonates very strongly with me. It literally means "meditation." Seated meditation, therefore, is called *zazen*, also sometimes referred to as *shikantaza* which means "just sitting." On the Zen view, there is no more to meditation than just that, only sitting. The etymology of shikantaza fleshes out the meaning which points to a deeper profundity.

    *Shi* means *tranquillity*, *kan* means *awareness*. *Ta* refers to the exact correct spot to sit, and *za* means *to sit* as explained above in the description of *zazen*.

This "just sitting" as tranquil awareness or "doing nothing" business is the essence of meditation but unfortunately not often stressed clearly enough in most contemporary teachings. In fact, Wally never described meditation in these simple terms as he was drawn to complicate the matter by introducing endless contemplation techniques one could employ while on the mat. I guess if teaching is your thing, this tact keeps you employed, if nothing else, doesn't it?

The first day of silent retreat I sat in zazen posture, for my back ached so when in lotus position, counting my breath for a full ten hours before I finally retired for the night. This was a challenge to say the least. Certainly, I had never encountered any activity that was more tedious, trying and deathly boring. After the first hour, I wondered how I was ever going to make it to the end of the day, never mind the week. But failure truly was never an option.

My self-imposed goal was to get to a combined eight hundred inhalations/exhalations without forgetting my count before moving on to simply following the breath. Between sessions, I did an Internet search on meditation.

I quickly saw that experts proclaimed the virtues of meditation in glowing terms and explained how it could improve one's life, and admittedly self-help was just the kind of thing I was looking for when I first sought a little information on the virtues of meditation. Fairly quickly though, it dawned on me that self-improvement regimes have nothing to do with enlightenment.

While teachers and pundits alike were extolling mediation's health benefits, I was only interested in discovering whether or not meditation was a bona fide spiritual technology and secondarily whether it was safe to employ. This is the typical kind of egoic (ego means one's sense of self, I don't mean having an excessively pronounced sense of self-worth here as some might presume) inclination that arises when novel situations are encountered. The ego seeks reassurances about safety and the quality and quantity of "pay-back" it can expect to receive when jumping into a new endeavour. Harm reduction and accruing maximum benefit is paramount when it comes to the "selfish gene" and seems a reasonable tact to take if the human species is to be preserved.

Specifically, I aimed to discover if rational, sober-minded folks, of course whom amongst I counted myself, bought into any of this stuff. In my mind, as often portrayed by the mainstream media, meditation was seen to be a somewhat off-beat, goofy, hippy-dippy counter-culture type of pursuit that looked pretty dodgy to me. The flake factor seemed pretty pronounced, so I was wary. My first broad search results were inconclusive, so I refined my investigation in order to try to discover whether or not there was any empirical evidence or support from mainstream science that could validate the efficacy of meditation. I have a university degree in the applied sciences, so I find value in quantifiable data and materialistic empirical repeatable results.

Was evidence available that demonstrated thoughts could be slowed down or even stopped? The results I came up with after more searching were again a mixed bag of opinions and were certainly inconclusive. One scientist even claimed that it was categorically impossible for a human being to exist yet experience no thought. What was I to make of that statement given the fact that the goal of meditation was the very thing this scientist refuted? Soon I was relieved to discover hard evidence to the contrary. Not only was meditation shown to be a varied and complex phenomenon, it had even been studied using the latest brain imaging technology available.

Several top-level studies undertaken by various American universities during the opening years of the 2000s showed some interesting results. Some studies were even undertaken with the blessing of the Dalai Lama, who it turns out is quite interested in science. The studies determined that various kinds of meditation affected the brain in distinctly different ways.

For example, expert meditators adept in focused, one-pointed concentration, when examined by the MRI, showed demonstrable changes in the networks of neural tissue responsible for modulating attention. Other test subjects, who practiced a more holistic, non-concentrative kind of mediation, demonstrated pronounced gamma brainwave activity which was quite out of the norm.

Those results were satisfying to me. This was the kind of evidence I could really sink my teeth into. Obviously, I could see that meditation was an accepted practice that had—if not rigorously, then at least at some basic level—been scientifically investigated. I concluded that it certainly wasn't *woo woo* stuff. Thank goodness for that.

During further pauses in between meditations, I discovered over the next few days more corroborating evidence that this meditation stuff was on the up and up. I chanced upon Jon Kabat-Zinn and references to his mindfulness centre. The concept of mindfulness was bandied about quite frequently in certain spiritual circles I soon learned and with good reason. It was a key component to promoting lucidity and clarity of mind.

Jon Kabat-Zinn is a professor of medicine and also is known for a stress reduction clinic as well as the Center for Mindfulness in Medicine, Health Care, and Society at the University of Massachusetts Medical School. His healing modality relies significantly on meditation. Again, this was further evidence that meditation was not for kooks.

Another piece of evidence that proved significant to me was a YouTube clip that showed writer and philosopher Ken Wilber modifying his brainwaves in real time, solely through the power of meditation. By now I had little doubt regarding the validity of silent sitting. It was clear it could be employed in various fashions to promote a range of effects. It certainly did not rely solely on the power of suggestion or the placebo effect as I once imagined it might. Yet, I was momentarily perturbed when a writer suggested that a series of severe grand mal seizures which Ken Wilber suffered could have been related to his meditation practice.

The ego (again the means by which the I-thought arises), ever on the outlook for threats to its safety and security, paused to consider this news carefully. Could this practice really damage my brain, I wondered? In the end, I carried on due to a lack of any substantiating evidence as well as the need to at some point inject a bit of faith into the process. I can report I certainly never suffered any cognitive impairment from meditation practice, quite the opposite in fact.

Some positive effects I found noted in the literature included lower blood pressure, improved emotional regulation, increased tolerance of chronic pain, improved sleep, greater attention to detail, decreased stress levels, reduced occurrence of depression, lower heart rate, decreased anxiety, lower blood cortisol levels, improved feelings of well-being, less anger issues and so on.

Of course, while of interest, these were not the kind of effects I was chasing. Of paramount interest to me was the fact that a strong meditation practice was noted as a significant factor in waking up, though at that point I had no idea how or why this was so. Once I verified that the process was safe and efficacious, I poured all my energy into becoming an adept meditator. For the most part, I left the Internet alone and got down to the business at hand using single-pointed concentration to calm the bucking bronco.

> Sometimes the questions are complicated and the answers are simple.
> Dr. Seuss

# Chapter 9

*Whatever you have in your mind—forget it. Whatever you have in your hand—give it. Whatever is to be your fate—face it!*
  Abu Sa'id (Sufi)

This single-pointed concentration business was apparently an important skill to master as far as Tibetan Buddhists were concerned. Apparently the degree to which *samatha*, which translated means *calm abiding meditation*, was "pointed" or greatly focused, the better.

I aimed to become the best one-pointed meditator possible in the quickest amount of time ever. My goal was to put those Tibetan monks to shame. Was I competitive and goal oriented? You bet! Arrogant? Not at all. I had been tested in life numerous times and knew my strengths and limitations very well. Great patience and perseverance were things I didn't lack.

I would meditate as many hours each day as I found productive and rewarding. At the beginning, and for a good long time after, this amounted to some ten hours daily. Any more than this became counterproductive. I stayed at this sweet spot for some months. If I could have improved my meditation situation by sitting longer hours, I surely would have. For some reason though more than ten hours felt intuitively counterproductive and experientially the greater fatigue was a detriment to the overall practice.

How much or little I meditated was entirely up to me. I simply aspired to accrue maximum gain. Counting breaths had been a good introduction to meditation, but now the challenging phase began, so I would like to presently describe it in some detail. Lama Wally pointed out that each of us has a "chattering monkey mind." What follows, then, is the means to quell thinking to a greater or lesser degree, but I posit never totally for in truth what is ultimately being pointed to in authentic spirituality can't be conquered.

Lama Wally never drew on personal anecdote to express the dharma. I found this tact very odd. He was, though, very fond of quoting scripture and citing tried and true spiritual *pointers* but to what end, I wondered? No one had explained to me the final goal of meditation. Retreat after retreat Wally stressed the importance of *samatha* but never explained why we did it.

This calm abiding practice is a well-known meditation technique not limited to Buddhist practitioners. In fact, paying attention to the breath is found in almost every major spiritual tradition, such as that of the Hindus, Sikhs, Jains, Sufis, Taoists, and even Christian mystics.

When the religions turned to matters of calming the mind, they all in some capacity used the breath as an object of focus. The practice was eminently pragmatic as the breath was always available no matter the circumstances. You needn't cart around a candle to peer at nor a mirror to cast your gaze upon or bring out a deity to behold. All you had to be was conscious, and this object of awareness would be forever available to you.

We were instructed to first find a comfortable place in which to meditate. Many retreatants were naturally attracted to the communal yurt which, when not serving as the lecture hall in the morning, was available as a public meditation space the rest of the time. Group meditation held no appeal for me. Similarly, guided meditation was of no interest. Furthermore, the various cushions spread around the yurt floor were useless to me due to my bad back. When forced to kneel in the yurt, I did so with the aid of a purpose-built, Japanese-style, small stool called a seiza bench that I placed under my rump in order to sit semi-supported in the zazen fashion. This allowed the seiza Zen posture to be adopted with much less pain. Normally though, I favoured the simple hard-backed chair.

Of interest to me was the fact that Buddha spoke of four permissible meditation postures. These were noted to be lying, siting, standing and walking. I never saw a need to sit in a contorted position battling pain. Apparently, neither did the Buddha. I had more important things on my mind than to try to be a good sitter. Presently that would be mastering one-pointed concentration.

The practice itself was simple enough though exceedingly monotonous. Sure, the mechanics of it, the watching the breath rise and fall again, could not have been easier to carry out, but it was no small matter to endure. Spending the better part of your waking hours occupied in this seemingly pointless pursuit was tedious beyond compare. Luckily, farm life had prepared me for such drudgery. The kind of perseverance rural routine demanded helped me become exceedingly patient as did martial arts training and earning a couple of university degrees. So I wonder if I suffered less than some meditators did. I was prepared to do this same routine for the remainder of my life, so it was imperative that I not allow it to get to me.

When I inhaled, I simply mentally noted "iiiiiiiiinnnnnnn." An exhale was mindfully noted as "ooooouuuuuttttt." I concentrated on this practice and never wavered. Never once did I let my attention drift by softening my focus. Not for a moment. To do so would have been to get lazy, and there was no place for that kind of behaviour in this most serious of affairs. To have the spirit of a warrior, at least in the early stages, was something that came naturally and served me well.

> A man may fulfill the object of his existence by asking a question he cannot answer, and attempting a task he cannot achieve.
> Oliver Wendell Holmes (writer and educator)

# Chapter 10

*I'm afraid sometimes you'll play lonely games too, games you can't win because you'll play against you.*
Dr. Seuss (writer)

    As the first five-day retreat began to wind down, I now had a good grasp of how this outfit operated and where my position in it lay. Basically, in the spirit of the old Zen saying, "Before enlightenment chop wood and haul water...after enlightenment do the same," I literally performed those duties as well as helped make breakfast, wash dishes, clean house, etc., and of course performed my main agricultural chores such as garden work, orchard and greenhouse maintenance, etc.

    When not engaged in *karma yoga,* a retreat centre euphemism for unpaid labour, I found some time to intermingle (usually pre- or postretreat due to the silence rule but some retreatants chose to not honour it) with the retreatants which gave me the opportunity to get to know some of the "players" of this little set piece at least in a cursory fashion. The full contingent of this little band of thespians included the main players, Lama Wally and me, supported by several monks, along with the chorus.

The retreatants comprised the chorus; members came from afar as well as locally. Some were short term, others the longer hangers-on. The song that collectively emanated from under their masks of persona was a strident, insistent, almost cacophonous drone. If you listened carefully, it was a lament to a human condition rife with uncontrolled egoic identification and projection, confusion, loneliness and unhappiness.

These choral members ran the gamut from the relatively well-adjusted professional, such as a life coach or accountant there for a week of R and R, to the stressed-out blue collar bus driver ordered to attend retreat by his concerned wife, to the short-order cook, to the counter-culture hippy types looking for a free ride, and finally to the locals and patrons who sometimes holed up for several weeks of downtime. Then there were the occasional long-termers who hung on for several retreats in a row or occasionally longer.

One repeat male customer was an unstable, directionless Bohemian who broke into my room in the middle of the night deep in the throes of a pronounced schizophrenic breakdown. Another unforgettable member of the chorus was a quirky economic refugee of sorts, a middle-aged woman who was severely malnourished due to a variety of food issues. She would corner me and babble on incessantly about the Divine feminine within and the power available to manifest anything our little hearts desired. This outlook seemed somewhat misguided as she didn't have two nickels to scratch together nor a home to call her own. Why in God's name didn't she practice what she preached and manifest this wonderful life she claimed was available to all? Perhaps something called reality stood in the way. And then there was one of the most memorable choral members of them all—the enigmatic Mr. Knap

Knap was a bit of an eccentric local fifty-something handyman type recently separated from his wife of some years. He carried the fair complexion, dirty blonde thinning hair, coarse beard and lanky muscular build his Nordic forefathers bore, which he informed me came from his father's side of the family. He also told me that his Swedish family name had previously been Knappa until it was sensibly Americanized to the shorter Knap when his grandfather immigrated to Canada.

I later discovered that he was a friend of Lama and his wife, Vicky. Apparently, Knap was living in a tent somewhere on the property. Try as I might, I never could locate his camp. When a man is well and truly lost, perhaps he can't be found. He seemed to have a great deal to hide, including a drinking problem. Alcohol was, of course, prohibited on The TSC grounds, so this in part may have explained his reclusive behaviour.

I met him the day before the first retreat was to begin. As if conveyed by some sort of supernatural means, Knap startled me when he suddenly appeared unannounced at my wide-open door. I wasn't expecting to see anyone since no one had greeted me to date, but he had not come for a social visit it seemed.

Chapter 10

Neither pleasantries nor even much of an introduction was offered. Knap simply came to the point and launched straight into business. He had a proposal, or more exactly a mandate, from on high for me. He put it to me that I would now be expected to prepare all the breakfasts for the upcoming retreat. He couched it in such a way that it sounded official and was not a matter of choice. "Ok, I'll be there early next morning as requested," I replied.

Later I discovered this was all a ruse, complete BS through and through. He volunteered to cook all meals for the upcoming retreat and then slyly got me to do his bidding. I was not impressed at all; not so much because I had to do the extra work, but rather because he had totally misrepresented the situation and lied to me. I informed Vicky about his chicanery. The Lama's wife did not want to hear this, and when I pressed, she simply elected to make an enemy out of me. Her unjustified disdain for me lasted many weeks. Later I found out why she was so unsupportive (and probably negatively influenced her husband's attitude towards me as well).

It turned out that Knap had done many thousands of dollars' worth of free...er karma yoga...carpentry renovations on her home. This explained her lack of support and resultant longstanding grudge against me. The Buddhist tradition was supposed to be about coming to terms with reality as it was, which in part meant being truthful. They always had such high standards, but I noticed few, if any of these Buddhists, actually lived by their creed. Hypocrisy ran rampant in this organization and its members. On a positive note, Knap seemed relatively free of hubris.

Getting to know him a little better over the ensuing weeks, I came to understand that no matter where Knap went, *he always lived a short distance from his home.* He told me that regardless of his location throughout life, he always felt a little unsettled, never truly at ease. During the last decade or so, he had lived in matrimony but recently discord had caused him to move out of the shared home into an adjacent carpentry shed for good. Presently, he was living rough in the bush. This might seem peculiar, but things like this are taken in stride on this island. I met a guy who bathed in a wood-heated bathtub which sat perched atop his cook stove which was itself situated smack dab in the middle of his kitchen, while I heard tell of another quirky character who electrified his house with power he illegally siphoned from the telephone line. Knap was no queerer than any of these folk, so his behaviour, if nothing else, was quite "at home" in this regard.

I asked Knap how long he had lived in the shed.

"Oh that, well, I didn't actually ever *live* there," came his curt reply.

"But I thought you just said that you...," but I couldn't finish my thought for he interjected, "Look it's real simple, okay? Yes, I stayed there for a couple years, but I most certainly never *lived* there...it's like I'm a tourist...forever a tourist, get it?"

"Sure" I said, feeling a bit chastised. "So where do you *tourist* now then?" came my sarcastic follow-up. Knap glared silently at me from eyes that reflected an unsettled mind, a man not entirely present, a man still in search of a home.

From what Knap told me of his spiritual journey, I concluded that he was still a seeker though now a pretty jaded and exhausted one. He was of the age that he had practically seen it all, yet apparently refuge still evaded him…as it does all of us.

Over the ensuing weeks, Knap would let his history slip out in dribs and drabs, just like Japanese sake is served. During his spiritual life, he had attended numerous meditation retreats and sat long hours. He claimed to be able to maintain silent sitting for twelve hours straight, which I found very hard to believe. Alas, despite such apparent effort, peace of mind still evaded him.

In fact, somewhat humorously, he told me that whenever he meditated for prolonged periods of retreat, a psychotic episode invariably broke out. He assured me that he had no problem with this kind of thing in the same manner an alcoholic once confided to me "I ain't got no problem when I'm drunk, none at all. It's other folks whose got the issue…not me."

As he spoke of his psychotic episodes, he seemed to come alive. Knap actually enjoyed them. He said that they were a liberating experience and often quite fun, an escape of sorts like the full bottle of sherry he pounded back every evening, I presume.

Knap seemed reticent to speak freely. Once, though, he said something to me that surprised me in the same manner one is startled when they receive an unexpected smack to the face, a wake-up call administered like a *Zen bitch slap*.

While walking to the beach one day in silence, the only time Knap let me accompany him anywhere, I couldn't take the quiet anymore, so I piped up with a question:

> So Mr. Knap, tell me…I mean tell me, what's this whole Buddhist thing really all about anyhow…fill me in will you? What's the big picture here?

A quizzical look appeared on Knap's face. "WHAT!" he bellowed like a forlorn bull. Apparently, I had asked a stupid question. He then added, "This whole Buddhist thing you ask…what the fuck are you talking about; what big picture?"

I replied a bit defensively, "Well you know…you know…what's it all about? Where does it all lead?"

Knap countered with a, "Well what do you think?"

So I blurted out the one thing about spirituality that I was pretty certain about. I told him that I thought it all came down to life being like a school of sorts where we get to have a myriad of experiences and learn many different things. As a consequence, we spiritually mature and eventually ascend to another higher level of reality when we are ready. Spiritual maturation led to a graduation of sorts. "That, then, would be enlightenment," I told him.

First, Knap guffawed and mumbled something unintelligible, which I expect it was not flattering towards me. Then he came to a halt and barked the wisdom of one who really knew a thing or two. "That's bullshit my friend, utter crap. And I am being polite here 'cause I like you." He kicked a crumpled beer can off of the edge of the tarmac and marched on.

# Chapter 10

I caught up with Knap. He scrutinized me as one would the village idiot. "Look, it's not like that at all," he informed me. "What you just said there about graduation and all—are you fucking kidding me or what…?" Then he stomped forward about ten more paces and halted yet again. While glaring at me some more, he asked, "So you wanna know where it all ends do you…what's it all about?" He pondered a bit more; then a slight grin appeared on his face, "Look I can't tell you where it all ends, but I sure as hell can tell you where it all begins..." He paused for effect and then with great satisfaction added, "By you not being such an asshole!" Then he laughed uproariously.

I was taken aback by Knap's vulgarity and sulked a bit by walking on ahead alone. Noting my discomfort, he caught up and added the following kindness with a wee grin. "Hey, DJ…that don't be such an ass thing I just said to you back there…Look…here's the deal…it takes one to know one, okay?"

Still…"what an ignoramus," I thought.

Of course, it was I who was the ignorant one there. In the coming months, as direct experience revealed itself to me, I came to recognize the wisdom of his words. But enough of Knap for now. Let me move on, and I'll tell you a bit about another member of the chorus—my "overseer."

The "Swami," as he was known about the centre, was an ex-Rajneesh/Osho (flamboyant and somewhat infamous Indian guru transplanted to the US during the early '80s) devotee and pretty much burned out seeker, an American expat who still carried his counter-culture ethos around with him like the greying tresses that flowed down his back. Presently, he made a living by growing Chinese medicinal herbs. "Swami" was a title conferred on him while he resided at the Osho compound. It was a term he now forbade anyone from using. Still, we used it behind his back.

I found Swami to be one of the coolest, most well-adjusted and rational members of the chorus I encountered along the way. Out of great admiration and respect for what the title of "Swami" actually denotes, plus a little bit of teasing as well, I shall continue to employ this title when referring to him just as I did back when I was getting to know him.

This wizened, grey-bearded, former New York City unionized carpenter appeared to have none of the supposed mystical/flaky trappings many ex-Osho disciples still project. Swami was down to earth, hip, and kind as well. He was the guy most interested in the farm side of the enterprise, so he naturally became my boss of sorts. We had a cordial working relationship while we spent time together improving infrastructure, etc. He came to me at times with new projects that needed attending to, like picking the orchard fruit that needed to be juiced, aiding in the building of a shower stall, field maintenance or spreading great mounds of gravel around.

A less prominent "choral" member included the LA real estate agent and ex-wife of a famous movie producer who camped out on the property for most of the season. She seemed to be a serious meditator and was one of the few who diligently followed the silence rule. Between retreats, she visited island art galleries and often took off to the bistro for fine meals and the odd bottle of locally produced mead. She was a fun gal to be around.

Then there was Mitra, who held a special place in my heart. She became a spiritual buddy of sorts and undoubtedly was a favoured choral member, though she was not much more than a peripheral player; in fact, I learned little about her personal life, yet she certainly played an important role in my awakening. Integral really, for you see she was the only person on the island I knew who had a certain aura of spiritual authenticity and authority. Her support was surely much valued for a while.

To jump ahead of the story for just a moment, I came to know Mitra's name through Bhikhu Fatty who told me in a rather sceptical tone that she had proclaimed herself *to be awake*. I knew the Lama held her in high regard. Though I knew nothing at all about her, something in her countenance caught my eye during a ten-day silent retreat we shared together at season's end. Her quiet dignity and poise stood out from the rest of the retreatants.

Mitra impressed me greatly with an authenticity rarely encountered. Now middle-aged, she still possessed the dark features, clear skin and high cheek bones prevalent amongst Persian beauties. Though still physically attractive, it was the Divine within that most caught my attention. I asked Bhikhu Fatty where she lived. I made an appointment to meet her at her house in the later part of the fall. It was then that she made a most unexpected admission to me.

Mitra told me she had caught sight of me by chance during the last major silent retreat of the year that we shared together. She knew me not at all, yet there was a flash of recognition she now reported to me. It seems she had previously encountered me weeks earlier in a dream. She was so amazed to actually see me in the flesh that she even told a friend during the same retreat how uncanny the experience felt.

Her name intrigued me. I wondered if Mitra was her real given name or rather an acquired fake spiritual nickname like so many aspirants seem to assume somewhere along their journey. She assured me that it was, in fact, the Iranian name that she had been given at birth. Its meaning became significant as time went along. I discovered the name "Mitra" was steeped in mythology and carried great religious significance.

In ancient Indo-Iranian mythology, Mitra was the God of Light. The name held similar connotations to the mystique the Christ name carried. Mitra was regarded as the Light, the Life, the Way and the Truth. Therefore, Mitra's name carried a history of great significance which was not lost on me. Could an awakened one really be here right in our midst, I wondered? What a thrill to even ponder such a possibility. What a rare gift if it were true. I certainly had to investigate further. I still craved guidance, and clearly the titular head of The Truth Sangha Centre had never lived up to my expectations. Maybe this was another possible spiritual entre. Perhaps one should not have such high hopes though. I have found that they often turn out to be misguided.

I assumed that anyone teaching the Dharma in the guise of a master, must naturally really be awake. This is where I hear echoes of Knap chime in. "DJ," he bellows, "There you go again being such an ass!" Well he'd certainly be correct on that count. I was so naïve and trusting in the beginning.

I always had thought, and quite rightly so, that if you taught surgery, you must be a surgeon by profession. It seems that this kind of logic does not apply when it comes to spiritual matters. Apparently, loads of chappies are traipsing about advising other fellows on how to cut deep into the marrow, perhaps even attempt lobotomies, yet don't have the faintest clue what the hell they are really talking about. This realization served as a wake-up call. I was starting to appreciate Knap's acerbic wit and wisdom a little more with each passing day.

Anyhow, I struck up a friendship of sorts with Mitra, and it was in this capacity, the capacity of a spiritual buddy, that I am eternally grateful to her. She offered me the support and interest only one who has gone before can provide. Though we met but a handful of times, her willingness to listen and her wisdom and stillness all impressed and inspired me greatly.

It was just the kind of tonic I had been keenly anticipating since bidding farewell to Mother Ayahuasca. Using a mixed martial arts metaphor here, Mitra became my *cornerman*. If you are unfamiliar with the fight game, the cornerman is your best buddy come fight night. He gives you essential advice, strategies and encouragement; puts ice on your battered chest; passes you the water bottle and may be called to treat your cuts with a dab of adrenaline chloride, thrombin or a dusting of Avitene when you need to get patched up real quick. I was so pleased at the time to chance across a mentor or *true spiritual friend*. It was with some astonishment then that several years later I came to discover that *Mitra* quite literally meant exactly that— "spiritual buddy."

The word "mitra" is commonly translated as "guru" in the expression *guru-devotion*, but it is formally rendered as "kalyana*mitra*" in Sanskrit and "geway-shenyen" in Tibetan and is abbreviated as "Geshe." The Tibetan term appears within the context of the Mahayana teachings for attaining enlightenment and is usually rendered in either language as *spiritual friend*.

"Mitra" in Sanskrit is the common word for friend. The root of the word, "*maitri*" means "love." "Love" here does not denote romantic attraction but rather the wish for others to be happy. It is a selfless desire which does not imply clinging attachment to the people one loves. Nor do such buddies desire anything in return, such as reciprocal love, affection, or appreciation. A spiritual friend then is someone with a purely altruistic compassionate attitude and probably quite a rarity in a field so full of hubris and gigantic spiritual egos.

Spiritual friendship, according to the Buddhist ideal, does not imply that the two people involved are equals or peers like two drinking buddies consider themselves to be in a Western relationship. Here, only the spiritual mentor is called the spiritual friend. Fellow Dharma students or fellow disciples may be spiritual friends in the Western sense of friendship, but they are not each other's spiritual mentors or guides. I infrequently interacted with Mitra as to meet often was not necessary. The fact that she cared and had my back was a great relief and comfort.

There comes a time in the practice that the heart-centred channel starts to open up. This is a movement away from the conceptual mind. It is sometimes called *Bhakti* or devotional practice. It was matters of this nature, for example, that I could discuss with Mitra. When the emptiness of the void began to appear, along with the concomitant terror it produced, Mitra was there to offer guidance and support as well. I think sincere seekers could benefit from this kind of spiritual buddy somewhere along their journey, and apparently Buddha concurs.

The following dialogue is reported in the *Upaddha Sutra* of the *Pali Canon* which involves the Buddha and his enthusiastic disciple Ananda:

> This is half of the holy life, lord: admirable friendship, admirable companionship, and admirable camaraderie.

The Buddha replies:

> Don't say that, Ananda. Don't say that.
> Admirable friendship, admirable companionship, admirable camaraderie is actually the *whole* of the holy life. When a monk has admirable people as friends, companions, and comrades, he can be expected to develop and pursue the noble eightfold path.


> You have your way. I have my way. As for the right way, the correct way, and the only way, it does not exist.
> Friedrich Nietzsche (writer and philosopher)

# Chapter 11

*But there is greater comfort in the substance of silence than in the answer to a question.*
Thomas Merton (Jesuit priest and writer)

After I got a couple of five-day silent retreats under my belt, several more things had become clear to me. Each retreat had a unique theme like "Compassion and Mindful Living," "Meditation Practice in the Modern Age," "Vipassana for Insight" or the "Mahamudra Retreat of Eternal Wisdom," and each lasted about a week or so, but a few special events could run almost two weeks. Most guests hailed from in province, though a few came from further afield including the USA.

The schedule for each day typically ran as follows:

> 7:00–8:00 a.m., Non obligatory group meditation in yurt
> 8:00–8:40 a.m., Breakfast
> 9:00–10:00 a.m. (often longer), Wally's Dharma talk
> The rest of morning reserved for meditation and a private interview with Wally.
> 12:00 a.m., Lunch (or perhaps later if private interviews ran too long)
> All meals were silent, and Wally never attended a single one, though a monk was often present to lead us in prayer or blessing.

After lunch, everybody had karma yoga to do. Some chores were fixed, others, like washing dishes or scrubbing the toilet, were assigned on a rotating schedule. When the chores were completed, more individual meditation practice was encouraged until the evening meal (light soup, considered by some not to be a meal).

Sometimes there was chanting practice in late afternoon.

> 6:00 p.m., Light (soup only) dinner
> 7:30 p.m., Occassionally silent group meditation open to the public

My personal schedule closely followed the above save for the fact that I meditated in private from 6:00–7:00 a.m. and helped prepare breakfast on many retreats. I never attended "extracurricular" functions that seemed irrelevant to me like memorising Tibetan liturgical passages, reciting prayers, chanting, or attending evening group meditation.

I was too busy engaging in endless hours of meditation to concern myself with such folly. None of that identity building practice seemed particularly germane to the waking-up process. Of course, meditation was entirely relevant and happened to be proceeding nicely at this point of the game. By the end of the second retreat, my single-pointed concentration practice of whole-heartedly following the breath was deepening a bit further each day. The unruly mind, likened to a wild stallion, had been settled a bit but certainly not yet put to bridle. The slow progress indicated to me that this process of pacification, of developing a quiet mind, would likely take some time.

When I began to meditate, I was shocked to learn how active my mind really was. A ceaseless and seemingly uncontrollable stream of babbling mental chatter spontaneously bubbled up, and there was little I could do about it. Once noted, I found the situation a bit unnerving.

We are all aware that certain forms of mental illness cause the afflicted to have visual hallucinations or hear incessant voices in their heads. The startling thing here is that meditation practice revealed to me, and by wider abstraction I presume the same applies to everyone, that I was suffering symptoms similar to those indicators of mental illness described above, yet I accepted this aberrant mental behaviour as quite normal. Through the awareness fostered by silent sitting, I came to appreciate that humanity is suffering from a certain level of cognitive dissonance. How can constantly being barraged by a mental movie without intermission, a talk show where the host never takes questions, always prattles on about the past or future and never once shuts up, be deemed quite normal? Worst of all, we can't even switch stations. If our radio ever acted up in that fashion, we would undoubtedly smash the bloody thing. Without question I always considered the thoughts that spontaneously manifested in my head to be "my thoughts." Now I was becoming more uncertain of this. I seemingly could not control them in any regard. What gives here, I wondered?

Through the practice of meditation, I was learning that a steady, unbridled stream of mind chatter could be slowed a bit through focusing attention on the breath, but it could not be abated entirely. Samatha was certainly something I had to work at, and I wouldn't say that it was fun or relaxing.

The good news was that at this juncture I could manage to meditate a full hour in one sitting and not find it the most dreadful thing imaginable. It was getting a bit easier to do, but still I wondered how meditation was prescribed as a stress reducer by health practitioners and life coaches around the globe when it seemed to produce the thing they promised it would alleviate. "Had they actually tried the frickin thing out for themselves?" I wondered.

At this point, focus on the breath could be maintained for many seconds, perhaps even a minute or more without getting lost in some mindless narrative. If the mind did begin to wander, attention was simply placed back on the breath when this loss of concentration was noticed.

Additionally, I made sure to keep my eyes softly focused on a point on the floor about four feet in front of me with the eyes neither too widely opened nor too closely shut per Lama's instructions. Also, I checked in with my hands from time to time. Over the weeks they had become ever more clenched due to anxiety. I made a point to relax them periodically. As weeks of meditation grew into months, my hands would eventually come to be habitually clenched in a panicked death grip of sorts. I don't aim to alarm you unnecessarily. This reaction to meditation is rather atypical.

I also developed prolonged headaches. This kind of malady was a result of intense concentration and was not unknown to me. Whenever great concentration was required, like driving through rush hour, or learning a new, complicated martial art *kata* (routine), invariably headaches arose. Headaches also probably arose in part due to the neurological impact concentrative sitting had on my wetware. Wally claimed prolonged practice could impact the structure of the brain, and I concur.

As I was a novice meditator, I found some of Wally's basic tips and pointers regarding this skill to be quite useful. However, I came to feel his words lacked a certain depth and vitality that I would have welcomed, as well as the wisdom that comes from one who knows through direct personal experience. But his preliminary basic pointers common to most Buddhist sects and meditation traditions were helpful enough.

For example, Wally pointed out how unsettled and unruly the mind truly is and promoted mindfulness and good meditation practice as a powerful antidote to this malady. It was the particulars steeped in a quaint and obscure style of delivery that I found often so inaccessible. His patois seemed about as old, staid and decrepit as the mouldering Tibetan relics strewn around the yurt's interior. Often his absolutist statements seemed more akin to articles of faith than a practical guide to awakening. I sensed agenda in his teachings or pointers. Much of it seemed designed to gain converts and, thus, further the power, prestige and membership level of his Kagyu lineage.

I recall Wally made a point of telling us we must prostrate ourselves in a bow towards him when he entered the yurt but not to make too much of an issue out of this act as it was simply a devotional bow meant to recognize the Buddha within us all. We weren't supplicating ourselves to him per se. I didn't quite buy that. The guy was clearly getting off on the adulation. I never did once prostrate myself to him. I figured that when that dude started bowing in my direction when I entered a room, I would then reciprocate in kind.

At one time, I used to engage in what I consider to be a truly mutually respectful bowing practice. I knew the real McCoy when I saw it. That was when my Japanese sword master, Watanabe Sensei, entered the room. That kind of deep respect is unmistakable. It was devoid of ego or hubris on both our parts.

The Tibetan practice felt more like a subservient relationship was being cultivated, one based on authority and a position of power. I prefer to keep Buddha's statement close to heart, "Be islands unto yourselves, refuges unto yourselves. Seek no external refuge..."

In other words, seek no authority outside yourself.

> Only that which is always with you can be said to be your self and if you look closely and simply at experience, only awareness is always "with you."
> Rupert Spira (non-dual teacher)

# Chapter 12

*The voice of beauty speaks softly; it creeps only into the most fully awakened souls.*
   Friedrich Nietzsche (philosopher)

Through the handful of useful pointers Wally provided, plus the revealing material I kept coming across on the Internet, as well as through my own growing direct experience of stilling the mind, I can report that several weeks into this enterprise I was starting to gain some small insight into things as they really were. For example, the Buddha's fundamental tenet had become quite clear to me, not as a point of speculation but simply as the plain honest truth.

The Buddha pointed out that life was inherently unsatisfying, but the good news was that there was a way out of this miserable situation. This, he explained, came by way of understanding "The Four Noble Truths" and then following "The Eightfold Path.". More to follow on this topic later. It was at this juncture that Wally introduced a new kind of meditation. This was walking meditation, and I took to it like a boar does to a new wallow. It was a nice change of pace to say the least.

This walking meditation was an enjoyable new practice, which is a high compliment given how dreadfully taxing meditation could be. Keep in mind, "enjoyable" is still a rather relative term. It did certainly break up the monotony of just sitting all day. The mechanics of this new practice, like its predecessor, were quite simple.

Fundamentally, it involved walking a short distance, say forty to fifty feet or so, and noting each foot fall very mindfully. At least that was the stripped-down version I employed. Originally, Wally suggested we keep a slow plodding pace while noting the rising, then the momentary suspension of the foot in mid-air and finally the falling in turn, but I simplified and sped things up a bit. Why not get some exercise out of it I figured. The effect was the same regardless of pace. It was merely another form of meditation that employed an object of concentration.

I particularly enjoyed the bit in the walking meditation when I had to turn around and head back in the opposite direction. I found the three step pivot required to accomplish this adjustment very enjoyable. Those short readjusting steps were often the highlight of the day. To carefully and with great determination note each footfall again and again was pretty boring just like seated meditation was, but to break the monotony with a little pirouette which shook the routine up, if only for an instant, was relatively speaking, a helluva lot of fun. And they say serious seekers don't know how to live it up!

Practically speaking, this form of meditation proved quite rewarding to me. My chattering monkey mind seemed to become more pacified while walking than when I just sat in solitude. It was undeniable that this practice was having tangible results for it was during just one such walk, fairly early on, that a most amazing experience occurred.

What unfolded was an example of the renowned and coveted *direct experience* I so longed to have. The profound insight that direct experience affords us is a rather rare occurrence and gets to the heart of the matter. These spiritual "aha" moments are the occasions in our practice when great truths are revealed by some capacity outside of our conceptual way of regarding reality. We "see" something that is unmistakably "just so." Whatever is revealed to us in this experience of direct knowing cuts through the illusory nature of the dream state.

So there I was out in the fresh air doing a mid-morning walk when I began to slowly recognize the words that came from the still, small voice of wisdom that rarely made its presence known to me.

It first quietly pointed out, "Take note, this is what quietude is." I barely paid it any notice. I took several more steps and again it piped up, "Hey, DJ, this is what silence is like, pay attention." I paused for an instant then dismissed any significance those words may have held and moved on. But it was insistent. In a more demanding manner the third time it finally got my full attention. "PAY ATTENTION; this is what TRUE SILENCE is!" And, by God, it most assuredly was. Boy, oh boy, did I ever get the message this time around.

## Chapter 12

I was quite taken aback by nothing more fantastic than a simple gap. I gasped in amazement, a gap in the eternal, infernal monologue. This was a kind of quiescence or stillness I had never experienced before. It was such a small thing, but when newly apprehended, it can feel truly revelatory. And to think, I was so unaware, so lost in the incessant mutterings of my mind, so trapped in egoic identification that something seemingly outside of my normal self had to pipe up and point this little pause out to "me" three times in a row before I finally got it.

This occasion was quite likely the first time in my life that I had ever been made aware of a momentary gap in the chattering monkey mind during normal waking reality. It was not much of a gap, mind you, but a gap nonetheless. There it was—*true silence*. This was NOT the kind of quietude ear plugs or a sensory deprivation tank can bring on. That was just a trivial muffling of background noise. No, this was rather the purest silence you will ever experience, the silence born out of a gap, the gap between you and the ineffable.

How marvellous. Eureka, this was the fabled *pregnant pause* long sought after by many but apparently rarely found. "Now we are starting to cook with gas," I thought.

I can assure you that from that moment on meditation became a whole lot easier to do. Soon the headaches became less pronounced and frequent. Slowly but surely the frequency and duration of the gaps increased. Though it would take some time, meditation eventually went from annoying to enjoying, and I mark this moment as the start of that trend.

It was around this juncture, too, that I also experienced a delightful little interlude featuring a friendly mouse. One day, I was meditating quite deeply in *zazen* on my concrete floor when some subtle point of awareness slowly drew me out of my one-pointed concentration. My eyes opened widely, and my gaze fell upon my left foot. Nothing really registered for some seconds. I continued to peer at my left foot, and out of the depths of consciousness a concept formed in my mind, "Oh look…there is a mouse dancing on a foot." And it was true. There really was a mouse doing a little jig on my foot. He seemed pleased with himself. Why not? So he danced some more.

As I came to my senses, there was a moment of recognition. I didn't flinch or move a muscle, but in my mind a thought welled up and solidified—"Shit, there is a damn mouse on my foot." That was all it took to solidify ego into a "self" and "other" which in turn ended the little party. No more fun and games. We have to get serious again here. I am a human, DJ; you are a mouse, vermin. So I went "Ah!" The mouse went "Ah," and off the little creature scampered. That is how emptiness can come to no longer dance.

> There is only the watching of this dance of life. No watcher. The mind is clear, empty space. The heart is connected to all that it sees. The within is the without.
> Scott Kiloby (non-dual teacher)

*A Fleeting Improvised Man Awakens*

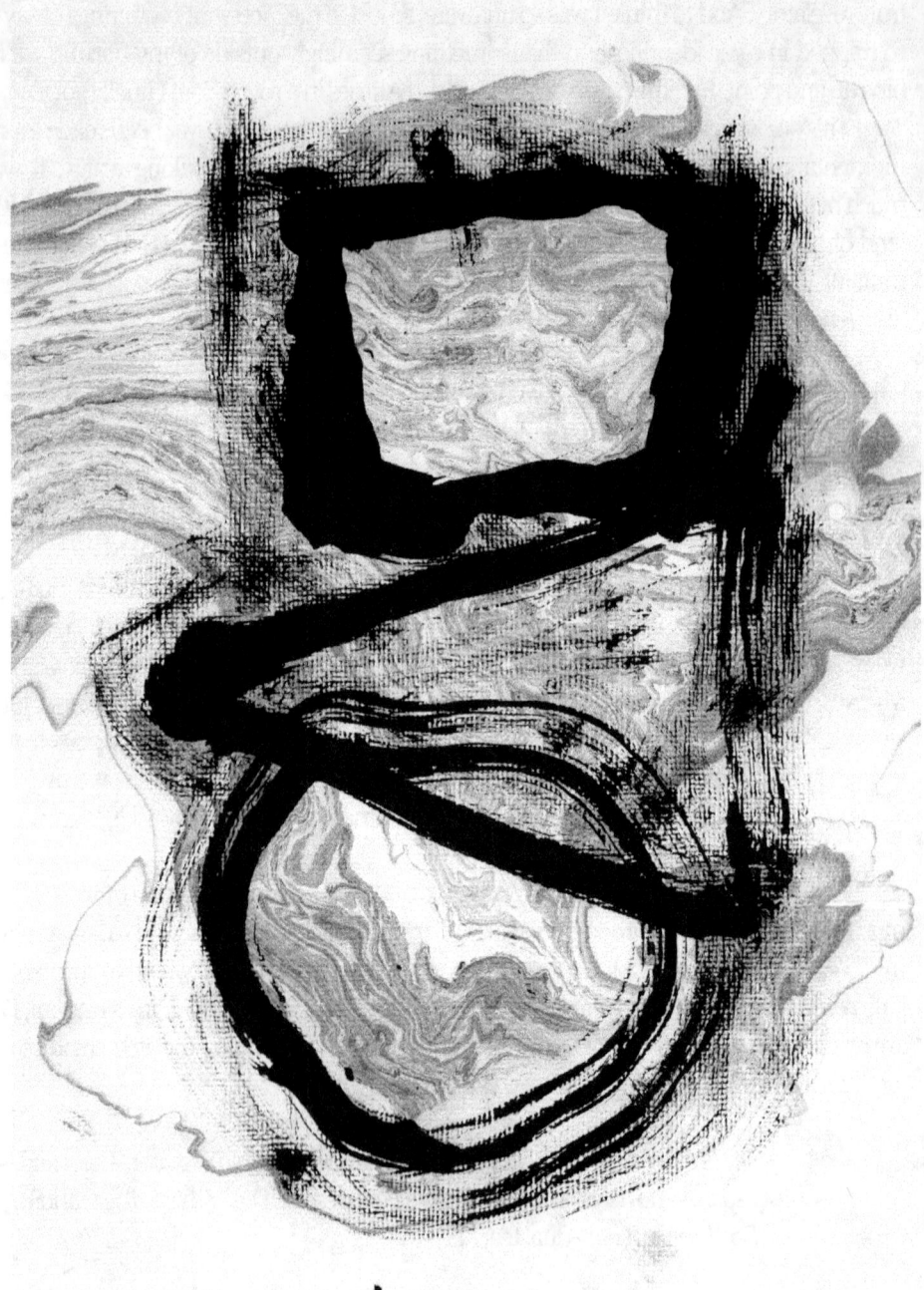

# Chapter 13

*Soon you will be ashes or bones. A mere name at most and even that is just a sound, an echo. The things we want in life are empty, stale, and trivial.*
   Marcus Aurelius (Stoic philosopher and Roman emperor)

   After the second five-day retreat concluded, I was called away from the hermitage to spend a few weeks helping a local woman do a landscaping project.
   I still managed to meditate some six hours or so a day during this period, without fail. When this term was almost over, I decided to check in with my dear, old friend "Mother Aya,"

the South American plant medicine that proved so psychologically abrogative when it came to negative emotional issues and detrimental mental patterns.

If you have read the first book, you will recall how I, or more exactly SWIM (it was SWIM all along I tell you!), employed this entheogen extensively during the early phases of the spiritual quest. Besides being the catalyst for tremendously positive and effective psychological healing, it also gave me glimpses of an ineffable mystery I could have scarcely imagined.

At this point, I felt little need to employ it as a spiritual tool. Still, I was most curious to see how my psyche would respond while under the influence of this powerful entheogen given I had a full five weeks of sustained meditation practice under my belt. As curiosity always got the better of me, I once again drank deeply from the chalice of bitter brew and humbly prostrated myself before *Pachamama*. As was often her wont, she again showed me something quite amazing and a bit disturbing as well. Those two suckers often went hand in hand when this wise teacher stood at the head of the class. She was often a stern headmistress but never cruel.

It was during the later portion of the Ayahuasca journey, the segment where I was usually most settled and at ease, that a *hohlraum*, German for "hollow room" or "empty space," appeared. It was an odd experience and was clearly informed by my recent spate of prolonged meditation practice.

In a sense, nothing strange at all was going on since what's the big deal…it's only an empty space that has appeared, right? Yeah, but surely not as you imagine. It's frickin E-M-P-T-Y!

Emptiness can be quite unsettling when you first bump into it. With my eyes wide open, I could see everything was now still and seemingly unchanging. Nothing had been physically altered in the bedroom I was in, but it now felt for all the world like material reality was rendered somehow insubstantial and hollow. As I said, that predicament, my friends, can be very unsettling at first. This feeling grew inexorably more uncomfortable and creepy as time, or more exactly the absence of time, didn't go by.

This is the reaction the ego undergoes when it is first confronted by sustained quietude. This stillness often unhinges us when first experienced, especially if it comes unannounced or if we have done nothing to prepare for it in advance. But I am not sure you can ever be totally prepared for this kind of experience even if acting from a position of great alacrity, at least not when it happens for the very first time. Some may not be unnerved, who knows, but I sure was.

Few thoughts arose, but several feelings persisted such as wonderment, clarity and lucidity. Everything in the room appeared sharply defined, crisp and clean, almost clinically sterile. I looked at various items strewn about the room as if they were curios displayed in a museum. They felt "dead" and without context. The overall ambience of this hohlraum, which was both full of objects to the eye yet at the same time seemingly stripped of content and essence, was a space devoid of color and life. It was a compartment marked by washed out sepia tones and apparent great age. It felt like everything was in stasis and had sat in this perfectly sanitized environment for an eternity in a space seemingly never once glimpsed by human eyes, since it felt like I was the only one in existence, and I certainly had never laid eyes upon such a hohlraum before! Why describe this lifeless space, this necropolis, as empty you may well ask?

Well, that was the part that disturbed me the most. The room seemed to lack a sense of content. The objects in it seemed immaterial. There was a sensed transparency of things though I could clearly discern form and function as always like, for example, a night table which sat in front of me, a chair to my right, and a painting hung on the wall. Yet each object lacked a certain sense of materiality and solidity. Objective reality seemed both genuine and illusory at the same time. To suddenly come to perceive the world in this way was an eminently weird thing to behold.

My mind was disconcertingly quiet and still too. Chatter was at a minimum. There was little inclination to objectify or reify reality. Thoughts at this moment neither conjured up a past nor moved to a future. There was just a sense of me, alone in this awe-full room. And this hohlraum seemed like it was the only thing that existed, had ever existed, and yet simultaneously didn't exist, and furthermore, it felt like I had been ensconced here for an extremely long time indeed. Yet at the same time it felt like I had just been parachuted down into this environment like a Special Forces officer would be inserted into the primordial Vietnamese jungle for his or her first mission. This is the kind of paradox non-duality can engender.

As the experience progressed, a sense of forlorn hopelessness and dread grew. How terrible to be alone in a world that was about as material as a transparent soap bubble. It was like the vacuum of space had sucked all the life out of the place. Nothing was going on, and this, clearly, was a disturbing predicament. In hindsight, what was transpiring was something akin to a state of being known as *bare witnessing*, which I later came to intimately know through my continuing meditation practice, as well as a slight impression of *pure beingness* or *emptiness* that would follow later as well.

In this trip, Ayahuasca caused a similar kind of neutral, detached, disengaged, almost disassociated witnessing to occur as is the case with classical meditative bare witnessing, but unfortunately too much of my ego remained in the picture to make it a pleasant experience. Too much of "the self" persisted, unlike what was to follow later, so in this case anxiety levels were really elevated. When *no-self* eventually prevails, there is no problem.

My experience seemed a bit reminiscent with the one that befell Suzanne Segal back in 1982. To give you a little background, this paradigm shifting event began for this American while she was about to board a bus in Paris. Segal experienced a sudden shift in her consciousness which was documented in her book, *Collision with the Infinite*.

In the book she described the first stage of her experience as "witnessing," since she was aware of herself and objective reality but also critically detached from it. This unpleasant situation caused great anxiety and fear to arise on the spot and for much of the remainder of her life as well.

I can well imagine Segal's angst since this kind of awakening experience was novel and caught her entirely off guard. In my situation, the sense of detachment did not provoke such an extreme reaction, probably in part due to my previous experiences with Ayahuasca and meditation. Her experience, as described in her book, seems horrific; an excerpt follows:

> The moment the eyes opened the next morning, the mind exploded in worry. Is this insanity? Pscyhosis? Schizophrenia? Is this what people call a nervous breakdown? Depression? What happened? And would it ever stop? ...The mind was in agony as it tried valiantly to make sense of something it could never comprehend, and the body responded to the anguish of the mind by locking itself into survival mode, adrenaline pumping, senses fine-tuned, finding and responding to the threat of annihilation in every moment. (p. 49)

Segal consulted mental health specialists specifically regarding the depersonalized state and dissociative disorders in general but decided that these kinds of syndromes were a poor explanation when it came to describing her own problem.

Segal had a background in the practice of yoga, so she wondered whether the terrible erosion of self could be the first step in a positive spiritual journey but dismissed it due to the following logic:

> The thought did arise that perhaps this experience of witnessing was the state of Cosmic Consciousness Maharishi had described long before as the first stage of awakened awareness. But the mind instantly discarded this possibility because it seemed impossible that the hell realm I was inhabiting could have anything to do with Cosmic Consciousness. (p. 49)

It came to pass that Segal's original conclusion was misguided. Her account of eventual spiritual awakening where the nihilism of no-self was replaced with the fullness of the unity experience makes for fascinating reading.

My experience was of a reality primarily drained of its colour, of life stripped of its story. It was certainly perplexing and very uncomfortable, but it did not unhinge me like it did Segal. If it had persisted, who knows?

On a positive note, I concluded that meditation was having such a strong effect on me that it seemed capable of altering the Ayahuasca experience in some pronounced regard. This impartial witnessing episode was like nothing I had experienced previously while taking any kind of mind-altering drug. So I got my answer. I concluded meditation was having an actual quantifiable effect on me.

I should add though that this kind of fleeting, state bound, drug-induced experience was merely an appetizer to the main course. Still, I don't consider it something to be entirely trivialized. The few occasions when my ego became sufficiently eroded to allow a momentary glimpse beyond the veil of illusion were always seen as singular experiences and something to be appreciated. But I tried not to get into the habit of overemphasizing them. To attempt to cling to or covet such transitory experiences merely exacerbated the waking-up process.

> What a liberation to realize that the "voice in my head" is not who I am.
> "Who am I, then?" The one who sees that.
> Eckhart Tolle (spiritual teacher)

# Chapter 14

*Who cares about an enlightened phantom? Only the other phantoms. It always needs a community of ignorant ideas and one of them maybe is a master-ignorant. The master of ignorance! There are no masters of knowledge. How can there be a master of knowledge? How can there be a master of Heart? You can only be a master of shit.*

    Karl Renz (spiritual teacher)

      After the three-week break, I returned to the hermitage rejuvenated and eager to discover what kind of spiritual revelation further long-term meditation would reveal.

## A Fleeting Improvised Man Awakens

I was taking in the view of the pond, which by this season resembled a muddy crater in the ground due to the late summer heat, while listening to a particularly noisy raven hidden somewhere amongst the nearby fir tree tops, when Bhikhu Fatty paid me a rare visit.

We talked of Fatty's time spent at Plum village, the French monastic centre headed up by Vietnamese Buddhist master, Thich Nhat Hanh. His association with a Toronto contemplative centre also came up. Though still a relatively young man, he had been occupied with this gig for most of his adult life. At times he seemed a bit weary of it all but appeared resigned to his fate. He asked me if I could water the few spindly tomato plants he was tending to in the greenhouse since he was off to a "street retreat" for a week.

This, he explained, was a Buddhist organized affair originally conceived of in the USA. It was designed to provide paying participants the opportunity to practice the dharma out on the mean streets of a large metropolitan centre. One was expected to get by much in the same manner as the homeless did every day sans the flowing robes, spiritual teachings and compassion for all sentient beings rhetoric.

Apparently, these hardy aspirants would be taking meals at the local soup kitchen and sleeping rough in the urban jungle. Begging in the tradition Buddha favoured would also be part of their routine. I recognized the opportunity for growth such challenging situations afford us. Furthermore, I was really intrigued given my penchant for practicing wilderness survival skills. Just think of it, *Survivormonk* cast into the fray with only his mala, begging bowl, robes and the dharma to ensure his survival. Now that is an interesting premise for a new reality TV show, don't you think? I promised to look after Fatty's plants, and he was off. Tomorrow, the next retreat would begin for me. I was anticipating its arrival for it would be the first one that Wally did not facilitate.

This retreat would be presided over by a recently transplanted Tibetan national, whom I'll refer to as Lama "Maybe One" since he is the same fella I posed the question to of, "How many enlightened beings have you actually met?" Apparently, this thirty-something Rinpoche was a well-studied Buddhist scholar hailing from a rare lineage. I relished the occasion to take in what I hoped would be a profound sharing from a "real live Tibetan master." As things turned out, this "real" Tibetan Lama inspired me less than Wally did.

I was beginning to detect a pattern here. These guys seemed to lack authentic wisdom so replaced their paucity of direct experience and insight with formalized teachings they had acquired from other equally unenlightened lamas or learned rote from their dusty old scriptures. I struggled to come to terms with this realization, and of course a certain level of disenchantment was growing. How was this situation tenable? How could these guys present themselves as authority figures on the fine art of waking up yet still be asleep at the wheel themselves? Well, there's your answer, and she responds to the name of Maya. It looked like my hopes had been rather misplaced.

"Fuck it," I thought. Buddha by his own example assured us enlightenment was indeed a reality, and I for one would settle for nothing less. These guys could go to hell with all their moral dictums, religious philosophizing and "compassion for all sentient beings" crap. If you think I am being too harsh, consider this case in point.

I had a young friend who lived for a time in the suburban house of a Tibetan Lama and his Canadian-born wife and kids. I was surprised to learn firsthand from my friend that this Lama was very abusive, both physically and mentally, towards his wife and children yet had on occasion taught at the very same hermitage I now resided in. Guess what his public message was? The same old crap...*compassion for all sentient beings and the merit in accumulating bodhicitta through good works and diligent practice*. What a sham! Apparently, Wally and his wife use to socialise with this creep. Eventually this guy's marriage disintegrated. Here is a tip: If you wanna know what a spiritual master's true colors are, just ask his wife and children. They'll tell you!

Still I had hopes, though more reserved, that further retreats might offer some kind of spiritual insight into the waking-up process. I can report though that I recall nothing relevant was gleaned from the five-day retreat I was about to spend with Lama Maybe One.

At retreat's end, Lama Maybe One performed some kind of prolonged ritual, known as *Chod*, which featured lots of noisy chanting, banging of gongs and drums, and burning of sacred objects. The performance was, just as the old Bard put it, "full of sound and fury" but in my estimation surely "signifying nothing." In a fashion reminiscent of quaint colonial regimental parade drills of yesteryear, Tibetan Buddhism was rife with pomp and circumstance. What this had to do with awakening was beyond me.

It was once put to me by one well versed in all things Tibetan, that this kind of animated ostentatious display, so endemic of Tibetan Buddhist tradition, was just as much about "Tibetanism" as it was about Buddhism proper. In fact *Bon*, the pre-Buddhist shamanic religious tradition, actually informs a significant portion of modern day Tibetan Buddhism. This fact shocked me. What did animism, superstition, fortune telling, casting spells, tantric sex and shamanism, versus what the Buddha taught, have in common? Nothing.

This fact provided another reason to grow ever more disenchanted. Apparently, the form of Buddhism that Tibet engineered from centuries past was severely adulterated with other influences besides the true dharma of Buddha. Yet it seemed that the masses could care less. The greater the level of exoticism these guys served up, the better. The spiritual ego seems enamoured by such spectacle. My private interviews with Lama Wally weren't any more rewarding either.

The time available was limited to only several minutes per day as all participants were obliged to shuffle through each morning. I held this brief daily interview session with little regard. The plain, honest fact was Wally was not a wise or particularly perceptive man, at least not as far as dharma transmission went. Consequently, he had few illuminating words of wisdom to offer me. Worse still, the advice he did proffer from time to time was often counterproductive or just plain bad.

For example, I would tell Wally meditation gave me headaches and caused me to have anxiety. He said it was "not supposed to be this way. It should be a pleasant, joyful experience," he assured me. But it wasn't. Therefore, he concluded that I must be doing it wrong. But in point of fact, that was not the case at all. For example, I know that my *satguru*, which means primary root teacher, whom I later drew much inspiration from, suffered headaches during his own journey. It is actually a commonly reported phenomenon among those folks actually awakening.

But no, since I was "doing it wrong," Wally would have me "argue with reality" and meditate in some other fashion. This was very misguided advice. In point of fact, a good definition of enlightened behaviour is when one no longer argues with the way things actually are. You try to pull a fast one on reality, and you'll always end up on the short end of the stick.

> Yesterday is dead, tomorrow hasn't arrived yet. I have just one day and I'm going to be happy in it.
> Groucho Marx (comedian)

# Chapter 15

*Life's a piece of shit, when you look at it. Life's a laugh and death's a joke, it's true. You'll see it's all a show, keep 'em laughin as you go. Just remember that the last laugh is on you.*
Monty Python (comedy troop)

Wally held only one Mahamudra (Sanskrit for great seal or symbol...in other words the fast track to enlightenment) retreat each season, and you had to earn the right to attend it by participating in several other shorter retreats. This invitation-only affair seemed to be intended for advanced students only. Besides the die-hard retreatants drawn from far and wide, some lucky locals would be invited to attend as well. One of them included *moi*. I was pleased.

It was during this special event that I first became aware of Mitra, though I only glimpsed her from afar. A two-week retreat required quite a commitment, so there was a heightened sense of importance about this affair.

Bhikhu Ananda arrived a few days in advance on one of his biannual visits. He was the highest ranking resident monk in the parent operation serving out of the USA. Furthermore, he was also a close friend to Wally and had done much to get the centre off the ground in the early days. He arrived early to ensure everything was copacetic. One cheery afternoon, he appeared at the door of my humble abode to introduce himself.

I was pleased to make Ananda's acquaintance. His effort at being sociable was a welcomed departure from the aloof, disinterested stance Wally maintained towards me.

Apparently, Monk Ananda was last employed as an accountant, though he was now some years retired. After reading his spiritual biography posted on the centre's website, it was clear that the guy had devoted a great deal of time and energy towards spiritual refinement. He knew a lot about Tibetan Buddhism and other forms of spirituality as well, and as I grew to better know him, it became clearer to me that it was important to him that you were aware of his spiritual bona fides and accolades.

For certain, Monk Ananda was an adept and shrewd game player, a clever and ambitious guy who had learned in due time how to ascend the ladders of spiritual authority and in turn used the prestige this office afforded him to gain certain advantages. Over time, I grew ever more wary of this man. I never quite trusted him. Others who knew him in the community confided to me that they regarded him in a similar manner.

Be that as it may, this initial encounter provided a fine opportunity to dialogue with someone of elevated spiritual authority, and hopefully elevated wisdom too. Expressly I told him that my meditation practice was improving but then asked him "to what end? Where was it heading? What was the goal?" I inquired. Nobody had filled me in on what I regarded to be a relevant piece of the puzzle.

Monk Ananda told me that "we should not be concerned with results." Goals were just another form of attachment, and Buddha had warned us against such defilements. But I was a goal-oriented guy, I protested. I valued results. Furthermore, I lacked much of a conceptual background to draw upon. "Sure I could become a great meditator but to what end?" I pressed again. "What is this whole Buddhist thing fundamentally pointing to? How does it lead us to discover the ultimate nature of reality?"

He replied:

> Well, I won't address all of that now, DJ, but I guess I can share one important bit of wisdom with you…speaking for myself, I might say that I don't think I actually exist. Perhaps that can serve as a key point of inquiry for now.

"You don't think you exist you say…hmmmm…seriously?" was the first thought that popped into my head as I went over in my mind again what I thought I heard this guy just say.

# Chapter 15

Once I confirmed to my satisfaction that he actually said what he did, I silently concluded—"Bollocks!" After a moment of further reflection came, "Well I'll be damned. I have heard many an asinine statement in my day, but that little gem pretty much takes the cake…what nonsense."

Without a doubt Ananda's proclamation was the single most ridiculous statement ever uttered in my presence for it simply flew in the face of reality. I wanted to shake some sense into this jester and say:

> Dude, get a grip will ya. You are sitting right in front of me; surely you are aware of this fact. If you are not jibber jabbering to me presently, then who the heck is doing so…?

But good manners prevailed, so I refrained from engaging him further on the topic.

Besides, deep deep down in my gut I knew very well this guy existed…just as it was evident so did I. It was *irrefutable*. If someone has the temerity to say "I don't exist," then they bloody well must in order to even utter such a piece of nonsense, right? So that was that. This guy was obviously either playing head games with me or else was simply full of crap. "That guy is best to be avoided," I concluded. My lord, "didn't exist," what was he thinking? He must take me for an imbecile.

Yet in an astounding turn around, I came to discover that Monk Ananda wasn't full of crap at all. In fact, he was right on the money. That was a shocker. What I was about to discover would put into question everything I assumed to be true. The resulting realization would become the foundation of a self-inquiry practice that would sustain itself until the end of my journey. The following anecdote describes how I came to stumble across one of the most incredible revelations that can ever befall a person.

The pivotal event began the next day during a break in my meditation when I decided to investigate all of this nonsense about "non-existence of self" directly. To accomplish this I understood that I needed to discover *who or what I was*. Before I could pose that question, something in me realized that this was a very serious endeavour to undertake. Somehow I intuited that this was not a trivial question to be brokered lightly. So I summoned the greatest sincerity I could muster, and with my eyes starting to mist up I threw the question, "Who or what am I?" out into the ether and waited for a response.

The question arose in the simplest most direct manner imaginable. I merely implored myself, or was it the cosmos, to tell me, "Really. I mean really, really, REALLY—who or what am I?"

Nothing. Nada. No answer arose at all. Silence. "Well…how terribly odd," I thought. So I tried again by being more specific.

"Okay then, how about a less broad question…so let me see, Oh, I know—am I my body?"

"Nope," came the immediate realization. Instantly I could see that whatever I was, I had nothing to do with flesh and blood. It was quite simply that obvious. I was not my body. Sure I "had a body," but I needed to discover who possessed it. Who was t*hat* guy?

Next came, "Was I my thoughts?"

Nope, not those either. I didn't need time to conceptually figure all this out. It was just a matter of fact that I instantly recognized that my thoughts were not me. Yes, I had thoughts, but again, who was the owner of them? Perhaps this is what happens when you get sincere and real quiet for a moment: great Truths are revealed. "So if I wasn't my body or my thoughts, then what was left? Who or what am I?" I asked once more. But again no answer was forthcoming. It was the damndest thing.

"Was I my..." but what else remained to be considered? I pushed on as best I might, but the obvious conclusion was beginning to disturb me greatly.

"Was I my job?" No that was only a title. "Maybe I am a crazy-ass adventurer?" No. The fact was that I had plenty of adventures during my travels, but thrill-seeking did not define who or what I was. What was I then? Every question resulted in the same lack of resolution. I remember thinking how crazy this was. I again tried a slightly different tact.

"Who was the one who claimed to have a body? Who was the possessor?" Again this elicited nothing. How could this be? How could I not know who or what I was? This was weird. It should be quite obvious and abundantly clear, in fact, in the same way that I instantly could tell you what the colour of my shoes are or what my favourite pizza topping is. This should be the most recognizable thing in the world. I should be able to tell myself (and yet another conundrum, who is this "I" that would be telling the "myself"...were there two entities here?) just who or what I am in less time than it would take for me to slice a tatami roll mat in half with my Japanese katana sword, yet this clearly was not the case.

In fact, all I could see was what I wasn't. If I wasn't willing to lie to myself and make up a little story, then I could not in any way affirm or ascribe any plausible positive qualities to myself. Yet clearly I existed. "So what gives then?" I kept asking myself. My inability to resolve this quandary led me to conclude that I must be doing the inquiry incorrectly.

I decided to let the matter rest. The next day I tried again and got the same result. I was more perplexed than ever but still held out hope I was missing something. But that is the point—I simply wasn't.

When Bhikhu Ananda put it to me that he didn't "think" he existed he hedged his bet a little. It is not a matter of "THINKING" or belief. I can categorically state for the record that I "KNOW" that *I don't exist*. Or at least not in the way I had previously presumed that I did. It is not a matter of speculation for me. The non-existence of a separate self is entirely apparent to anyone who cares to sincerely investigate the matter. Of course, this statement is beyond belief, so you'll just have to go and check it out for yourself.

If you care/dare to reach the same conclusion, then with all of your heart simply posit the same question and see what you come up with. Who or what are you REALLY? So hats off to Ananda. What a wonderful, terrible revelation he turned me on to. With further investigation over the months to come, I came to see with one hundred percent certitude that the perception of self is all smoke and mirrors. Buddha elaborates with his Anattalakkhana Sutra. This discourse on the not-self characteristic elegantly describes what I learned:

> Thus, monks, anybody whatsoever—past, future, or present; internal or external; blatant or subtle; common or sublime; far or near; everybody—is to be seen as it actually is with right discernment as: This is not mine. This is not myself. This is not what I am.
>
> Any feeling whatsoever—past, future, or present; internal or external; blatant or subtle; common or sublime; far or near; every feeling—is to be seen as it actually is with right discernment as: This is not mine. This is not my self. This is not what I am.
>
> Any perception whatsoever—past, future, or present; internal or external; blatant or subtle; common or sublime; far or near; every perception—is to be seen as it actually is with right discernment as: This is not mine. This is not myself. This is not what I am.
>
> Any mental processes whatsoever—past, future, or present; internal or external; blatant or subtle; common or sublime; far or near; all mental processes—are to be seen as they actually are with right discernment as: This is not mine. This is not myself. This is not what I am.
>
> Any consciousness whatsoever—past, future, or present; internal or external; blatant or subtle; common or sublime; far or near; every consciousness—is to be seen as it actually is with right discernment as: This is not mine. This is not myself. This is not what I am.

And that was where Buddha left it hanging. Absolute negation. Self was not found in any of those five characteristics we presume to locate ourselves in. He never went on to point out where self actually resided. He left us dangling. He simply pointed out that if one cares to investigate reality as it truly is, "self" is not locatable anywhere.

I was once told by someone who should have known better that Buddha really meant that the sum of the parts constituted the whole. "Sure self can't be found in each disparate constituent part or faculty," this ignorant fellow conceded, but then went on to elaborate that "Buddha meant that if we take all five of the factors together as a whole," one surely could then find a *self*.

The problem with that faulty bit of critical thinking is that Buddha never stated nor implied any such supposition. Furthermore, all that that foolish man had to do was check in with reality itself; he, too, would have directly discovered *anatta*, Not-self. But he was a philosopher schooled by the Jesuits, so he knew better. "Never let reality get in the way of a really, really good yarn," these guys always seem to maintain.

The afternoon before the special Mahamudra retreat began, Wally handed out the manual which covered most of the material he would speak about. I must admit a sense of growing anticipation had begun to grip me. I was finally going to get to hang out with the *big kids*. It was to be an intensive two weeks of silence, something I had not experienced yet. I relished the chance to sit with seasoned meditators and be exposed to the so-called, *fast track to enlightenment*. One thing though greatly disturbed me. The course book warned the student not to share the information contained in its pages with anybody. It was to be a *secret teaching*. I was appalled. If something wasn't open for any and all to consider, I wanted no part of it. The caution that was given smacked of spiritual elitism. This new information really gave me pause. Should I even attend?

The situation, though, quite quickly resolved itself. The morning of the retreat, Wally informed me that I would not be permitted to attend Mahamudra. I would, however, be invited to take all meals and have private interviews with him. In addition, Monk Ananda would be my new mentor for the duration of the retreat, but there was to be no Mahamudra, no "secret teachings" for poor old DJ☹.

I was more than slightly put-off by this turn of affairs. Later, I discovered that it was Ananda who put the bug in Wally's ear. Bhikhu Ananda considered me to be too much of a spiritual green horn, which explained the rescinded invitation. In retrospect, it was the best thing that could have befallen me. I had almost two weeks of uninterrupted, hardcore meditation ahead of me. Perfect, just what the Buddha ordered. And as an aside, I can report that the next year when I did get to attend Mahamudra, I found it highly disappointing.

Ananda told Wally that I needed to perfect greater one-pointed concentration so advised more samatha meditation was in order. "I'll show that little prick," I thought. I was determined to become the best damn concentration meditator possible. I would continue to pour my heart and soul into the endeavour.

I found getting very still and quiet to be a revolutionary act, much like telling the truth is. The next two weeks would pry me farther away from delusion than ever before, to the breaking point and beyond in fact. I wanted nothing more than to go deeply down the rabbit hole, but one should be careful what they wish for, shouldn't one?

> Why are you unhappy? Because 99.9 percent of everything you do is for yourself—and there isn't one.
> Wei Wu Wei (writer)

# Chapter 16

*And this "knowing" is our self, aware presence. In other words, all that is ever experienced is our self knowing itself, awareness aware of awareness.*

Rupert Spira (non-duality teacher)

  I am the kind of guy who requires nine hours of sleep to feel well-rested and refreshed in the morning, so my schedule was simple. Nine hours of sleep left me fifteen hours per day in which to meditate and do my chores. Ten hours of that time was taken up by meditation. In the five hours that remained, some of it was spent doing work, some on internet research. No other distractions were entertained. Long gone was the inclination to listen to the radio, take in a podcast or watch a movie for pleasure. I had well and truly reoriented my whole life to serve one purpose and one purpose only—*waking the fuck up!*

I previously reported on the rare "gapping out" phenomenon that occurred while I meditated. These gaps in thoughts continued to appear, but they were sporadic and of short duration, perhaps a second or less it seemed. This "pause," while jolting, lacked any discernable qualities. More interesting still was another phenomenon that was beginning to make its presence known.

This was something Wally termed *bare witnessing*. His recognition and labelling of this cognitive state was the most helpful comment he had offered in ages. At least he gave me a point of reference for it.

This bare witnessing or bare attention business was a bit familiar as something quite like it had occurred during that strange Ayahuasca episode I described earlier. Unlike that experience though, this time it was not a brief, one off event.

Rather, with ever deepening intensity, my outlook during meditation was becoming more like that of a dispassionate spectator watching meditation unfold while not really being engaged in the practice per se. It felt like I was one step removed from the proceedings. Oddly enough, this peculiar feeling could also be brought to bear during my daily routine if attention was placed there.

For example, I recall feeding some fresh meadow grass to a horse in its paddock and feeling entirely disengaged from the event. You see, I wasn't actually feeding grass to a horse. There was simply a silent observer watching a horse being fed. If life was being lived like the pages of a novel, then I was just reading the book of myself. I was one step removed from the doer of the deed.

To return to meditation practice proper for a moment, during this long retreat the breath was still being utilized as an object of focus which was tedious work. The long hours spent sitting made it a struggle, but the new bare witnessing effect ameliorated the drudgery a little bit. It was no longer such a pronounced personal struggle. There was much less irritation about those "damned uncontrollable thoughts" and more just a bare disengaged witnessing of whatever arose.

In the witnessing, I was *de-habituating* the tendency of the reflexive mind to claim ownership of an experience. In a dramatic way the experiencer, DJ, was uncoupled from, or ceased to so strongly identify with, any experience that arose be it immediately informed by the five senses or rather instead by thoughts of past or future arising out of the virtual realm of the mind. During these times, it was like I experienced only the unfiltered and raw, or "bare," five senses. No stories or narratives were then created about reality after the fact.

The Zen master Suzuki Roshi captured the essence of what I am pointing to here when he said:

> The air comes in and goes out like someone passing through a swinging door. If you think, "I breathe," the "I" is extra. There is no you to say "I."
>
> What we call "I" is just a swinging door, which moves when we inhale and when we exhale. It just moves; that is all.

Whereas before I might have said after long hours of sitting, "I'm getting really bored and agitated," I now believe that kind of notion was significantly disempowered. There was enough distance between the witness and the witnessed to see that what was happening was not actually personal. By shifting identification away from "me," the one having the experience, reality became more immediate and less open to interpretation.

For example, the thought might arise "It seems that the stomach is churning" rather than "I'm hungry." Or "The feeling of sleepiness is apparent" rather than "I'm exhausted." It seems that my long hours of meditation as well as continued self-inquiry practice encouraged such depersonalization. Bringing the thoughts back to the present moment, which encouraged awareness itself, was a strong tonic to my mind's enchantment. This brings up another topic which goes hand in hand with bare witnessing.

That is *mindfulness* which is the practice of paying *attention NOW!* We can appreciate how important attention is to awakening when we recall the old Zen story below:

> A student said to Master Ikkyu, "Please write something of great wisdom."
> Master Ikkyu picked up his calligraphy brush and composed one word: "Attention."
>
> The student said, "Ha, Is that all?"
>
> The master then wrote, "Attention. Attention."
>
> The student was not pleased. "That doesn't seem profound or subtle to me."
> This poor monk knew not how deep the master's wisdoms lay for in response, Master Ikyu wrote once again, "Attention. Attention. Attention."
>
> In growing frustration, the student demanded to know, "What does this word *attention* mean?"
>
> Master Ichu replied, "*Attention* means *attention*."

Mindfulness or the habit of cultivating attention is not simply a Zen practice for it is paramount to many spiritual traditions. Wally mentioned the importance of it from time to time in much the same manner Star Trek's science officer, Mr. Spock, used to bid people adieu, "Live long and prosper." But I thought the follow-up question always begged to be asked— "Fine and dandy, Spock, but how, HOW?"

Similarly, I often wished that Wally would have utilized clever means to impart to us by what manner we could actually cultivate the *attention or mindfulness* he promoted. Just being told to "be mindful" didn't cut it.

Wally's habit of throwing in a random "be mindful" or "be present," while offered with good intention one presumes, was of little practical benefit. Once I chuckled to myself when I thought, "There goes Wally again doing his best impression of the *Reminder Bird*." That was the creature whose mindless, repetitive directive island residents were supposed to heed. It originates from the pages of the utopian novel, *Island*, written by Aldous Huxley.

"Attention, attention," squawked the silly bird at the brow-beaten islanders as it autocratically sat upon its lofty perch, unaware of its inconsequential nature. This kind of reminder was ineffectual for it lacked strategy. If only Wally could have fleshed out his advice with some practical techniques or personal anecdotes instead of sounding like that mindless bird brain, he might have helped us.

A teacher must be willing, as well as able, to point out to students again and again just how inattentive, unfocused and scattered their thought processes really are. Then the master must pragmatically demonstrate to students how they can call forth pure presence into their own practice and strive to mindfully maintain it whenever possible. It's essential for the guru to invite seekers to know this for themselves, to comprehend how unsettled and scattered the mind really is.

Lively discourse and motivational strategies will excite the student's imagination and help instil a certain faith in the practice. Then it is up to the aspirant to fully engage in the practice of mindfulness for him or herself.

I discovered several teachers online as well as in print that proved very inspirational in this regard. People like Michael Kavanagh with his book, *The Awareness Method*; Scott Kiloby and Rupert Spira with their terrific YouTube presentation; or Adyashanti with his insightful satsangs all immediately come to mind though there were others as well. Buddhistgeeks.com, for example, often featured podcast guests that had a clever way of pointing out mindfulness strategies.

I found the practice of mindfulness rather revolutionary. I realized how I used to take a walk in the park for an hour and not actually notice anything. In effect, I hadn't even shown up for the experience. Due to mindfulness, I now started to make an appearance every once in a while and engaged with existence directly. This was eminently refreshing.

Communal meals provided another excellent opportunity to practice being present. At the beginning, I found it so odd that many retreatants chewed each mouthful for what seemed like an eternity, and then paused to set down their fork in order to remain still and silent for an even longer period of time. I was stymied. What was the point, I wondered? How pretentious and contrived this kind of mindless inactivity seemed.

Given a bit more time though, I came around and learned to appreciate the *power of presence*. Soon I was extending my meal time for up to an hour with the best of them. It turned out that the practice these diners had been engaged in was no phony ploy to appear spiritual. How misguided I had been in my original estimation. Rather, it was a strategy to reengage with life, existence itself, and that is a bloody marvellous thing!

I began to relish my meal for the first time in ages. I mean, I really started to savour flavours, feel textures, and revel in aromas and even experience other subtle nuances I had never even been aware of before. A veritable feast for the senses was being served up nightly, and I had been oblivious the whole time.

In mindfulness practice the world was slowly coming alive again. It gave me a sense of coming out of a fog bank. Little details began to be noticed. The experience was akin to the Zen tea ceremony, and its constant invitation to "pay attention."

For example, I noted the pretty batik pattern on the hand-dyed napkins and the artistic, bejewelled silver work on the rings that held them rolled up. Similarly, the exquisite shape of the hand-thrown ceramic water jug sitting on the dinner table delighted me, and the bright hue of Ananda's robe became alluring as well. I even noted how most retreatants took care never to clang their forks on the bottom of their plates. The silence was conducive to such mindfulness practice. Since we couldn't chat, we didn't have to keep up appearances and worry about presenting an attractive persona. With no need to make a favourable social impression, my dinner table mind was free to notice what was unfolding right in front of it.

This kind of new-found awareness, of course, extended outside of the retreat as well. When I waited in a bank line, more often than not, that was what was really going on. There was just a guy standing in line disengaged from the normal mind chatter of past and future. There was much of interest to be found in that simple experience. I was just a feller standing in a line, yet how sublime it could be!

I encourage you to try it yourself sometime. When you are in a cue, actually *BE* in line. BE Present. Note the appearance of the customers in front of you, be aware of snippets of conversation, the colour of the velvet rope, the construction of the imposing vault door, note the bank's long-term mortgage rates, and the teller's beautiful smile, but let it go no further than that. Resist the urge to add the incessant narrative commentary that usually immediately follows such observation. Be present. Disengage from the past and future. I learned from various sources how important it was to be in the moment, or perhaps more famously, recognize the *power of now*.

There have been whole books devoted to the topic of mindfulness. It's mentioned in the mainstream media with greater frequency. I'm told modern mental health practitioners expound its virtues as never before.

If this topic is of interest, these sources are very easy to come by. In fact, talk of mindfulness seems everywhere these days from local yoga studios, to professional athletic associations, to health clinics. Everybody and his brother seems intent on getting a piece of the action. I don't intend to turn this tale into a how-to book, so I will leave it at that for now. Here though, I'll let Buddha chime in with a little advice on the subject. He is reputed to have pointed to the heart of the matter with the following excerpt from the story of Bahiya.

Bahiya, you should train yourself in this way:

> With the seen, there will be just the seen; with the heard, there will be just the heard; with the sensed (touched, tasted, smelt) there will be just the sensed; with the cognized, there will be just the cognized.

If mindfulness is taken entirely to heart in an experiential manner, it may make nirvana, or liberation, much more likely to follow. This, of course, is the summum bonum of Buddhist praxis.

Developing a great one-pointed practice was important to me. I felt I needed to validate myself and prove Ananda wrong. So I went looking for inspiration in the Buddhist library. "Just what were the characteristics of single-pointed concentration," I wondered? More importantly, how could I judge my competency? I felt that as the days went by, my ability to stay focused was increasing in leaps and bounds. But I needed feedback.

However, eventually this kind of self-centred egoic drive has to be abandoned. Any desire initiated from the ego will only reinforce dualism and the dream state. In the early preliminary stages though, my goal-oriented outlook was typical of the behaviour many seekers exhibit in their drive to attain accomplishment, self-improvement, excellence and ultimately recognition. Spiritual materialism must eventually give way to a selfless inclination to discover Truth for its own sake.

However, at this stage, I still had the goal-driven, naïve enthusiasm of the spiritually immature. Following my urge to discover how accomplished I had become in samatha practice, I eventually located a Tibetan Buddhist source which was pretty dense but comprehensible enough for me to understand that by the authors' reckoning there were nine stages or sign posts of meditation/mental development. I took it to be a gauge of sorts which I (my ego) found most appealing. Of course it did. It revelled in merit making. It perpetually sought distinctions of honour to impress others just as it had done since grade school when ink stamp impressions and golden star stickers were sought after or the Cub Scout days when merit badges were *de rigueur*. That kind of conditioning starts very early, doesn't it? Fortunately, I would soon learn that this attitude would retard awakening. I will share with you in the next chapter the outline of the nine stages of samatha meditation.

> Awareness cannot be taught. Awareness simply throws light on what is, without any separation whatsoever. Activity does not destroy it and sitting does not create it.
> Toni Packer (spiritual teacher)

# Chapter 17

*Separation is a kind of optical delusion of consciousness...The true value of a human being is determined by the measure and the sense in which they have obtained liberation from the self.*

Albert Einstein (physicist)

    I cogitated over the following nine factors of meditation and tried to make sense out of them. This is what Tibetan Buddhism, as presented by the hermitage website, had to say about the workings of the mind and meditation. I have made this excerpt more concise in the hope that it will be a little more comprehensible.

### 1st Stage in Stabilizing the Mind

The meditator simply begins to chase the untamed mind. In the first stage our mind is completely under the sway and allure of the five sense objects and mental-emotional events. At this preliminary stage mental disturbance is the rule and the flame of the fire of effort must be very strong.

### 2nd Stage Continuous Stabilizing

The meditator fixes his mind on an object of concentration. The breath is the primary focus. The hope of taming the chattering monkey mind commences here. One must use remembrance and watchfulness to bring the object of meditation close. Things are beginning to move in the right direction.

### 3rd Stage Habitual Stabilization

The power of recollection rises and comes from the "memory" nature of mind. The meditator can distinguish the subtler forms of distraction and weakness. The mind comes ever more passive. Here, especially, the meditator seems to enjoy the state of "spacing out." The meditator thinks that he or she has attained an ideal calm. Everything feels good. In fact, this is really a distraction, a subtle daze. The knowledgeable meditator knows that there are two levels of "passivity": a basic form of "spacing-out," which seems very pleasant but is obviously a distraction, and a far subtler form, which seems to be a peaceful state of mind, but which is really a disguised form of depression. This must be watched for by careful introspection.

This stage can be mistaken for progress, and since this subtle weakness does not disturb concentration, it relaxes the meditator and seems pleasurable. Yet it is a disturbance nevertheless for later it will make our minds weak.

### 4th Stage Near Stabilization

At this stage distraction and fogginess have diminished by half. With the power of watchfulness and alertness the meditator firmly understands what is being done and what is occurring. The mind is quite obedient. At this point concentration on the breath is possible for about fifteen minutes.

### 5th Stage Habituation

Through immersion in the power of watchfulness, distraction and fogginess are almost completely gone; the mind is not under the leadership of scattering distractions. Remembrance is not so necessary now, but since subtle distractions grow stronger, the power of diligence/perseverance must be applied. The long effort against the invasive distraction of the five senses and any inner events may too quickly relax the effort of the meditator, and the subtler forms of distraction may wax stronger, and thereby the intensity of clarity diminishes. No other thoughts, even those of Dharma or meditations on Samsara, etc., can be allowed to interfere with concentration!

One experiences steady concentration for a half an hour, and the breath-object is very "close" to the mind; the mind is peaceful with no distractions.

6th Stage Pacifying

The allure of the five senses are now gone. Gone also are the other distractions of the inner emotional and mental events. A very energetic concentration has arisen. Concentration without any disturbance is possible for at least one hour.

7th Stage Thorough Pacification

After long persevering practice, the meditator reaches complete pacification of the mind which "rests" naturally. It concentrates on its own. Concentration comes immediately. But still, the meditator observes as in the case of bare witnessing. Concentration is possible for about four hours. There is only the slightest trace of disturbance. The subtlest sinking and scattering may continue to arise. Should they begin to arise, they can be eliminated with little effort.

8th Stage Becoming One-Pointed

Spontaneous concentration is now present until the meditator wishes to stop it. As the concentration progresses, so does the clarity of the object concentrated upon. One's sense-media are not needed and do not intrude. The mind breaks into spontaneous meditation immediately. Concentration for one or two days without a break is possible. The mind can now remain continually in absorption on the object of concentration.

9th Stage Entrance into samadhi

The meditator is totally non-dependent upon the senses and in perfect equanimity. The path has ended. At this stage there is no limit to the length of fixed concentration. According to the meditator's feelings, his mind and the object become one. The ninth stage of *samadhi*, or mental absorption, is attained through the power of total habituation, a familiarization and integration in Calm-Abiding.

That concludes my condensed excerpt of the nine stages of samatha which Tibetans hold will eventually lead to *samadhi*.

I reckoned I ranked at about a six on the above meditation scale by the time the Mahamudra retreat was nearing completion. I was now meditating for long spells of time, up to three hours in one sitting. I had confidence that the eighth stage, my goal of one-pointedness, was not really that far off. My ego was pleased with the progress. It could not be denied that I was becoming a good meditator. Yet my striving to attain success was soon to weaken. What I discovered would eventually relegate spiritual materialism to the rubbish bin of the deluded self.

Here I am in part alluding to the important concept that everyone has innate Buddha nature, but we quite simply have not realized this fact yet. This fundamental aspect of reality, also referred to as "Buddha-mind," was apparently closer than close.

This idea was supported by other traditions as well, such as the modern age *Neo-Advaita* Movement. These *non-dualists* repeat a mantra of "there is nowhere to go. Nothing to discover. You are already THAT."

If that were the case, then quite obviously wherever I might have ranked in the meditation scale above, ultimately it could have little bearing on the outcome of my awakening. I could appreciate how such striving and attachment to goal-oriented success must be counterproductive in fundamental ways. If the outlook was always future oriented, always "becoming," then there would be no room for "became" or more pointedly simply "am."

To drop into the moment is to simply realize what is already present right here and now. I was beginning to understand that as long as I perpetually sought happiness somewhere "out there," it would always lay undiscovered right beneath my feet. As long as I sought fulfillment elsewhere, Spirit would never manifest itself in the moment. That notion made a lot of sense to me. I heard the story of the "The Diamond in Your Pocket" as told by spiritual heavyweight Gangaji on the internet one day, and it illustrated this predicament quite wonderfully.

The story chronicled the tale of the wily pickpocket and the even cleverer diamond merchant. No matter where the thief looked, he could never locate the treasure for the merchant had secreted it in the one place the thief would never think to look, the crook's own pocket. This is the same kind of message relayed in the spiritual novel, *The Alchemist*. In this story, a young man dreams of finding great treasure in a far off land. Inspired, he sets off to seek his fortune. Many trials and tribulations ensue. The quest concludes with the revelation that "that which was sought was already and always back at his original departure point" right under the spot where the hero originally dreamt of the treasure that inspired his quest.

My original goal to discover the ultimate nature of reality now suggested it could be a lot closer at hand than I first presumed. There was also the suggestion that it was something or someone I already was. This puzzled me but was not dismissed outright. To my mind it seemed inconceivable that I was already THAT. Yet could so many wise ones be deceiving themselves?

## Chapter 18

The treasure hunt thus became the focused search to discover "Who/what I am." This drive differed substantially from the original quest. The search would now be redirected from looking "out there" to "in here," from seeking some kind of objective resolution to one that entailed discovering the "grand subject," no-self or non-dual awareness. Undoubtedly, the drive to awaken was morphing into the search to realize the ancient Greek Delphic maxim, "Know Thyself," which was also incised over the Oracle's door in the movie *The Matrix*.

Among the growing pool of information I had begun to accumulate, one distinction really stood out. It seemed spiritual traditions stressed either the progressive path (step by step progress) or else the more speedy direct path to spiritual enlightenment. From what I could tell, the direct path was what I seemed more attracted to. A lot of the stuff I disdained about religion seemed to be included in the progressive path. This slow plodding outlook seemed to be the one favoured at The Truth Sangha Centre.

| **Progressive** | **Direct** |
|---|---|
| Teacher dependant | Greater independance |
| Devotion to a path | Pathless path |
| Slower | Quicker |
| Self-centred | Non-self oriented |
| Building up ego | Breaking down ego |
| Appeases the mind | Uncertainty, challenging |
| Established doctrine | Non-scriptural, experiential |
| Often group oriented | Solitary, independent |
| Self-help | Self-annihilating |
| Affirm | Question |
| Effort required | Non-doing "doing" |
| Focus spiritual practice | Awakening centred |
| Lifestyle important | Lifestyle less important |
| Meing | Being |
| Seeking | Stopping, resting |
| My will be done | Thy will be done |
| Habituating mind | Realizing MIND |
| Rigid | Open beginner's mind |
| Goal oriented | TRUTH oriented |
| Panders to dream state | Abolishes delusion |
| Disempowerment | Self-empowerment |
| Conceptual beliefs | Knowing |
| Self-improvement | Letting things be |

| | |
|---|---|
| Spiritual materialism | Non-grasping |
| Seeker wants answers | Unmanifested realized |
| Dualistic identification | Non-dual awareness |
| Content | Emptiness |

It would take many more months until all of the above distinctions of the direct path numbered amongst my own. Still, I would say I was experiencing a growing disenchantment with the "big picture" Tibetan Buddhism had to offer. I realized at this point that the progressive path it attempted to instil in the seeker, as well as the politics and platitudes it pushed, were not at all to my liking. Still, I held out hope that Wally had some special teachings that he might share with me. In retrospect, I now see how my coveting these teachings was a ridiculous desire given my disdain for keeping secrets, but that is delusion for you. Maya is relentless.

Furthermore, coveting Wally's special teachings was equally absurd for in essence who or what you are is really an open secret available for all to discover for themselves. It has nothing to do with acquiring new conceptual information, but at that point I was still naïve enough to think that the so-called "secret" teachings Wally shared with favoured students might be of value to me.

It seems to me that this is just one ploy amongst several that the Kagyu lineage employed to entice students to stay the course. Bhikhu Fatty once shared with me the fact that the "home office," as he more or less put it, had set a kind of quota for Wally to fill. Increasing enrolment and gaining "converts" was apparently something the establishment desired. No kidding. More Kagyu devotees meant a stronger presence in America which ultimately favoured donations and cash flow. Wally once suggested that I accompany Bhikhu Ananda back to San Francisco for specialised training. Of course, to do so meant I would have to formally become a monk, which obviously wasn't ever going to happen.

Besides, I was too busy devoting all my energy to becoming the real McCoy. I had begun to get the distinct impression that I was the only guy in the whole joint that actually sought genuine enlightenment. I don't mean this to be a mark of distinction or as a kind of self-aggrandizement. It is just a fact.

At The Truth Sangha Centre, all manner and kind of agenda were going down which had precious little to do with truth-realization. Most common seekers aspired to become a better Buddhist, or at the least give off the impression that they were devout followers, rather than attempt to realize their own innate Buddha-nature themselves.

Of course, the impression Wally gave of that likelihood ever transpiring was not favourable since he reserved enlightenment for the greatest of the great, the rarest of the rare. You had to be an exalted super being, *Ubermensch*, God-like Divine Avatar instead of just the plebs and rabble that gathered at his feet. Of course, I can't stress enough how inaccurate this kind of belief is. Everybody awakens in the end, but this kind of attitude may help explain ignorant chaps like Lama Maybe One and Wally who treat this sentiment as a kind of self-fulfilling prophecy.

Around mid-retreat, I had a curious exchange with Bhikhu Ananda. He gave me some discouraging advice regarding my hard-core meditation practice and gung-ho attitude in general. I mentioned my bare-witnessing experiences to him. I talked of my three or four-hour sits. He felt I was exerting too much effort in this regard and advised that I should slow things down a bit, relax more, be less of a maverick and embrace the progressive path to enlightenment. Hoorah!

I told Ananda how I felt compelled to spare no effort in my great desire to awaken. Furthermore, I explained that I was sincerely "going for this thing" come what may. He proceeded to get agitated, almost personally offended by my eagerness and talked of a "brass ring" that I shouldn't be trying to grasp. What nonsense, I thought. This guy didn't have a clue and apparently not much authentic spiritual experience either. To say my earnestness was dead wrong was missing the point. As certain famous spiritual sources stress, "One must strive for enlightenment in the manner a drowning man struggles to catch his next breath of air." My attitude exemplified this ideal, and it was totally spontaneous and natural. Again, more poor advice on how I should resist what was.

But I realize that there is a caveat to be considered here, one that Ananda failed to successfully articulate. This drowning man in peril I just mentioned is of course driven to get his next breath at all costs, but it is through instinct, the will to survive, not the ego, that he is compelled to do so. Similarly, enlightenment must be sought without the clinging, grasping nature of the ego being at the root of it. At that time, I lacked the ability to conceive of these kinds of pointers, and so too, apparently, did Ananda.

If I could meet Ananda these days, I would inform him that my sincere, take-no-prisoners kind of attitude back then was born out of a simple wish to wake the fuck up. Nothing else. I can't explain where this urge originated. In fact, in retrospect it seems quite irrational. Who in his right mind would continue to follow a path whose attested goal seemed more and more unlikely to earn the aspirant any kind of pay off or reward whatsoever?

> …something that is worth nothing, that can't be proved to anybody…it is actually a completely illogical thing to do. It is not justifiable by any rational terms. That is probably why you do it.
> Joe Simpson (extreme mountain climber)

## A Fleeting Improvised Man Awakens

# Chapter 18

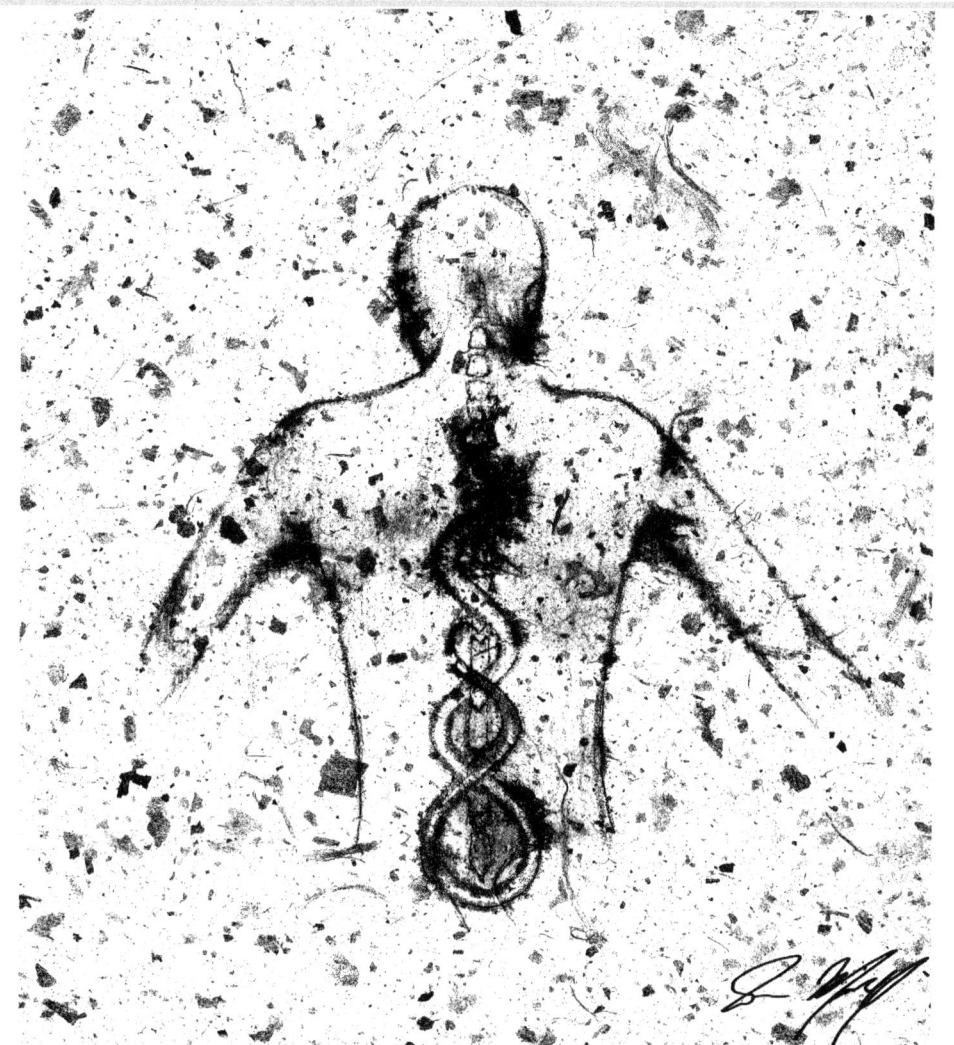

*There is no true self. There is self and no-self. The deepest truth of any person is no-person. It's not fear of death that drives humans, it's fear of non-being, oblivion.*
Jed McKenna (spiritual teacher)

Around the eight-day mark, it seemed that the majority of the Mahamudra retreatants were all pretty much glassy eyed and stressed out or just detached and spacey. I was having my issues as well. This experience had become exceptionally trying and was inexorably wearing me down meditation by meditation, like a sand castle being eroded by successive ocean waves.

I once shot a documentary movie in the late '80s about an ultra-marathon bicycle race called "The Race Across America." At the time, it was billed as "the world's most gruelling sporting event." Participants were expected to ride coast to coast in less than seven days. It was a pretty fantastic display of human endurance. Judging from the condition of those athletes, I daresay my own present travail was on par with that event. Yes, my mind was calming down, but still the *samatha* technique required great willpower and fortitude to maintain over the long haul, and frankly, I was running out of steam. Carried out at the one-hundred-percent concentration level I elected to hold, I assure you this experience was the single most unappealing and trying endeavour I ever engaged in.

I once survived alone in the bush for two weeks with no tent or shelter save the one I constructed, no sleeping bag or blanket, and no food other than that which I procured for myself. I lost about fifteen pounds in the adventure. This retreat was far tougher than the gut-wrenching hunger pangs and discomfort I suffered during my fortnight of wilderness survival.

Now just over a week into the retreat, but feeling it was a lifetime, I had grown ever more weary of the monotony (remember I had been more or less keeping this pace up for weeks on end already), and I have to admit at this point I longed for it all to come to an end. But still, I was not about to give up.

I had never quit anything and was not about to start now. If awakening was not soon in the cards then a serious meditation routine would probably be with me for the rest of my days. I was not about to fail this test, particularly as this one seemed to mark the measure of my mettle as never before.

I once almost quit a self-organized bicycle tour through the Chinese side of the Himalayan mountain range. The first few days were particularly gruelling to the unconditioned cyclist that I was. I thought once about just collapsing on the side of the road and calling it a day, but it didn't happen that way. I pushed on using the last of my reserves and wobbled into a Chinese guest house completely spent.

The problem with the present situation, unlike the anecdote just described, was the fact that this one had no end in sight. Sure the formal two-week retreat would come to a close, but I would continue to soldier on with exactly the same meditation regimen the next day. There would be no respite for me, quite possibly ever. Can anyone see the problem here? I didn't at the time. My exuberant enthusiasm was a bit naïve for it was unsustainable over the long haul.

By the terminal stage of this retreat, my body was becoming a mess. It longed for the strenuous daily exercise it was accustomed to, and I suffered from a relentless headache and a backache that was only relieved when sleep caught up with me, and even this was in short supply due to my early rising to get in an extra hour of meditation before going off to prepare breakfast. I was also quickly losing muscle mass from the low-calorie, protein-deficient vegetarian diet. Combined with the loneliness long-term solitude brings about, as well as my increasing disenchantment with Lama Wally, Bhikhu Ananda and the whole shitty Tibetan Buddhism deal in general, things were starting to feel like I was once again facing those incredibly daunting Chinese peaks.

Though now I couldn't say, "Just a bit further…push on a little more old fella and you'll be fine…your goal is in sight." My prospects held no certain end game. Perhaps it was time for a break, though even a pause in my practice seemed inconceivable. I could not even consider a brief respite for who knew where this kind of precedent would lead? I was truly caught between a soft cushion and a hard-backed chair. I was mentally spent but had to forge on regardless.

Routine-wise, things were pretty much as they had been for the last six weeks or so: focus, concentration, non-identification with thought, gap, bare witnessing—the standard practice.

Though now as I sat on the afternoon of the eighth day, a very odd phenomenon started to express itself. A persistent little narrative started to creep into my awareness, and I was having great trouble putting it aside. In fact, it felt like "Another" was directly addressing me. Not the ordinary voice inside me but a character completely separate and unfamiliar. Was I going bonkers?

I had never experienced this kind of sensed presence before in my life. Incredibly, it was like another person was in the room addressing me directly. This sensed presence seemed external to me and was quite matter of factly carrying on a monologue in a natural-sounding female voice. For some unknown reason, I felt at ease with this presence, and she certainly knew me well. She presented as a kind of gracious, maternal and kindly presence seeking to offer me solace.

She was not at all like I imagine aggressive schizophrenic voices must sound. Though I could not perceive the figure visually, the feeling of a sensed presence was uncanny. Most odd was the fact that it felt like another person was actually there in the room beside me giving me reassuring advice. This pleasant female personage was carrying on just like a flesh-and-blood woman would.

I tried to ignore her for that seemed to be the best course of action, but she was very persistent. Previously, all the thoughts that welled up into my conscious mind during meditation had been my own. That is, they were in "my" voice. This lady was a bit of an interloper, though I felt she meant me well.

Strangely, I got the impression that this character was a *travel agent* by profession. She regaled me with tempting travel destinations I might find interesting or deals I might like to snap up. Oddly enough, she also commented on how well my meditation practice was going.

Her positive feedback was difficult to ignore. She seemed most impressed with the gaps in my thoughts and encouraged me not to break my routine for even one moment. "You are better than that...stronger," she said as she extolled me forward. She affirmed the fact that I was no quitter and said that "I must go on regardless" though she appreciated how exhausted I was. Then this very animated presence pointed out to me that my fists were once again clenched in an anxious death grip. They almost always were.

Though I was doing my best to try to ignore her, she was correct about my hands. Momentarily I focused on relaxing and relieving the built up anxiety in them. Attending to mounting stress levels during meditation was something I had to remain vigilant of, so I was glad that she had pointed this issue out to me.

As I focused on relaxing my grip, the "agent's" presence vaporized. Poof. Gone. I enjoyed the silence. She meant well, but I was glad she evaporated back into the ether. Now here is the really interesting point about what had just transpired. I had just experienced the classic *Third Man Factor*.

This kind of experience is well-known to occur to mountain climbers, adventurers, lost hikers, shipwrecked sailors and others placed under extreme mental and physical duress. It is a fairly common occurrence amongst those placed in a life or death struggle or when subjected to extreme isolation for instance, but it is not so widely written about. For more information on the third man syndrome, see the book written by John Geiger entitled, *The Third Man Factor: Surviving the Impossible*. Here he chronicles episodes just like the one I encountered. Apparently this phenomenon is a coping strategy the mind employs when times get dire. This "companion" is sometimes physically seen while on other occasions merely sensed and offers words of encouragement and support to help the victim get through his or her ordeal. Everybody reports this presence as being seemingly quite real and something far more than just a mere mental hallucination. Some apprehend it in the guise of a deceased loved one. Others put it off to a guardian angel. I appreciate why this position is held. It does seem like some kind of sentient being, separate from yourself, is truly offering you solace and aid when you feel alone against the world. Leaving the "Third Man" behind me, next something equally unexpected transpired, and once more I had no conceptual framework with which to make any sense of it.

I have since learned that what was about to transpire is known as a classic *Kundalini awakening*. At the time, it was a rather "shocking" episode. In a moment you will come to see how I mean this figuratively as well as quite literally. I count it among the odder spiritual experiences that arose during my awakening journey. Apparently, certain spiritual types hold this kind of episode in high, almost reverential, regard. For me it was just another experience in a long line, though quite unusual to be sure.

This arising was a relatively brief, though very intense, experience and had a visceral, somatic element to it which made it unique for me. Most of my epiphanies arose in the conceptual realm. This, however, was grounded solely in the body, so this arising was more a case of *anschauung* (sense impression before ideas) than anything else. I identify very little with my skin suit, but this experience could not be quickly put aside like I had just done with the sensed presence recently dispatched. No, this very visceral experience was of an entirely different nature.

Unexpectedly, the affair began with a moment or two of peace as the "travel agent" winked out of existence. Then a subtle tingling in my lower back arose that registered as a kind of gentle spasm which after a few seconds spontaneously erupted very violently into a paroxysm.

From the bottom of my vertebral column near my tail bone and emanating from the sides of my back inwards towards my spinal column, a kind of electric shock-like feeling or energetic arising occurred. This shocking effect, simultaneously combined with muscle spasms along the whole back, seemed to continuously energise itself in a repeating pattern. This energetic movement traveled from the base of my spine, up the vertebral column and then exploded in my head multiple times in a row.

Some who undergo this kind of Kundalini awakening report concomitant joy or bliss, or a white light, while others become fearful and anxious. For me it was simply a strong energetic arising with no other feeling attached to it. It didn't seem spiritual at all. Overtly, I had done nothing to bring it on (though exhaustion was undoubtedly the causal factor) nor was there any way to stop it. It spontaneously petered out eventually on its own accord just as it had begun.

It seemed to me that certain seekers made way, way too big a deal out of this phenomenon. I felt many were coveting the signs or symptoms of awakening rather than appreciating the deeper implications that lay undiscovered below. Mistaking the side effects of awakening for enlightenment itself is all too common in the Truth game.

It's like mistaking the attractive, iridescent mother of pearl oyster shell for the greater treasure hidden within. The "pearl of inestimable value" can't be grasped for it is what you already are. Your true nature is not an experience to be had but more akin to that which is aware of all experience. To go chasing Kundalini or seek any particular kind of spiritual revelation is to remain as delusion itself.

Yes these experiences, and I am documenting some of my own right here in this book, are at times dear to one's own heart but of no real import. They arise and fall away again, come and go just like the tide, but what all truly enlightened sages constantly point to is the perennial wisdom beyond such trivialities.

Incredibly, that kind of totally authentic wisdom would momentarily announce itself to me for the first time just as I was recovering from the impact of the Kundalini experience. Like a man destined to meet his fate on the electric chair but the keeper fails to apply enough amperage the first time around, so too spirituality sometimes elects to give you another immediate jolt when the first application didn't quite finish the job. I was about to receive another zap! This time the amperage would be increased tenfold and would not entail another Kundalini experience but something far stranger.

> Recognize everything as a lie, especially the one who recognises everything as a lie.
> Karl Renz (spiritual teacher)

*A Fleeting Improvised Man Awakens*

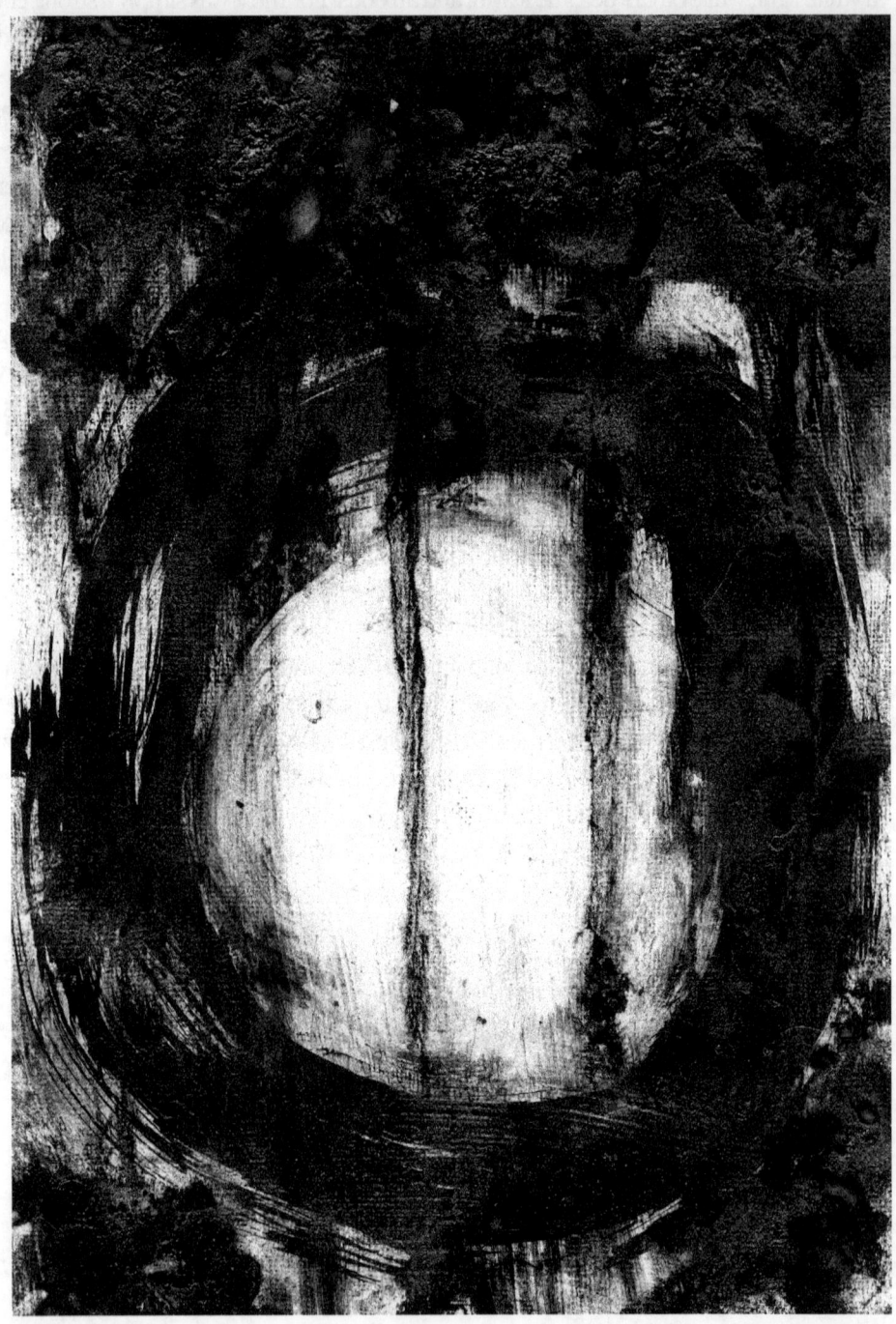

# Chapter 19

*A guru or a teacher can only take you to the edge of their courage.*

Benjamin Smythe (spiritual teacher)

Moments after the Kundalini arising ended, several thoughts entered my mind. Chiefly amongst them was, "What the hell just happened there?" No answers were forthcoming. This frustrated my mind for it always sought to impart meaning to these kinds of mystical experiences. "What did it mean? Was this experience relevant? Was it spiritually edifying?" These kinds of questions often arose, but in this kind of experience confusion usually prevailed.

This kind of episode was entirely outside my limited reality tunnel, perceptual periscope or purview, so I had nothing to relate it to. Once again I was left dumfounded.

"Ok, forget all this weird shit...that's quite enough for one day," I exclaimed probably aloud as I was pretty freaked out by now. "So let's get on with the matter at hand," I concluded. Meditation it is.

But at that moment, I felt wearier than ever. I was tired beyond compare in fact. There had just been an immense energetic arising; some kind of zenith had been reached, and now I was on my way back down. I felt spent. Finally I had reached the breaking point. Weeks and weeks of unrelenting concentration practice had taken their toll. I needed a break, but it was more than that. In my frustration, I actually considered the unimaginable—giving up...or rather was it giving in... if only for a long-overdue, short respite.

To be clear, I wasn't considering giving up the whole enterprise. The quest would go on, but I felt so weary that I finally admitted to myself that a little break was in order, a break from it all, from the whole shebang.

That was a novel proposition because as I described earlier, I was no quitter. Though in a very limited way, this was precisely what I was now contemplating. Giving up, even for just a minute, had never been an option. But it sure the hell was going to happen now.

I needed a time out. Something in me came to its senses like a concerned fight coach who has finally admitted that his boxer is utterly exhausted and beat insensible so wisely turns to his cornerman and says those fateful words no pugilist or coaching staff ever wants to hear, "We gotta yank the kid outta the ring right now for his own good. Go ahead, throw in the fucking towel." This was no request. It was a demand. I had to escape now!

But in this break there was not the desperate measure a fleeing prisoner employs. I had no escape plan or preconceived destination in mind. In fact, I didn't want to escape to anywhere. I wasn't seeking a break from anything in particular. A clear desire arose in my entire being and was articulated in my mind very succinctly as—"I need a break. I just need a fucking break right now." And with great authority the next thought was, "I mean right now, and I *don't want to meditate* anymore, but I *also don't want to 'not meditate.'* I just want a god damn break from it all!"

This was a surprising thought for I am very sure that such a notion, neither engaging in a *doing* nor a *not doing*, had ever arisen before in my life.

Of course, certain spiritual traditions utilize such pointers to foster awakening, but this was unknown to me at the time. I wasn't being spiritual now. I was just a guy who had been pushed a little past his breaking point and finally needed to take a moment. What transpired next was not so much like "taking a moment" but more like falling into the moment proper or being the moment itself. The state about to befall me was even weirder than the *Third Man episode* and *Kundalini arising* combined.

When the decision to quit was finally reached, what followed next was quite natural. I simply closed my eyes and laid my head back on my meditation chair as the coach yelled, "time out." The effect was astonishing.

In about the time it takes for a grenade to explode, my world was shattered as if hit by a concussive shock wave designed to level everything in its path. Shiva, the Hindu God known as "the destroyer of worlds," sat on the sidelines just to ensure the job was complete. This thing had gone full nuclear. Kabam! Existence wiped clear away. Holy fuck…

MEDIC!

An intensely silent gap in my thoughts immediately arose of about five to six seconds, which was much more pronounced than any of my typical "gapping-out" experiences to date. Then an immense feeling began to overwhelm me. I stress the notion of "feeling" here for the ensuing incident was devoid of pretty much all thought. The impression engendered was like a great pool of water was being emptied. The egoic conceptual mind, duality itself, was instantly drained away, self was eradicated, leaving…what? Well, God only knows. Some call it the void.

This existential experience caused me to recoil in shock as the feeling of emptiness continued to grow. It struck me hard as if a swift side kick to the solar plexus had just been delivered by a mixed martial arts champion. Non-conceptual in nature, it was a very visceral experience. Emptiness itself lasted but a few seconds, and then the rising anxiety was relieved as I instantly came back to dualistic reality. The speed with which the experience ended, and also began, was surprising, much like the rapidity with which an inhaled DMT hit could transport you to another realm. The fact that reality could be entirely obliterated that quickly truly took my breath away.

I regained my composure and took a moment to wipe the sweat from my brow. I paused for about fifteen seconds, and despite being somewhat unnerved and shaken by what had just transpired, still the thought arose, "That was weird, wonder if I could do that again?"

With that I closed my eyes, settled back once more and was instantly "evaporated" again. Though to be clear, conceptually this disappearance of self was not known to me in that moment. I only came to recognize this fact and label it a no-self or no-mind experience well after the episode ended.

The feeling was precisely the same the second time around, though even more pronounced, and again I became anxious quite quickly. This experienceless experience of the vast and spacious "wide open nothing" grew ever more apparent. Holy shit! Super, super weird.

This type of feeling is not defined in any dictionary for it is the result of duality collapsing in on itself or alternatively non-duality blossoming which, of course, defies all definition. What was transpiring was not born out of a materialistic objective experience so my mind was unable to fathom it.

The vastness I felt certainly wasn't like the feeling engendered when I sat in an empty auditorium. That feeling of being in a cavernous space is simply caused by my eyes and ears beholding a large cavity in a building. This profound spacious feeling was more a result of being the expanse itself. The feeling being spontaneously generated was arising out of nothing at all, but what a grand nothing this was—unimaginably huge, immensity beyond compare.

I distinctly remember having the mental image of putting a hand to forehead to, in effect, "shade my eyes" while I attempted to peer out into the dazzling, illuminated, inky blackness of space in order to try to ascertain the limits of this expanse. This inclination was just like trying to find the horizon on a brightly lit beach. But there was neither horizon nor anything else whatsoever to get my bearings on. Ever try to peer into the eternal? I guarantee that will give you pause. This realization freaked me out once more. Again, I pulled out of the experience and ended it for this session.

Instantly, I came to my senses, and the first thing that struck me was:

Wow! What a transition from the clarity of whatever that was back into the dullness of my human mind. Man, oh man, am I ever a dull and befuddled wretch.

In retrospect, I can tell you that the momentary clarity of what I now know to be *no-mind*, was only recognized as I transitioned out of the brief *no-self* experience. Over and over I asked myself the same simple question, "Am I really that dull?"

The movement from a sense of clear mindedness to a fuzzy, foggy and unfocused stream of consciousness was akin to the startling change in definition and resolution that occurred as moving pictures went from the archaic celluloid hand cranked black and white moving pictures from early last century to the HD digital Dolby full surround sound and high definition colour extravaganza of today's video. Then move that distinction up by an additional factor or two. The contrast was just that stark and vivid. One moment mental clarity beyond compare, the next a feeling like I had just suddenly been dumped into the murky, dumbed-down, numbed-out cranial cavity of a prehistoric Palaeolithic cave dweller who had been thumped over the noggin once too often.

Also of note was a sensed vibratory "sound-like" effect that momentarily enveloped "me" during this letting go experience. The vibration produced a peculiar feeling that I couldn't quite put my finger on. Due to the short duration, I could not clearly discern what this oddly sensed sound feeling was.

To experience the Third Man syndrome, a Kundalini awakening and then something even more intense back to back to back was rather overwhelming, yet still I was undaunted. I remember pulling out of the last experience thinking, "Well, that seemed easy enough to induce, I'll check it out once again early tomorrow, but for now I am done." I broke the meditation a bit early in favour of some fresh air.

I walked but a few steps to get under the forest canopy full of towering firs and aromatic red cedars. The undergrowth was comprised of swaths of sword fern, salal and Oregon grape, and here I paused to consider further what had just transpired. I couldn't make sense out of any of it. Primarily, I recalled the feeling of trying to peer out through the inky miasma and sensing a vastness beyond measure. I attempted to discern a boundary, verge or limit to this realm, but in the moments afforded me it seemed I was nowhere at all. The ominous feeling and disorientation evoked was entirely disconcerting. This had to be the strangest awakening experience to date.

As I walked on, I knew the experiences were significant, but in what regard I could not fathom. Later that day upon further reflection, I wondered if I had bumped into so-called "Buddha-nature." "Was this really what serious seekers were chasing?" I wondered. Had

"True-nature" revealed itself? I would consult the Lama on the matter the next day as I was expected to go to his daily private interview anyhow.

Meeting next morning, I explained to Wally what had occurred. He agreed that it was significant and was undoubtedly an instance of Buddha-nature just as I had presumed. When I told him how dumbed down I felt when I was slammed back into my corporeal body and what an incredibly dull chap I truly was, he pointed out that "It's not just you, DJ. Your friends, mother and father, all humans are in this state." I sat silently nodding when he then added, "All the time. Everybody is in the exact same state of unawareness, ignorance and unclarity that you have just described."

That surprised me quite a bit. I told him about this feeling I had had, the sound, though at this time I had not identified it as a sound as such. It presented more like a feeling. The best way to describe it was to recollect a memory from childhood. I told him about being in the back of a station wagon during a rainstorm. We kids were in the rear, lulled to sleep by the driven water splashing off the floor creating a soothing, drone-like effect. I asked him what he made of this. He provided some useless mumbo jumbo about the nostalgia of childhood blah, blah, blah. In fact, I later determined exactly why my mind had such a recollection. As my ego struggled to make sense of the "soundscape" experience, it recalled the closest aural experience it knew of.

You see if Wally had actually had any direct experience of the kind that had just unfolded for me or had met others who did, he would have recognized that I had experienced *anahata nada*.

*Anahata nada* is a Sanskrit term which means the "struckless sound," the sound not caused by two things hitting each other, a sourceless sound, the eternal hum of creation or, as Hindus put it, the *OM* of the universe. It is a well-documented, though relatively rare, phenomenon.

> Listen to the secret sound, the real sound, which is inside you.
> The one no one talks of speaks the secret sound to himself,
> and he's the one who has made it all.
> Kabir (Indian mystic/poet)

I recollected the sound of water splashing on the undercarriage of a car because in a sense the feeling is a bit akin to that. Some say it sounds like bees buzzing, but for me *anahata nada* most closely resembles the hiss one hears when you put a large seashell to your ear combined with the white noise and static you get from a TV receiver not tuned to a specific channel. I imagine it could be misdiagnosed as tinnitus by health care professionals, but I assure you it is an entirely different thing altogether. As I write these words, I can perceive it right now if I turn my attention towards it. It became my constant companion a few months after the incident I just described ended, and it never left. *Anahata nada* could have always been present for all I know. My mind may have just been too noisy for me to previously notice it.

The next morning, I arose expecting to be able to reinvigorate the strange spacious clarity of the previous day as easily as I could find the "bare witness" of my usual meditative practice. That was something that had struck me about the previous day's experience; it seemed to be effortless and quite natural. On the previous day, the second time I invoked the stillness, it came back almost instantly, just as a well-trained dog would do if called. I was sure I could *do* it again with the same ease.

But being under the misguided belief that this phenomenon involved a "doing," it failed to reappear. Try as I might during many episodes of meditation over numerous days, I could not get it to come back at that time.

Monk Ananda had warned me against trying. He advised it would be counter-productive. I ignored his advice as I expected it to just spontaneously arise again with great ease. But, of course, it never did (only in the short term that is, it later became the norm), for what was required here, and this is quite essential to understand, was not a doing but more of a non-doing.

I had stumbled across this phenomenological expression of "pure awareness" or "be-ingness itself" rather than a "doing." The previous day it happened quite by accident, simply by naturally adopting an authentic naïve attitude of complete equanimity and surrender. Or to put it more plainly, during the episode of the previous day I simply gave up. For a moment, the desire to cease meditating came to mind, but the opposite was true as well. Absolutely giving up included even NOT wanting to NOT meditate, utter non-doing. With that ethos a totally novel non-doingness manifested. In this case, the Truth of Being revealed itself due to the radical letting go that extreme fatigue induced.

When people ask me how they should meditate I say "don't" as in "do not meditate," as in "do not do." There is no room for "doing" in True meditation. Of course, some people think the idea then is to strive really, really hard to perfect this "not doing" attitude, which of course is just more doing. True meditation is all about "being." Even the slightest whiff of doing is too much if awakening is your true goal. Of course, this truth was unknown to me at the time, so for the next few days, until the retreat came to a close and a little after, I tried hard to bring back my Buddha-nature, but of course it was all to no avail. For the second time, Bhikhu Ananda was proven correct. Attempting to grasp and cling to such events is pointless.

The Great Mahamudra retreat of 2008 finally came to a close. Lunch was served, and this was the only occasion when guests could chat freely. I focused my attention on a middle-aged, urbane, white-collar guy who sported a sophisticated French accent. I had met him two weeks before just prior to Mahamudra beginning.

Then he had spoken highly of the merits and great revelations the previous year's Mahamudra retreat had afforded him. He spoke of profound awakening experiences, visions of Green Tara and ecstatic openings of the heart chakra which were sublime beyond compare. He was looking for more of that he assured me, a lot more.

I had to admit it sounded pretty good. But this miserable character that now stood in front of me was an entirely different being. He was bummed out and a little pissed-off as well. It was clear by his bitching and moaning that he felt that this year the goods had not been delivered. "My God," he exclaimed, "what a disaster this retreat was."

He further elaborated:

> I didn't see a deity of any kind this year, not a one, just nonsense from grade school and even weirder shit. It was like I was on LSD or something. How pointless. Can you imagine, not a single Tara? I'm telling you, well, anyhow, and no heart opening either, crown chakra activation, Kundalini, nothing!

Boy was he ever displeased. I put on my best game face and tried to sympathise.
 That's too bad," I said. "But how about your meditation? How did that go?" I asked.
"What do you mean?" he retorted.
"I mean was your mind quiet? Did the chattering stop for a while?"
Silence and a quizzical look of bewilderment was all he offered in response.
I tried to make myself clearer, "Did you have many thoughts arising? I mean, well, I mean… well, it musta been pretty quiet right?"

The Frenchman now acted as if that darn fool Pierrot, the clown, of the *Commedia dell'arte* fame had somehow materialized right in front of his chair and was asking him the silliest questions. Through no fault of my own, for I felt my questions were sincere and in good humour, I could see my discourse was now irking him mightily in a manner akin to that damned redneck at the zoo who consistently insists on poking the grizzly bear with a stick, which is not a good idea, so I excused myself.

Of course, this was an example of what happens when you go chasing great spiritual experiences for their own sake. If you do, dissatisfaction will surely be the eventual outcome. As Buddha always said of such impermanent experiences, "They come and go but are ultimately inherently unsatisfying and empty."

> True humour is indeed laughter at one's own self, at the Devine comedy, the fabulous deception, whereby one comes to imagine that a creature in existence is not also of existence.
> Alan Watts (spiritual philosopher and scholar)

# Chapter 20

*The scientists of today think deeply instead of clearly. One must be sane to think clearly, but one can think deeply and be quite insane.*

   Nikola Tesla (pioneering scientist and inventor)

   With the Mahamudra retreat period now under my belt, I simply went back to my room and sat again in silent meditation. There would be no respite for me. I did, however, decide to introduce a small modification to my routine. Henceforth, I would cut my hours down from the typical ten hours per day of sitting to a more reasonable eight. It was clear that ten or more hours per day could not be sustained indefinitely. This pace was just too darned exhausting and demanding. I found that eight hours, just like the favoured "just right" porridge in *The Story of the Three Bears*, hit the sweet spot nicely. Soon after the retreat ended, Fatty came to my door, and we socialised and decompressed a bit.

I enjoyed the opportunity to engage in these sporadic tete-a-tetes. Long periods of seclusion can take their toll, and that seemed to be the case for the both of us. Fatty seemed to be suffering from the effects of the long retreat. In fact, he apologised for being particularly gruff with me at one point during the proceedings. These monks always made a big production if you disturbed their silence, this despite their mantra of "compassion for all sentient beings." Go figure.

I once accidentally disturbed Bhikhu Ananda near the tail end of his solitary, one-month, silent meditation retreat centred on the theme of *compassion and loving kindness*. He was set up in a private hut near the back of the property where no one could disturb him. Unbeknownst to me, he had come to take a shower in the public bathhouse. I enquired within, thinking it was someone else. After he washed up, he challenged me about disturbing him and was frightfully rude about it. WTF? One month in isolation meditating on nothing but the topic of compassion *for all sentient beings* and that outrageous behaviour was the best he could muster? Such inquiry had apparently created a very miserable, uptight and unloving individual.

These Tibetan Buddhists, be they Western or otherwise, admittedly put on a really good game face when out amongst the masses. How they acted out of the public's gaze was often an entirely different matter. In short, I got the distinct impression that most of them were surely as screwed up as we all were.

The situation described above with Ananda was yet another example of a guy arguing with reality. I disturbed him, so he felt he had to point out how this should not have been so. I should not go around interfering with his peace. Yet clearly I had. And of course he suffered then for his position taking since reality will always prevail. There will always be moments where things don't go your way, and consequently there will always be moments where you get pissed off. The number of times I heard an ascetic complain about a disturbed meditation at the centre became quite a laughing matter for me.

I recall one incident where a decades-long meditator had his sit interrupted (thank God it wasn't me this time), and for days afterwards he would tell anyone who cared to listen how horrible the experience had been. He was so over the top with his "that jerk who interrupted me caused such a shock to my system...well, it took six days for me to recover...blah ,blah, blah," that my silent response was "Why don't you get a life buddy; you need to grow a pair and get off your bloody high horse."

Note to Buddha:

> Hey, my friend, you gotta add high horse to your list of lofty places your monks need to avoid. Apparently, chairs and beds ain't the end of it.

# Chapter 20

I found the Tibetan Buddhist lifestyle attracted a lot of passive aggressive and often quite neurotic folks on the one hand and downright nasty flakes on the other. Few seemed like the kind of people I would willingly want to share a picnic with though, of course, socialising was not on my agenda anyhow. Surprisingly, it now seemed to be on Monk Fatty's.

With the sweetest smile on his face, Fatty changed the subject and confided a secret to me. "Heh, DJ, remember that Asian-looking girl from the Vipassana retreat?"

"Of course I do," I replied. "She was into that Shambhala warriorship stuff, quite the looker too, eh?"

Fatty then surprisingly added, "Well, yeah, anyhow, her name is Joy, and by the way we are getting married."

I spluttered, "You are getting what…married…how?"

Fatty merely smiled at me. Forgotten now was the stress of the Mahamudra retreat. This new topic of conversation completely rejuvenated the man in the same manner watering wilted greenhouse lettuce brought the plants back to life.

I asked, "So how did you two meet?"

"Well," he replied, "I had a dream about her during the retreat, and in the dream it was clear that we should marry and that was that."

"Did you tell her that story?" I asked.

"Yep," came his pleased reply.

"And she accepted your proposal just like that?"

Again he replied, "Yep."

"Good for you…how about Wally?" I asked.

Fatty told me that Wally understood well his desires to enter into matrimonial bliss since the Lama, himself, had given up his robes long ago to marry. So blessings were given, and Bhikhu Fatty would soon be on his way to a better place I presumed. A couple of years later Fatty, now known as *David* for he went back to using his original given name since a monk must give up both his monkly title along with his robes, became a proud papa. I bet he got more out of that experience than he ever did from Buddhism.

Just before the last retreat of the season began, I decided to check in with Ayahuasca once again, and the decision turned out to be a good one.

Just a note here: Buddha had no prohibitions regarding the use of mind-enhancing drugs just as long as the experience did not cause *mindlessness* or *heedlessness*. Ayahuasca promoted quite the opposite effect so there was no guilt or trepidation on my part when I decided to have another session with dear, old Pachamama—this time on hermitage grounds. I am sure Gautama Buddha would have approved. It sure beat all those privations he put himself through. I did it very discretely so no one was ever the wiser, just in case it offended the sensibilities of the more ignorant.

As I recall, the single most spiritually relevant incident that transpired during that trip was the simple revelation that came to me in a kind of homage to the famous maxim "Be careful what you wish for as it may come true." Here it was slightly altered to "You should have been careful what you wished for (enlightenment) for it now most assuredly is going to come to pass." This revelation was presented in pretty much those exact words by an exceedingly authoritative presence.

Well, I tell you it is precisely that kind of admission that will really put the fear of God into you—quite literally. After the Ayahuasca session ended, I mulled that statement over again and again. The more I thought about it, the more unsettled I became. I discovered that it was one thing to entertain the noble quest, to aspire to reach the loftiest of spiritual heights but quite another to be told that it was a done deal. Yikes!

I had come to implicitly trust the wisdom, vision and advice Ayahuasca had provided in the past. It seemed like the plant was inviting me to state for the record my intention to awaken, and thus the implication was that it would most assuredly come to be. Frankly, that kind of direct admission scared the shit out of me.

Up to this point, I still had an "ejector seat," an "escape pod," in other words a little wiggle room left if I wanted to bail. Mother Ayahuasca, always on the lookout to ferret out insincerity and delusion, knew in this case this was the one "button" of mine that really needed to be pushed. I think she sensed a modicum of trepidation and indecision, so in her way she was helping me "get real." Would I bite?

I started to consider things more deeply, "Is this something I really, really wanted? I mean not to entertain the idea of enlightenment but to actually become the enlightened one?" The immensity of that notion took me aback. I began to wonder if I should think twice about this enlightenment gig. After all, I still knew so little about this way of being. Probably in part Ayahuasca was attempting to challenge my ego by showing it the enormity of what was really being called for here.

"Best to think this over much more carefully," I concluded. "I mean, we can't be too hasty on matters like this, can we?" What a Nancy pants my ego turned out to be. It gets a little hot in the kitchen and look who thinks about making a beeline for the exit. In fact, the next chance I got I asked Wally about the ramifications of the Ayahuasca incident, though I did not mention how it came about.

"Is this really a good thing to desire?," I inquired. He remained silent and was seemingly perplexed by this line of inquiry. I guess it was quite a thing to ask of a Lama seeing as his job, his whole raison d'etre, was seemingly at least partially premised on the very notion. "I mean what is the downside to this enlightenment thing?" I inquired further.

This raised an eyebrow, if not his ire, towards me. Basically Wally outright dismissed such a ridiculous question. His disdainful attitude was akin to "Of course awakening is the greatest thing since processed cheese slices." Then he added, and I'm paraphrasing a bit, "Don't be ridiculous. What is there to consider here, DJ? Stop being such a dope."

I was beginning to feel a bit sheepish at this point. To offer me a sense of "comfort" Wally added:

Chapter 20

Look, DJ…though reserved for the most exalted and rarest of beings ever to dwell in this corporeal realm, still we must all aspire to cultivate great bodhicitta with all our heart, receive merit through fostering compassion towards all sentient beings and realize the six (or was it ten, I forget now) *perfections* and wipe clear the ten *fetters* of the mind while attempting to attain the primordial ground of being where the clear light mind of awareness will abolish the five *hindrances*, the five *faults* and render the eight *antidotes* and four *immeasurables* irrelevant.

Whew!

With such wonderfully reasoned and reassuring advice (not), what the hell had I been thinking about? Now I could see it clearly. Of course, who wouldn't welcome enlightenment when you put it that way. Case closed. Wally cleared that one up "real good" for me, "real, real good." Again, I could see it would be left entirely up to me to get to the bottom of this matter.

After a day or so of deep introspection, I basically said, "Screw it" and decided to stay the course come what may. Try to scare me with your "Be careful what you wish for, blah, blah, blah crap…" In for a penny in for a pound. I would continue to wholeheartedly pursue this increasingly irrational journey to its natural conclusion or die trying. Which funnily enough was the exact same outcome.

>Sit down, shut up and ask yourself, "What's true?" until you know.
> Jed McKenna (mythical truth teller extraordinaire)

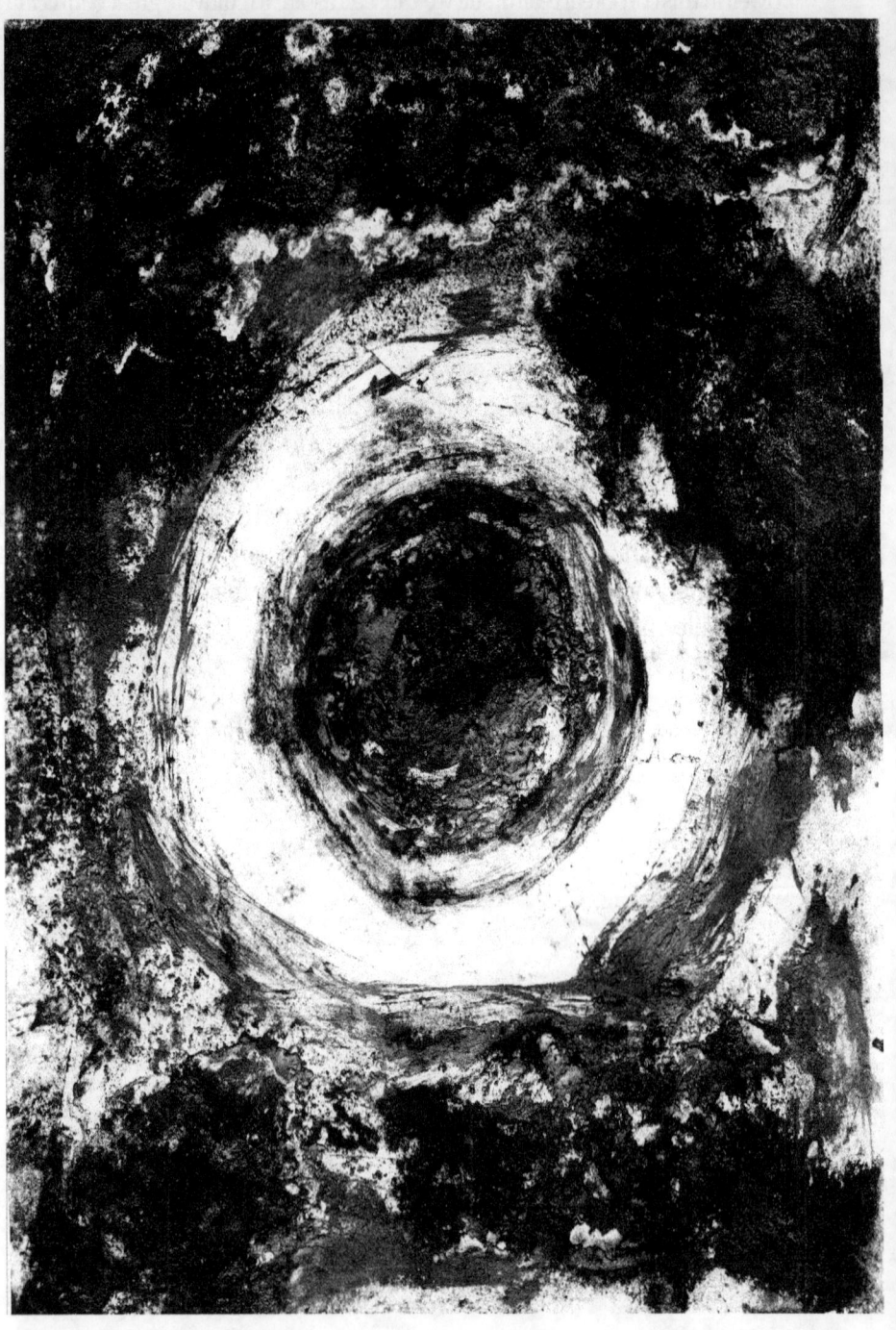

# Chapter 21

*There is beauty where there is no "me."*
　Toni Packer (writer, teacher)

　　　The final five-day retreat period of the season, led once again by Lama Maybe One, came and went with little fanfare save for one important event. I got to appreciate how wise my *inner guru* really was. I learned of the existence of this curious phenomenon (personified often as the inner sage, inner master or inner guru) directly from reputable sources on the Internet. This spiritual guide apparently resides in each of us. For millennia various sources have held that it is the wisest teacher of all. Originally, I thought the idea pretty outlandish. "Your own personal savant." Who could imagine such a thing?

Then a source of guidance, akin to intuition but seemingly able to share wisdom entirely outside my purview, started to pipe up. At certain times in the past it had presented itself in a guise I failed to recognize, such as when I was told by this wise presence while standing in a university cafeteria line not to continue to seek the path of wealth and privilege I was on at that time or more recently when I was stopped mid-stride during walking meditation and instructed to pay attention to *the gap*. Now, through the incident about to unfold, I could no longer mistake its identity.

This wise one actually made its presence known to me through a direct experience that transcended my conceptual mind entirely. This phenomenon pointed out things that I couldn't possibly know or even imagine. One might simply put it off to a subconscious part of my brain becoming more intuitive and intrusive, yet it seemingly had knowledge I had never been privy to.

Sadly I presume, few seekers know of its existence, and even fewer pay it any heed. I think our ego has to be sufficiently weakened for the message to get through. I assure you that there is a profound pool of wisdom awaiting discovery. This inner guru announced its presence rarely. It was intimately aware of the details of my journey and seemed to be close at hand, but its source of origin remains unknown to me. Quiet the monkey mind sufficiently and you too may become aware of it for yourself.

In what was to be its first officially recognized appearance, I sat in the yurt listening to another hackneyed teaching given by Lama Maybe One, hoping he would soon wrap it up so I could get on with the real work of bare witnessing and mindfulness practice, when suddenly the wise sage announced its presence.

I recall the experience quite vividly, for what it was about to reveal to me was so profound in nature that it revolutionized the very essence of my practice. No one up to this point in my journey, though relevant sources later emerged, had ever disclosed to me what I am about to describe.

Rather, somehow something (deep inside me…deep outside me?) knew precisely what I needed to discover at the exact correct moment. It was quite uncanny. What follows is pivotal to the rest of my journey for it pointed directly to "Beingness" or "presence" or "stillness" which is requisite to the awakening process.

As Lama Maybe One's tedious discourse continued full steam ahead at the front of the yurt, I was so exasperated that my eyes began to wander around looking for something, anything, of interest to relieve the tedium.

First, I noted the Tibetan artwork. Vibrantly hued, multi-coloured Tibetan *thangka* paintings, quite reminiscent of stained glass window panels, stood out as did other curiosities, mostly poorly discerned due to my lousy vision.

At the far end of the room, I spied a rather large sphere that I took to be a globe of the earth (in fact upon later inspection it turned out to be a drum). This presumed "globe" seemed to be one of those large free-standing antique pieces with a frame made of finely crafted hardwood. I didn't observe it for much more than several seconds before the wise one piped up to shatter my reverie.

Directly it opined (of course I am paraphrasing a bit here since it was a direct experience, but the gist is nevertheless accurate):

> So it is clear that you are getting really good at this meditation stuff. You are becoming a fine one-pointed concentrator indeed. And surely in twenty years you will be at the top of your game, a world class concentrator par excellence, maybe the best darn one-pointed meditator in the whole land. But to what end? Is that what is being called for here? Is that really what this affair is all about?
> No, it is not! To believe that is to miss the mark. And to miss the mark is to sin. That is not the way. Try this new course of inquiry instead.

It then proceeded to introduce me to a new form of meditation and, by wider abstraction, a new way of beginning to relate to the world at large, or more pointedly a new way to BE in, but not of, the world--embodied as just *Being existence itself*.

Then WIT (Wise Ineffable Teacher) said, "DJ, behold again that globe over there you were looking at." WIT then explained that rather than fixing my gaze about four feet in front of me as I usually did, I should instead not exclude anything from my outlook. I should simply apprehend the world in its entirety and include everything in my gaze. WIT called for the exact opposite form of identification the one-pointed meditation embraced. A holistic appreciation for all that existed in its entirety was to be fostered instead of a tiny speck of reality. Inclusive rather than exclusive, non-judgemental, WIT stressed that the practice of objectifying reality through the object of meditative focus (concentration on the breath) was no longer prudent.

I found that I instantly comprehended the non-discriminatory appreciation of reality through the metaphor of the globe that WIT had so wisely drawn to my attention. As the two-dimensional, abstracted piece of symbolic reality we call a "map" is to concentrative one-pointed meditation, so too this new meditation practice could be seen as the unified three-dimensional world of the globe. In other words, WIT was telling me "Where you once saw the crescent, you shall now see the whole of the moon."

WIT then introduced a further pointer, "You know that feeling you get…that special one, the one that comes when the gaps between the thoughts appear?"

I said, "sure, yeah, yeah, of course." I knew exactly what WIT was pointing to.

And then as if two friends were sharing a secret, WIT gently poked me in the ribs to get my attention and related a most beautiful pointer, "That's it. Just cultivate that. Find that feeling and run with it."

"Really…that's all it is? That's all I need to do, just 'cultivate,' that feeling" I inquired. (WIT carefully chose the term "cultivate" rather than 'do so and so').

"Right," came WIT's certain retort. "That's all it is."

I recall those exact words clearly—"Just cultivate that feeling."

"Okey-dokey, my friend. Roger on that one; DJ over and out."

That was the end of WIT's concise and revelatory transmission. It was always such a thrill to receive this kind of direct experience. Transcending the egoic mind to have authentic Truth reveal itself was the quintessential awakening experience. What a privilege and a blessing.

To the confused seeker that I still was, this kind of pointer was truly spot-on, certainly the best piece of advice that I could have received at that point in time. Rather than give my mind some philosophical tid-bit to chew on or suggest yet another useless conceptual idea to speculate about, WIT got right to the point and steered me in the direction of a new way to relate to reality.

That kind of advice bypassed the ego entirely. My "adviser" knew something that I apparently did not. Thoughts are the problem, not the solution. So it pointed out to me the feeling of "pure Beingness" that would occasionally arise in the gaps between my thoughts and suggested I try to cultivate that instead of concentrating on an object. I would say that this new juncture marked the beginning of the end for poor old DJ. Discovering *Beingness* is just that seminal in the awakening process.

So what, then, you may well ask does this *beingness* feel like? How can one ascertain it? Well, in a paradoxical way the thing that would try to pay attention to it, is the thing being pointed to here. Awareness. When attention begins to turn in on itself, some call this the act of cultivating *presence* or *beingness*. Of course, I knew naught about this at the time…I simply trusted WIT implicitly. Later, I found a passage in the "Diamond Sutra" that proved most illuminating:

> He should not dwell in forms when giving rise to that mind. He should not dwell in sounds, odours, tastes, tactile sensations, or ideas when giving rise to that mind. He should dwell nowhere when giving rise to that mind. If in that mind he has an abode, then it would be the non-abode.

This new direction quickly added another layer of vibrancy, lively presence and clarity to my practice. Soon these kinds of qualities would come to completely replace the doing and striving I was so fond of.

I immediately did as I was instructed right then and there in the yurt. I diffused my attention and cultivated a holistic, unfocused vivid sense of *the feeling of the gap* as Lama Maybe One yammered on in the background. Man if that guy only knew what I was experiencing, I doubt he would ever be moved to say another word about Tibetan Buddhism.

The effect was immediate, pronounced, extremely profound and startling. Momentarily an almost giddy feeling overwhelmed me. Then the non-objective, non-perspective, non-point of view—sometimes referred to as *awareness itself*, or *presence for its own sake*—arose, and I knew without a doubt that this was it. I had discovered True meditation. Wow! This is what my practice had been sorely missing all along.

I immediately appreciated how cultivating this "special feeling" was the key to it all. Later, I learned several labels or terms exist to describe this state of being. Among others it is called *pure beingness, pure awareness, emptiness, no-mind, no-self, true-nature, Buddha-mind, true-self, abiding as non-duality, sitting as the ground of being,* or simply *being as the void.*

By sitting with what was, by not attempting to interfere with or modify anything, neither focus attention on my breath nor try to stop my thoughts, a spaciousness and clarity of mind naturally manifested quite unlike anything I had experienced to date. This new practiceless practice was so simple and uncontrived to carry out that I marvelled at how easy it was.

Though I will state that at this point things were certainly now trending in the right direction, there was still a lot of "me" that had to continue to be burned away. This process would come to a close all in good time.

It was surprising how carefree, how much in the flow, this new style of meditation felt. The ease with which the meditation now proceeded seemed almost like "cheating."

My eyes could be wide open or closed; it really mattered not. The meditation room similarly could be brightly lit or dark, perfumed or dank and musty. It just didn't matter anymore. I discovered that my state of BEING was not dependant on my surroundings or outside influences. My attention remained focused on nothing in particular. I was both hyper aware and totally relaxed at the same time. Early on I scoffed at such a possibility for I wondered how it could be possible to be incredibly alert and yet so relaxed, as to be almost asleep, at the same time. Yet the further I let go into this non-meditation meditation, the more pronounced this reality became.

As the non-practice deepened, awareness simply noted a thought which then died out on its own accord in the same manner a fire dampens down when fuel is withheld from it. I might hear a bird outside. This was vaguely noted, but no story followed. Then silence would reappear. A compressor on the fridge would turn on. Same thing, just a noting of the sound and nothing more. No narratives arose like how noisy the black ravens were today or how disturbing electrical appliances could be. Such observations simply stemmed from senses doing what they do.

Never would I return to a meditation based on noting my breath. Neither would dedicated, purposefully contrived periods of insight practice be carried out. If insight arose, from now on it would do so by its own devices.

I found that this new kind of objectless meditation could be performed "out in the world" as well. This awareness that "I" was seemingly cultivating (but later understood to be present at all times, so "I" was not really cultivating anything at all) could be brought forth any time I wished. I could mow a lawn or walk in the woods, and if sufficient attention was paid, there it was—pure presence. In the early days of this new way of promoting stillness, I noted my senses growing ever more acute.

For example, the meadow grass appeared much more sharply defined and in focus, the dinner gong could now be heard from over half a kilometre away which astounded me and even things like mundane cracks in the muddy road took on a new found sense of significance.

These were exciting times. Reality became more immediate and intimate. As when I was a child, again with great pleasure and glee I became an explorer of a most magnificent realm.

I shared the good news with Ananda, but he was unimpressed. In fact, it was a matter of contention with him. He told me I was doing it all wrong. He reported this to Wally who in turn asked me to stop the new technique. He strongly advised me to go back to my old meditation routine.

What nonsense! I, of course, ignored this and any other future advice these two buffoons would offer me. As things progressed, I became acutely aware that the two guys had no experience in these matters. It is often the case that people operating or leading spiritual centres have no understanding or way to deal with seekers who are actually undergoing authentic and dramatic awakening experiences. It is shocking, but true, I am afraid.

One nice effect this new-found meditation had was that the headaches left me. They were instead replaced by a feeling of pretty intense pressure in my frontal lobe region. Also a peculiar feeling arose like bugs running through my hair (a very weird sensation since my scalp was clean shaven). I could have sworn cockroaches were having a fiesta on the top of my head each time I sat in silence. On the Internet, I saw reports of others with similar symptoms. It's actually quite common. Some say it feels like someone is gently patting your head.

Soon this queer, creepy, crawly feeling subsided, and then the pressure at the front of my skull shifted to the rear. Oh well, such are the vicissitudes of waking up. I never made anything out of them unlike Kundalini aficionados who speak highly of such symptoms.

To further elaborate on Wally's and Ananda's admonishment that I was *doing it all wrong*, I have several points to add. First, I took it upon myself to search in one of their beloved Tibetan meditation texts for some information on how my new holistic meditation style might compare to known techniques. Low and behold, I found the confirmation I was seeking.

There was a whole section devoted to an advanced form of meditation called *meditating without an object*, and the description of it precisely matched what I was presently doing/non-doing. How then was I erring, I wondered?

I reckon that a great deal of what is wrong with Tibetan Buddhism has a lot to do with all the degrees and manner of resistance they engage in. You know you have a problem when they are compelled to adjust and correct things with their, "right action," right speech," "right livelihood," etc., etc. Once you awaken these "right" qualities or attributes naturally well up on their own accord...not the other way around. First, get the "right view," and all else will naturally fall into place.

More ridiculous still are mandates like monks being required to sleep on low beds. The prohibitions seemed almost endless. Waking up has a great deal to do with not arguing with what is. Who cares if your robes are not of a certain hue or length, your bed a certain height, or your room a certain dimension? Again, who cares? Oh, how could I have forgotten, it's you Tibetan Buddhists, right? I assure you that the Absolute cares not a whit. Distinction making only leads to more of the same.

*Chapter 21*

I was reporting positive spiritual transformation. For the so called "authorities" to advise me to resist such blessings and do things another way seemed at the time, and even more so now, very foolish advice indeed. The consideration under scrutiny here is the difference between entertaining how it "should be" versus how it actually is right here and now. I have found that the present moment is always a beautiful thing indeed.

> Until the whole world is free to agree with you or disagree with you, until you have given the freedom to everyone to like you or not like you, to love you or hate you, to see things as you see them or to see things differently—until you have given the whole world its freedom—you'll never have your freedom.
> Adyashanti (spiritual teacher)

# Chapter 22

*Dare to look at everything around you without fear and without formula…and it won't be long before you see.*
　Anthony de Mello (Jesuit priest, writer and public speaker)

　　By now it had been weeks since Ananda vacated the premises. Fatty would be gone for good in a few days as well. Even the more frost-hardy garden vegetables such as broccoli and kale had pretty much called it quits for the season. Soon the early morning frost would give way to winter's ice and snow. Things had gotten very quiet now that the retreat season was over. Swami made the rare appearance only for practical reasons, like the day he showed up to repair the water pump. Otherwise, I was left to my own devices.
　　Continuing my Internet investigation, I had by now learned that the spiritual landscape was much broader than I first imagined. Over the past months, I had spotted a lot of rubbish,

but there were real luminaries out there that deserved consideration. Lots of new concepts awaited assimilation. To be clear, I was not looking for spiritual entertainment. Anything that appeared spiritually edifying got my utmost attention, the rest I ignored. So how does one discern authentic spirituality from the plethora of irrelevant material that abounds?

Well, in general I might say that as one increasingly aligns with the Truth, the Truth gets easier to discern. It's a bit like our intuitive faculty. The more attuned to it we become, the stronger it gets. How do you explain that? There is a knowing that exists outside the conceptual mind. Truth recognizes Truth.

I am talking about appreciating the difference between knowing and believing. Beliefs were useless by this point of the truth game. *To know* meant to discover something for myself.

Those teachers that pointed directly to Reality in a heartfelt manner while having an open, sincere and uncompromising attitude devoid of egoic projection, self-interest and hubris were the only ones worthy of my consideration.

The field was flooded with self-help gurus and feel-good showmen keen on whispering sweet little platitudes into our ears while extracting coin from our pockets. It was evident that these smooth operators had *their*, rather than *our*, best interest at heart. The spiritual marketplace, rife with its pretenders and even worse, did eventually cough up an authentic teacher or two.

Some of these guides were famous, others much less so as pedigree mattered not when it came to Truth telling. The wise ones seemed to have a firm finger on the pulse of Reality, and intuitively I could detect someone who was speaking from a place of authenticity. The situation was a lot like a farmer going to a rural sales barn to pick up some new heifers. In any lot of cows, an experienced stockman or drover could instantly discern the few good head worthy of consideration. It takes time and experience to develop this kind of keen eye, but once you find it, there is no doubt that it will never lead you astray. The Truth is easy to discern in a similar manner once you become aligned with it. I wondered then why so many seekers got so easily bamboozled by the BS. I'll put that one down once more to good old Maya.

Talking about getting aligned with the truth, during a casual chat not long before he left, Bhikhu Fatty let slip (monks were encouraged not to speak to others about their spiritual life…God only knows why.) that Wally had once again been pestering him about his lack of *samadhi* experience. "Have you had *samadhi* yet?" I pressed Fatty for further details. "What precisely is it?" I asked.

Fatty explained that Wally often stressed the importance of attaining this illumined state, but since he had never had this kind of experience himself, Fatty could not elaborate. "Well, oh well, finally something I can sink my teeth into," I rejoiced. Getting this *samadhi* thing was instantly elevated to the top of my to-do list. Obviously then, the man to ask was Wally. You may recall that he was the guy who prefaced his spiritual outlook with "Book learning bad…face time with the great guru good!" So the next chance I had, I asked the Venerable Rinpoche to fill me in. "What is *samadhi*?" I directly inquired. His answer surprised me greatly.

Without batting an eyelid, he referred me to a title, a goddamn book. Can you believe it? Wally suggested that I check out a certain passage from the *Autobiography of a Yogi*. The problem with the passage, presented in excerpt below, is that it has nothing at all to do with *samadhi*. Nada. Here then is an excerpt which portrays a Master, by way of a laying on of hands, giving his student his so-called "heart's desire"—*samadhi*. It really is a preposterous example for reasons I will elucidate in a minute.

"Poor boy, the mountains couldn't give what you wanted." Master spoke caressively, comfortingly. His calm gaze was unfathomable. "Your heart's desire shall be fulfilled...He struck gently on my chest above the heart. My body became immovably rooted; breath was drawn out of my lungs as if by some huge magnet. Soul and mind instantly lost their physical bondage, and streamed out like a fluid piercing light from my every pore. The flesh was as though dead, yet in my intense awareness I knew that never before had I been fully alive. My sense of identity was no longer narrowly confined to a body, but embraced the circumambient atoms. People on distant streets seemed to be moving gently over my own remote periphery. The roots of plants and trees appeared through a dim transparency of the soil; I discerned the inward flow of their sap.

The whole vicinity lay bare before me. My ordinary frontal vision was now changed to a vast spherical sight, simultaneously all-perceptive. Through the back of my head I saw men strolling far down Rai Ghat Road, and noticed also a white cow who was leisurely approaching. When she reached the space in front of the open ashram gate, I observed her with my two physical eyes. As she passed by, behind the brick wall, I saw her clearly still.

All objects within my panoramic gaze trembled and vibrated like quick motion pictures. My body, Master's, the pillared courtyard, the furniture and floor, the trees and sunshine, occasionally became violently agitated, until all melted into a luminescent sea; even as sugar crystals, thrown into a glass of water, dissolve after being shaken. The unifying light alternated with materializations of form, the metamorphoses revealing the law of cause and effect in creation.

An oceanic joy broke upon calm endless shores of my soul. The Spirit of God, I realized, is exhaustless Bliss; His body is countless tissues of light. A swelling glory within me began to envelop towns, continents, the earth, solar and stellar systems, tenuous nebulae, and floating universes.

I'll leave it there. It's a pretty fantastic tale, no? That wasn't even the half of it. This supposed mystical foray into the spiritual realm continues on and on with ever more amazing descriptions of wonderment, cosmic consciousness and bliss. How Wally could have mistaken this claptrap for *samadhi* is beyond me. Of course, if he never had the experience himself, then passing this dreck off as the real thing would make perfect sense. This is just the kind of fantastic nonsense the ego loves to entertain in its quest to maintain its everlasting state of delusion.

The plain honest truth is that the higher forms of *samadhi* are not experiences at all. And unlike this imaginative tale so rich in mystical underpinnings and wonder, *samadhi* in contrast has a paucity of detail.

This imaginative description is either a complete fabrication or else born out of an altered state of consciousness that has nothing to do with the Absolute ground of being at all. Perhaps the author entered the pre-dream, hypnagogic state. Being a proficient, lucid dreamer myself, I could well imagine this could be the case. A big tip off that indicates why this description has nothing at all to do with true letting go is the fact that the author presents a God external to himself. In legitimate *samadhi*, there is no "you" and no "God" either. I don't discount the fact that this tale could be an inspirational account of a mystical moment. But mysticism is far removed from waking up! My description of *samadhi* to follow should clear up why this account does not pertain to *samadhi* in the slightest. I think it was very telling that Wally did not offer me his own personal account of the phenomenon.

Though it would be a while before I cultivated my own *samadhi*, I immediately discounted the previous description. It was just so frickin apparent that that account had nothing to do with the realizations Buddha prescribed. A couple of months later, I asked Wally again to give me details on *samadhi* in the hopes that he had forgotten our first exchange (at this point I was wondering if he was purposely antagonising or confounding me), and again he referred me to a passage in yet another book. That suggested passage was as equally off base. Using the direct approach to try to confirm if Wally had any personal experience, I asked him how many times a week he experienced *samadhi*. He seemed to be shocked at my temerity. After a long pause, he muttered something about "infrequent occurrence due to lack of time available to meditate."

In my experience, *samadhi* required no time at all to "turn on," so to speak. I simply reclined on my meditation chair, placed identification nowhere/everywhere and in two to three seconds—bam...*samadhi* extraordinaire. Further details soon follow.

> Be "You." Do not do as others do or as I do. That is a lot of dodo...and we all know what that smells like.
> Puppetji ("wizdumb" master)

# Chapter 23

*The world is illusory. Brahman alone is real. Brahman is the world.*

Ramana Maharshi (non-dual guru)

Of course, if the Buddhist tradition had worthwhile advice to offer me, then I was all ears. If instead it came from the Hindu *advaita* tradition, that was just as well too. In fact if it was helpful, I could care less where the source of guidance originated. I was not attached to any "ism" in particular. Who cares what style the rod and reel is just as long as it lands the whoppers, right?

During my Internet investigation which employed the page rank algorithm system of the "Digital Delphic Oracle," colloquially known as the *Google search engine,* I was given access to all manner of marvellous forms of media that would have led the ancients of old to deduce that magic was somehow being surreptitiously employed.

Heck, I was even of an age such that back in 2008 YouTube, podcasts, blogs, social media, Skype and Java-enabled websites still seemed sufficiently high tech to be wondrous. I was truly fortunate to have such a cornucopia of information at my disposal.

In the early stages of parsing the net, I naturally kept the focus mainly on Buddhism, if for no other reason than I presently resided in one of their institutions. One thing I quickly discovered about the tradition was the fact that Siddhartha Gautama Buddha was not the inventor of meditation as I had originally and erroneously presumed. In fact, meditation predated him by centuries. He did, though, have a unique slant on some fundamental truths.

Several times I went back to Gautama Buddha's core teaching on suffering. Here he explained to the assembled monks how life was inherently unsatisfying. What follows is the gist of his observations.

Of note is the fact that Buddha's very first sutra, sermon or teaching, ever given was on the topic of dissatisfaction, and it is arguably his most important tenet. It is called "Turning the Wheel of the Dharma" and it is found in the *Pali Canon* which is considered to be the oldest and probably least corrupted of all Buddhist teachings.

The *Theravada* tradition uses this canon as its source material, whereas the Mahayana path follows much later texts. Tibetan Buddhist source material differs as well. It is placed under the umbrella of Tahayana, so its doctrine is quite different from the following outline I will now present which is the earliest, and therefore probably most germane, text regarding what the historical Buddha was actually pointing to.

I don't recall Wally ever speaking about the Eightfold Path, for instance. Tibetan teachings are much more complicated and to my mind less direct than the Pali Canon source material. Still, even that is a bit specious for it was written some five hundred years after the death of Buddha. Who knows what the old boy really said? Anyhow, the following are claimed to be his first instructions on the path to awakening. I figured it must have been kind of important, seeing that it was ostensibly the first thing on the man's mind after he woke up. He told the five assembled monks kneeling before him that they should consider the profundity of the Four Noble Truths as I have summarized below:

Suffering (or Dissatisfaction) Exists

> Chasing after sensual delights and expecting them to bring lasting pleasure will always lead to dissatisfaction in the end because these things are all subject to the miseries of birth, old age, sickness and death. These states are impermanent. None of them offer any lasting sense of fulfilment or peace of mind. Even when happiness arises, it soon fades.

# Chapter 23

## The Cause of Suffering

Being unable to find contentment with what we have or who we are, greed or desire and suffering in its myriad forms is the automatic result. Thus, selfishness and greediness are the roots of our perennial dissatisfaction. Therefore, we find no peace in the world.

## End of Suffering

If one truly understands how suffering arises due to these selfish attitudes, they can then be liberated from these tendencies, and hence all suffering and dissatisfaction will come to an end. Then that individual will experience a happiness that is far greater than their ordinary pleasures and a peace that is beyond words will be born.

## The Middle Path or the Nobel Eightfold Path

The way to find satisfaction is through the eightfold path which leads to the end of all suffering. If we avoid harming sentient beings, if we sharpen and focus our minds, and if we gain wisdom, each of us can reach perfect happiness, the end of all misery. This path comprises:

Right Understanding or View
Right Thought
Right Speech
Right Action
Right Livelihood
Right Effort
Right Mindfulness
Right Concentration

That then is Buddha's first teaching in a nutshell. I won't get into the specifics of the later points here for I never much bothered cultivating "right" outlooks myself. I was sincere in my attitude to awaken, and that apparently was sufficient.

I had little time to try to perfect moral behaviour and be a better person for, after all, waking up really has precious little to do with how we treat ourselves and others or conduct our daily affairs as we move through the vicissitudes of life. True spirituality is a far, far more radical proposition than that.

I suspect in practice these kinds of codes were designed to make well-behaved and responsible monks rather than liberated beings. Be that as it may, I think I found some wisdom in the guiding philosophies of the Four Noble Truths.

I found the part about life being inherently unsatisfying quite true, and the explanation Buddha provided for this predicament also seemed to hold. To not be satisfied with the current state of affairs did, indeed, cause anxiety and stress. Wants and desires and attachment to material possessions did lead one down the royal road to misery.

The fact that Buddha offered a way out of this pickle, and that he personally discovered this reality for himself, proved quite inspirational to me and certainly worth my full consideration. Getting rid of attachment of any sort, endeavouring to remove the grasping and clinging tendencies of the ego, seemed to be one of the most important concepts open for further consideration. With that ideal foremost in mind, I continued to peruse the Internet.

In the early weeks, I had spent quite a lot of time on The Wanderling's "Awakening 101" website sifting through reams of great information. One section grabbed my attention. It featured biographical accounts of actual contemporary awakenings. These accounts purported to describe the real thing and were a lot more accessible than stuffy old Tibetan texts for sure. Two accounts were of particular interest to me.

The first was "A Child of the Cyber-Sangha" which featured the account of a young man who found knowledge and inspiration predominantly through information he gathered over the Internet. I share now several pertinent excerpts to give you a taste of Cyber Child's experience:

> I discovered that anything that can be distinguished is not really me. Everything that is conditioned, subjected to cause and effect and thus impermanent, is not who I really am. That all the thoughts, feelings and views that we harbour have nothing to do with me. Even my body is not really me. There is no 'I'...The 'I' as such is nothing more than a set of ideas, thoughts and views which are being continuously sustained by dwelling on them and holding on to them as real. Once the false 'I' is seen through, the true self manifests.
>
> My true self is awareness or consciousness...and is not bound by anything at all. I call it the Unconditioned or Essence of Mind. What I mean by Essence of Mind is that when you take everything in the mind and strip it away, *then* there is just this, the essence, left.
>
> It is not bound by space, so it could be called infinite, yet this is not really true as it cannot really be said to have any spatial limits even if this limit is infinity. Thus my true self expands everywhere in all directions, yet it is nowhere to be found.
>
> It is not bound by time, so it could be called eternal, yet this is not really true either, as it is utterly beyond any time limits even if this limit is eternity. My true self was never born, never ages and never dies. Yet to say that I will live for eternity is not true either, as it is utterly beyond time. Perhaps the closest thing would be to say that there is just this utterly unchanging moment, yet this also fails to hit the mark as it could imply that it is static which it is not. It is beyond static and moving. Thus before the world was, I AM. Not before the world, I was, but before the world, I AM.

First off, that is an excellent account of what awakening really feels like. To the neophyte seeker in me, I found it an exciting but also unexpected and puzzling account. I had never in my life come across a report of what true awakening was like written in such a direct, graphic, lucid and no-nonsense manner.

Cyber Child's words were very lively and attractive to me. I was inspired and motivated to try to find further testimonials in this vein. Somehow I knew that he was telling the *Truth*. As I continued to read his account, I grew ever more impressed, but I did not know why, for his testimony seemed almost incomprehensible. Yet I knew beyond a shadow of a doubt he was pointing to something profound, revolutionary. But what was it? I read further to try to make more sense of it:

> It is not bound by any conditioned phenomena (which constitutes all of existence—the entire universe). Since all conditioned phenomena are in a constant state of flux, the Unconditioned could be said to be unmoving, yet this is not really true since it implies something static. Let it be understood that it merely does not participate in the flux of conditioned existence, and this absence of flux is called unmoving.
>
> It is not bound by the senses either…it could be said to be silent, yet this isn't really true either. Rather, it is the absence of sound and silence. It cannot be seen, heard, smelled, felt, tasted or cognised in any way…there is just this awareness of the senses.
>
> It is not dual in any way. Thus it could be said to be non-dual, yet this isn't really true either. Rather, it is neither dual nor non-dual…thoughts will never be able to capture your true self. True freedom means that everything merely is as it is…There is no "should"…True non-"shouldness" means taking in both "should" and the absence of "should" and let everything, even your "shoulds," be as it is…

Fascinating. There were no *thou shalt* nor *thou shalt nots* to be found anywhere in his account of seeing things as they really were. This kind of talk excited me beyond compare. This Cyber Kid goes on to conclude with:

> Since it is not bound by time or movement in any way, it is always present…you are constantly pulled around by your thoughts and views, yet your true self remains utterly unmoving…nothing changes at all. If anything changes it is merely that you are now aware of the fact that things are as they are, and that it has always been so. There is nothing to be realized.
>
> …nothing mysterious about it. Do not imagine that this unconditioned awareness is somehow apart from the world and daily life. On the contrary, it could be said that one is even closer to life than ever before…Yet there is just this awareness, there is nothing to be aware of…

Of course, my mind was once again drawn to try to use reason or logic to figure out what the heck Cyber Child was talking about. The thing I still failed to grasp at this juncture was that waking up has nothing at all to do with reason or thought. So, of course, I couldn't think my way out of the confusion Cyber Child's words had fomented.

Looking closer, it seemed like Cyber Child was negating everything that could come to a person's mind, which left me no place to stand at all. Bravo!

That is what a great Zen master does. When you have finally given up trying to figure it all out, liberation will naturally ensue. If you dwell solely in the conceptual realm, illusion is sure to prevail. If you want to wake up, you have to cease deriving your sense of self from within the narrative of "I." This is not a doing but more of an undoing or non-doing,. More along those lines to follow as my tale continues to unfold.

There was another contemporary account of awakening from the vaults of the Wanderling's website that grabbed my attention as well. Whereas Cyber Child presented a baffling, though seemingly not unpleasant, portrayal of awakening, the next piece I will now discuss chronicled a disturbing and rather frightful account of enlightenment. It unsettled me so much that, much against my better judgment, I sought out Ananda's take on its depressing viewpoint. Of course, his opinion was of no help whatsoever as he just glossed over the whole thing and dismissed the account as irrelevant. "A consequence of poor practice" he informed me, but I knew better.

Unfortunately, the link to this piece is nowhere to be found on Wanderling's site these days so I cannot share it with you as I have forgotten the author. Instead, I substitute several excerpts from Steven Norquist's essay entitled "What is enlightenment, no, I mean really, like what is it?" which is an account of what he realized upon awakening. When I first chanced upon it, its nihilism and sense of dread struck me in exactly the same manner the missing account had. Here are a few excerpts to give you a taste of what I am talking about:

> …even though there is much activity in the world, there are no doers. The universe is, in a sense, lifeless…
>
> …consciousness is not Aware of the universe, consciousness is aware as the universe…There is no observer…existence is an automatic machine-like emergence out of Universe/Consciousness and is following a strict non-chance pattern. More importantly, no one is performing any of the above…
>
> Stuff is happening but no one is doing it. Emergence proceeds and consciousness is aware.
>
> …The reality is, the body exists, the thoughts exist, the memories exist, and that is consciousness, and that is all…
>
> So in order to keep the illusion of personality, of the idea that there is something or someone, they invent stories, or theories, or ideas, wear special clothes, perform certain rituals, and so on. They teach this stuff. But the truth is so simple, it is laughable…

> …Enlightenment is not about morality or vows, it is simply existence in the truth, that is all…
>
> …Enlightenment carries no requirements and expects nothing; the universe manifests, and just that is enlightenment.
>
> We don't seek enlightenment to be happy or to give our lives meaning or to feel bliss or ecstasy.…

That is pretty heavy stuff, isn't it? Not what most seekers want to hear? Funny thing is, I wouldn't argue with the guy as to the veracity of his account nor his conclusions, though on some points I would language it quite differently. I found Norquist's admissions very provocative, a take-no-prisoners, nowhere-to-take-cover kind of engagement. I rather liked it.

I believed Norquist was speaking from experience. I had little doubt about that. I found it difficult though to reconcile his dreadful view of non-duality, of the awakened state, with the majority of far less depressing spiritual outlooks. How was I to account for the discrepancy between viewpoints? The answer is not a simple one, so I think I will leave it there for now. The complexities of what are under consideration here may become more apparent later in the book when I reveal the subtleties of my own awakening.

Reading the Wanderling's rambling website from the vantage point of the spiritually immature was an adventure unto itself. What a rollicking good time I had exploring its haphazard, unorganized, cross-linked pages. True to its namesake, I simply wandered around from link to link in the same fashion I would have if visiting a foreign museum with no English descriptions or signs to aid my comprehension. I never got lost in the confusion, for I had no idea where I was headed.

This organic approach suited the explorer in me. I found his emphasis on Buddhist material most rewarding, though he was not at all exclusive in this regard. The references he provided to the Hindu philosophy of *Advaita Vedanta* (non-duality) opened up a whole new realm for me. *Advaita Vedanta*, and to a lesser extent *neo-advaita*, which is a modern, far less scripturally oriented equivalent and thus an increasingly popular tradition in the West, really opened my eyes to a kind of spirituality hitherto unimagined.

No matter who was espousing the *Advaita* core teaching of "not twoness" (literal translation), better known to us as non-duality, its approach seemed eminently simple, rational and reasonably prosaic. Its emphasis on finding "the True Self" or cultivating the "I-amness" appealed to me. Through *Advaita,* I learned of the "open secret" and a concept popularly referred to as "oneness."

Further, I soon discovered that its emphasis on *monism* was not unique to this tradition. Its central tenet that the seeming multiplicity of existing things can ultimately be reduced to a single unified reality or indivisible substrate, ran through the discourses of many philosophers, metaphysicians and several theologians too.

The ancient Greek Philosopher Plotinus and his *Monad* concept is a case in point. Plotinus' view on monism held that the Monad was a supreme totally transcendent ONE which was prior to all existence. *Advaita Vedanta* holds this as well with its idea of "the ONE before a second." Several pre- and post-Socratic philosophers as well as a few religious traditions such as Islam, Sufism and Christian Gnosticism pointed to a similar idea also.

*Advaita Vedanta's* long history reaches back to some of the first recorded texts in history—the Vedas. *Advaita* is the oldest school of *Vedanta* and is rooted in the *Upanishads* and the *Bhagavad Gita,* which is considered to be the fundamental religious text of the Hindus. A core teaching in those texts is the idea that *Atman* is *Brahman*. Brahman here is the Absolute substratum on which all phenomena are experienced; the innermost Atman, the real self, is identical to Brahman. Brahman could be thought of as the cosmic soul and Atman the individual soul. Ultimately though, all distinctions break down when True self is realized. All is found to be divinity or pure Spirit itself. I found the Sanskrit term *tat tvam asi,* "That Thou Art" or "You Are That," to be a nice reminder here.

Similarly, *Maya* was another helpful concept. As you have probably gathered by now, it means the worldly play of illusion or ignorance in our lives such that the unity of Brahman remains obscured to us mortals. Thus, seeing through Maya's ability to create duality is paramount to awakening. To know Brahman is to experience the removal of ignorance of your own true nature. Therefore, to know Brahman is to be Brahman. Liberation then consists of a practical path which is not intellectual but experiential. This notion was appealing for it echoed the original impetus of my quest—namely to get up off my fanny and find out a thing or two for myself.

I remember coming across two wonderful *Advaita* pointers that helped me better appreciate what this path was really about. Both descriptions illustrate the inherent *Oneness* behind and beyond all things. I present them here for your consideration. The first example is the clay pot metaphor.

> Clay is the fundamental substance comprising the pot under consideration here. The perception of a pot is found in noting its *form and function*. The color, feel, smell, and sound of the pot is ultimately dependant on its more fundamental "clay" nature. Clay was there before the pot came into being, and clay will be there even after the pot returns to dust. To perceive "the pot" is to experience a temporary entity which is based on something more fundamental, though not really evident at the time it is being considered.

In a similar fashion, "human doings" fail to realize that reality is inherently relativistic. What you make of it boils down to point of view. As Friedrich Nietzsche opined, "There are no facts, only interpretations," which is similarly echoed in the words of the beloved Roman emperor and much admired Stoic philosopher Marcus Aurelius who wrote, "Everything we hear is an opinion, not a fact. Everything we see is a perspective, not the truth."

If you see ceramic ware, I can't argue with that, but the clay knows better. If "clay" had a point of view it might say, "Clay is clay is clay—it's all clay, all the time you dummy. Transmutation is simply impossible." The pot manifests due to a simple trick of the mind.

*Advaita Vedanta* holds that pure Consciousness is like the clay in this example. Everything in this world is mere form and function like the pot. The substance behind all objects is Brahman, sometimes also called your "true nature."

The next example is the rope/snake metaphor.

> In the dim light, a rope appears as a snake to a weary traveller retiring for the evening. The general size, colour, texture, shape, etc., of the rope appears to be that of a snake due to lack of discernment on the part of the lodger. Though a "snake" appears to the groggy onlooker, in truth the rope is unaffected by the guest's erroneous perception. The snake has appeared simply due to a lack of full knowledge or ignorance on the part of the onlooker.

This metaphor is commonly used to point out our own confusion regarding reality as it truly is. Consciousness or True nature is free from any qualities. It is changeless, indivisible, homogeneous, isotropic, eternal, whole and without a second. This explains why *Advaita Vedanta* literally is commonly called non-duality here in the West. Now I'd like to draw your attention to two of the most famous non-dualist gurus of the last century. I found their pointers to be most helpful in my own awakening.

Here I am referring to Ramana Maharshi and Nisargadatta Maharaj. The Bible mentions there once being an age of giants, the so called "mighty men of renown." Well, these two guys, and a select few others, were my spiritual goliaths, and it was upon their shoulders that I was fortunate enough to stand.

Ramana Maharshi died in 1950, so no one these days can actually recount sitting with him at his ashram. Still his teachings endure through contemporary works of his time or through those penned by various students after his death.

Ramana Maharshi's initial awakening is attributed to a rather odd experience from his youth. One day at the age of sixteen, and quite out of the blue, he turned his attention towards matters of death. He was gripped by fear as he imagined himself to be dying. Then, he wondered what it was that actually passed away. Through this spontaneous inquiry, he realized *THAT* which transcends life and death entirely. In other words, he discovered what he called his "true self."

Eventually, taking up the role of a guru, Ramana Maharshi presented as an unassuming and reserved figure. Apparently his quiet, humble presence was often all that was required to induce insight in his students. Sitting as stillness and silence was a central strategy he encouraged his followers to adopt. He also promoted the practice of self-inquiry if silence alone was insufficient to induce clarity of mind. By inquiring into "who or what am I?" the hope was "true-self" would be realized. You may recognize that this is precisely the same inquiry I spontaneously took up with great vigour.

This "authentic I" was, in contrast to one's normal experience of a perceptible objectified relative reality, not an experience the individual had per se but rather an impersonal, all-inclusive, undifferentiated aware consciousness, in other words, pure beingness itself. He stressed that this kind of realization had nothing to do with the individual small "s" egoic self. This he pointed out was essentially non-existent since it was only a fabrication of the mind to begin with and thus had no tangible qualities. He maintained that the True-Self is always present, but ONE is only consciously aware of it when the self-limiting tendencies of the mind are seen through. Permanent and continuous Self-awareness is known as Self-realization.

Self-enquiry into "Who am I?" places attention squarely on the inner awareness of "I" or "I amness." Ramana Maharshi frequently recommended it as the most efficient and direct way of discovering the unreality of the *I-thought*.

Ramana warned against utilizing self-enquiry as simply an intellectual exercise. Properly done, it involves fixing the attention firmly and intensely on the feeling of "I" without utilizing the conceptual mind. Attention must be fixed on the "I amness" until the sense of a personal self disappears, and the True Self is thus realized.

Ramana's written works contain insightful descriptions of the results of self-enquiry such as verse thirty of his book *Ulladu Narpadu (Forty Verses on Reality)*:

> Questioning "Who am I?" within one's mind, when one reaches the Heart, the individual I sinks crestfallen, and at once reality manifests itself as "I-I." Though it reveals itself thus, it is not the ego "I" but the perfect being the Self Absolute.

I appreciated very much what Ramana was pointing to here. Whatever this awakening thing was, it was clearly something "I" embodied and not something I thought about. It was more subject than object. This came as another huge shock to me. Increasingly, wherever I turned I could see that the crux of this spiritual journey had little if anything to do with "me," DJ, discovering some truth or great revelation. Apparently, it was not about gaining new wisdom or knowledge. It seemed more about discovering who I truly was. This concept became even clearer when I delved into the works of another great *Advaita* master—Nisargadatta Maharaj.

Nisargadatta died some three decades after Ramana passed away, which meant he lived long enough into the twentieth century that YouTube now features videos of the great man actually teaching. His style of presentation seemed much more impassioned and animated than I imagined Ramana's might have been. At times he even seemed a bit bombastic towards his more recalcitrant students, yet I sensed a great underlying compassion about the man. Unlike Ramana, who lived most of the time in a temple just as one might expect of a great sage, Nisargadatta owned a tiny convenience store in Bombay where he sold cigarettes and other assorted sundries until 1966 when he retired. Even after closing up shop, he continued to receive eager students in the small mezzanine room of his upstairs flat for twice daily teachings. Here he gave satsang (gathering in Truth) in the form of question and answer periods until his death in 1981.

The following anecdote describes how he came to awaken:

> When I met my Guru, he told me: "You are not what you take yourself to be. Find out what you are. Watch the sense 'I am,' find your real Self." I obeyed him, because I trusted him. I did as he told me. All my spare time I would spend looking at myself in silence. And what a difference it made, and how soon! This brought an end to the mind; in the stillness of the mind I saw myself as I am—unbound. I used to sit for hours together, with nothing but the 'I am' in my mind and soon peace and joy and a deep all-embracing love became my normal state. In it all disappeared—myself, my Guru, the life I lived, the world around me. Only peace remained and unfathomable silence.

Nisargadatta reminds me quite a bit of an old Zen master. I have an antique Zen calligraphy scroll which says, "The Way is revealed by that which lies directly underfoot." Nisargadatta echoes this Truth when he states:

> Once you realize that the road is the goal and that you are always on the road, not to reach a goal, but to enjoy its beauty and its wisdom, life ceases to be a task and becomes natural and simple, in itself an ecstasy.

Like a sage Chan or Zen adept, Nisargadatta also strives to always point to the core of the matter and has no time for the nonessentials. He stresses the wisdom of doing nothing, of abiding as pure beingness itself. Fundamentally, cultivating the sense of "amness" or resting as spacious non-dual awareness is precisely what he calls for at every moment. I think his following words wonderfully illustrate this point:

> A quiet mind is all you need. All else will happen rightly, once your mind is quiet. As the sun on rising makes the world active, so does self-awareness affect changes in the mind. In the light of calm and steady self-awareness, inner energies wake up and work miracles without any effort on your part.

Or this gem:

> Truth is not a reward for good behaviour, nor a prize for passing some tests. It cannot be brought about. It is the primary, the unborn, the ancient source of all that is. You are eligible because you are. You need not merit truth. It is your own....Stand still, be quiet.

Or this one:

> It has nothing to do with effort. Just turn away, look between the thoughts, rather than at the thoughts. When you happen to walk in a crowd, you do not fight every man you meet, you just find your way between. When you fight, you invite a fight. But when you do not resist, you meet no resistance. When you refuse to play the game, you are out of it.

This last one has always struck me as being particularly beautiful:

> Wisdom is knowing I am nothing,
> Love is knowing I am everything,
> and between the two my life moves.

> Blessed are those servants whom the master finds awake when he comes.
>     Luke 12:37

# Chapter 24

*Truth is the timeless awareness within you right now that is looking through your eyes. This awareness is beyond ideas. Therefore, the truth is beyond ideas.*
Scott Kiloby (non-dual teacher)

    The decreasing daylight and fall rains had cast a certain dreary pall over the hermitage. On a positive note, my silent sitting was getting ever more settled, but unfortunately the headaches returned once again, though not as severely as before, along with a constant but not overly intrusive dizziness that accompanied me wherever I went. It was clear to me that these physiological responses were among several symptoms indicative of the demolition project at work. Identification with the narrative of DJ was inexorably relaxing its grip.

At this point, I was transitioning out of the silent witness phase. My ego seemed to be sufficiently degraded, my objectless meditative practice sufficiently invigorated, to have just "presence itself" begin coming to the fore. This way of being is a radically different way to relate to the world for it is more like not relating to anything. I was transitioning out of a someone meditating (i.e., DJ or the silent witness who passively stood to the side of the experience), to just pure meditation itself. Here meditation occurs but no one is doing it. It sounds preposterous I know, but I assure you this is quite possible. Later still, I couldn't even say whether meditation itself was going on or not, but that is getting ahead of "myself."

During these depersonalized meditations, the germ of a thought would appear in consciousness, but awareness would catch it dead in its tracks. Once a thought was noted, it instantly vanished under the hot spotlight of awareness. Then a gap would once again preside, perhaps lasting ten or twenty seconds, sometimes even a minute or two. Then another lazy thought would float by in order to try to seduce me once more into identifying with the DJ story. But again, it would be vaporized out of the clear electric black sky of awareness in the same manner a skeet shooter blasts a clay pigeon into smithereens. As far as delusion is concerned, clarity of Being is a most formidable weapon. The actual practice of *just sitting* was getting so much easier since there was so little "doing" involved in it now.

This growing sense of ease in my meditation practice was put to the test one day when I visited a noisy public pool full of rambunctious kids and bellowing coaches. It was quite impossible to carry on a conversation due to the echoing reverberations of the barking coaches and the screaming kids. Yet, I immediately fell into a delightful hour-long meditation in which I was as peaceful as a slumbering baby, though actually I was wide awake. Several times I interrupted the silence to ascertain if the noise level had actually abated because I was puzzled by how unperturbed I was.

Weeks later, I continued the experiment when I sat quietly in an auditorium full of more than one hundred boisterous guests awaiting the speaker. Again I was oblivious to the entire hullabaloo. The silence that is already and always here is a most profound thing to discover. Some recognize it to be true nature, though I was not yet aware of this fact myself. To me this silence was still a state-bound experience that came and went. Maya's play of duality still prevailed.

Though I am not sure of the exact date, I know that sometime in the late fall I had a peculiar experience during routine mediation practice.

Deep in the throes of a normal hour sit, my mind suddenly flashed to a vivid image of the old Viking curmudgeon himself, Mr Knap, who had long ago vacated the hermitage property. I had not recollected that guy in ages and to have his image appear so clearly in my mind's eye during meditation seemed extremely odd. The vision of Knap faded and on went the silent sitting.

*Chapter 24*

The next day I answered the centre's phone. It was a next-door neighbour enquiring about the details of Mr. Knap's passing. The news came as a bit of a shock to me.

"Dead, you say?" I asked. "I know nothing of the matter. When and how did he pass?"

Apparently, Knap had perished in a car accident seemingly at the exact time his visage flashed into my consciousness. Strange. Maybe the weary wanderer was letting me know that he finally made it home at long last. Whatever the case, the sudden passing of Knap did cause me to reflect once again upon Buddha's pointer about impermanence.

Buddha's constant reminder about the impermanency of things was a great topic of self-inquiry. In fact, the last sentence he uttered right before passing away spoke directly to this matter, "All component things in the world are changeable. They are not lasting. Work hard to gain your own salvation."

We imagine ourselves to be permanent beings separate from the rest of existence. On some level the impermanent nature of reality is seen to be an unpleasant fact best ignored. Our obsession with youth culture and enduring beauty is a great case in point. We look at the world around us and believe it to be solid and fixed. Typically, we abhor change. Thus we like to imagine ourselves to be a changeless, permanent creature who will endure forever. The wisdom that Buddha is calling for is to see that permanence is an illusion, and thus separation is also an illusion.

> Truth, she thought. As terrible as death. But harder to find.
> Philip K. Dick (writer)

*A Fleeting Improvised Man Awakens*

# Chapter 25

*Enlightenment is often misunderstood to be a matter of personal achievement…But there's no person there! There's not even a "there" or a spatial location where a person can reside. There is no individualized or separate "you" or "me", no goal, no task and no achievement.*

Greg Goode (non-dual teacher)

The cold, crisp autumn days had turned even colder with the first light dusting of snow which marked the beginning of winter proper. The woodstove fire had to be stoked all day now if the cold was to be kept at bay. Trips to the dilapidated outhouse, referred to as a "bucket biffy" by the locals, now proved to be a bracing jaunt indeed. At this juncture, I was wondering if my outdoor water source would freeze up soon since I still had no indoor plumbing. None of these matters really worried me much as my eye was still firmly on that *brass ring* that Ananda warned me not to covet.

Though the cold had settled in, spiritually speaking there was no need to turn up the register for things had already begun to heat up dramatically by their own accord. Quite soon a "spiritual chinook" of sorts would begin to blow in.

The warm, dry "snow-eater" chinook winds so familiar to Western Canadians living in mountainous regions are pretty dramatic meteorological phenomena. These warm, thawing winds are driven over a mountain top and are capable of melting a foot of snow in a day once they reach the other side of the barrier.

> Be melting snow.
> Wash yourself of yourself.
> Rumi

The rapid increase in temperature these Chinooks are capable of producing is a good metaphor for the kind of sudden heating up my spiritual practice was about to experience, though this rise in temperature would pale in comparison to the conflagration I would shortly thereafter encounter.

In a few months, I would be squirming under the searing heat of unadulterated Truth. Here I am talking about a growing wildfire that would eventually become so intense as to consume everything. This is the inferno that rages through the forest, levelling all in its path but also consuming the ashes it leaves in its wake so that nothing remains. Rupert Spira offers some sage advice regarding what I might term the *spiritual quickening,* "At the heart of experience there is a fire that burns all we know, that turns all things into itself. Offer everything to this fire." While Rumi offers, "Set your life on fire. Seek those who fan your flames." St. Teresa of Avila similarly adds, "In order that love be fully satisfied it must lower itself to nothingness and transform this nothingness into fire." And finally Friedrich Nietzsche adds a pointed observation regarding this metaphor, "You must be ready to burn yourself in your own flame; how could you rise anew if you have not first become ashes?"

Oddly enough, even Adolf Hitler chimes in with a similar sentiment, "If you want to shine like the sun first you have to burn like it," though I suspect that he was coveting a rather different outcome than I was.

Thus far, the measure of my spiritual awakening had roughly followed a bisected parabola of sorts if charted on an x/y graph. Here I am referring to half of a parabolic curve looking quite reminiscent to the outline of the iconic Canadian hockey stick.

In standard x/y graphical form, the bottom of the graph where one would imagine the blade to begin, marks duration or time spent on the journey while the rise of the graph, marked by the rising handle, would indicate spiritual maturation. The first half of the journey saw a slightly rising, slow, but steady maturation over time. Now it was set to begin a rapid ascent, not

*Chapter 25*

exponentially so but still a very dramatic rise was commencing. The plotted points eventually came to resemble the arc of Canada's most beloved piece of sports equipment.

I would presently place my progress at just about the halfway point along the bottom, which is the place where the blade meets the handle. From here a steep increase of spiritual maturation commences, marked on the graph as the spot where the handle starts its rise up. From this point, the increase over the last six months or so was tremendous as is the rise in the height of the stick versus the rise in the blade.

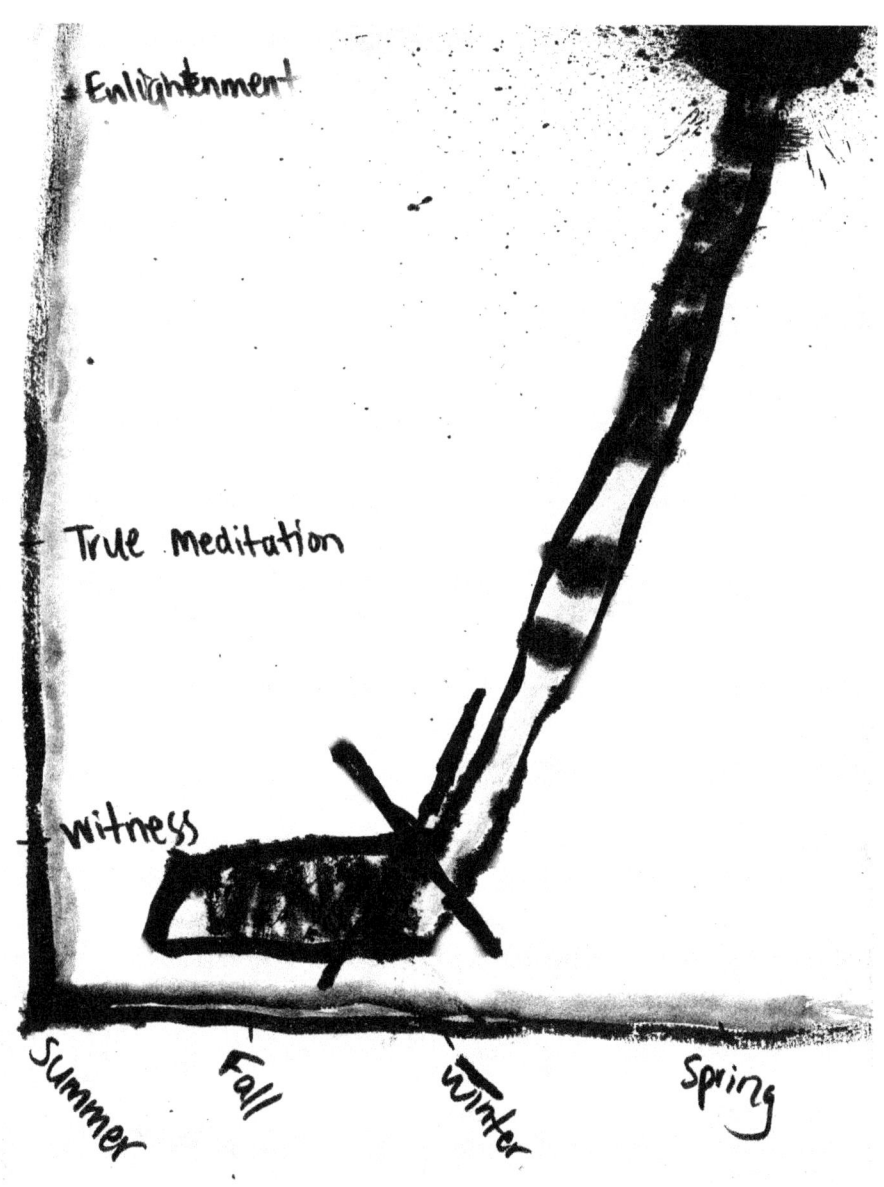

To begin to explain this spiritual quickening, I need to discuss the concept of *presence*. I might describe my spiritual maturation as the movement from "meing" to "being" which came by way of presence. In the beginning, during the forceful object of concentration phase, awareness or presence was essentially lacking. Or more precisely, awareness of awareness was not being experienced. Awareness itself is always present, but self-identification looks outward to objects to erroneously inform itself as to who or what it is. With presence, the focus shifts inward towards the subject. This is the stage in which self-identification begins to disappear. This last phase, which comprised the remainder of my journey, would take about half a year to complete the transition from objectification to total *I-amness* or pure subjectification.

Counter-intuitively, when all that remains is the pure subject, no sense of self remains, just wide open spacious awareness, Buddha's *anatta*, the Not-self. But I have gotten way too far ahead of myself once again.

Suffice it to say that this terminal stage was just beginning to present itself experientially. Conceptually speaking, I still had only a vague notion of what was about to befall me. People like Eckhart Tolle have made a career out of explaining the importance of being in "The Now" but that seemed like a state of mind that I had to work to achieve.

Even the profound wisdom offered on a YouTube video by that great *neo-advaitist* teacher, Jean Klein, remained obscure. He talked about finding "presence in your absence." This pointer resonated with me, but I was not yet truly aware of its full ramifications.

Most wonderfully and wondrously, at this point of the game it began to matter much less what my conceptual mind knew or knew not. "The Work" started to drive itself forward on its own accord, and insights were growing ever more prevalent. It was direct experience and the continued letting go that mattered most. Wisdom was spontaneously revealing itself. It didn't matter much now what others had to say about awakening. The point was what was it that I was directly discovering?

Well, for one thing my meditation technique was about to be tweaked once again. Though more exactly, I might say my "non-meditation" technique, for that was the direction the present movement was inexorably headed.

To be clear, when I say "non-meditation" it was not that I was no longer sitting in silence. On the contrary, I was still putting in a solid eight hours every day. What I mean by non-meditation is that there was less of a sense of me, the meditator, meditating or a growing sense of no one doing anything.

This transition was marked by the reappearance of WIT once again. The sage advice given this time was concise. I needed to "let go even further into my meditation practice." My meditation was still not "natural or care-free enough," the wise one informed me. The implication was that there was still too much of a "doer" striving to do a good job. This juncture marked the point where real letting go commenced.

As soon as WIT pointed out the issue to me, the required adjustment was immediately made. Somehow the body/mind complex intuitively knew how to further relax into beingness. A new, though at this point quite subtle, feeling of spacious awareness could be detected if attention was placed in that direction. The effect was pretty uncanny. This further "stepping back," so to speak, would over a relatively short period of time finally remove the last vestiges of the witness. This new phase marked the blossoming of pure presence.

Over the next few days of this even more relaxed method of silent alert sitting, further neurological effects were noted. The pressure in the back of my skull relieved itself. The dizziness stopped entirely, as did the headaches which had plagued me for so long. None of these symptoms ever resumed.

With further relaxation into the depths of being, my meditation became far, far less of a chore. I might even go so far as to say it was starting to become a rather pleasant affair. Whereas previously I had mostly kept my eyes open to maintain an attentive state, now it mattered little if they were open or closed. For the most part though I kept them shut, as I seemed to be able to let go that much further this way...but never to the point of inattentive drowsiness. My mind was beginning to abide in a deeply relaxed state, seemingly one step removed from sleep, but at the same time it was entirely attentive, alert and aware. I think it was at this point that I began to cultivate what is called "the equanimity of a Buddha in repose."

That is a fancy term, but all it means is that meditation was simply becoming a wide open, intimate, vibrant field of still presence/awareness. Thoughts, when they appeared, simply arose and fell away again, but they had nothing to do with "me." Gaps in the thought stream were more pronounced than ever, tens of minutes long in some cases. In fact, it was becoming progressively more difficult to distinguish how long the gaps actually were. The meditation situation was now more the case of thoughts appearing in the gaps rather than gaps appearing in the thought stream.

While meditating, I was much less inclined now to try to analyze what was transpiring. Previously, I had made the effort to try to figure out what was occurring stage by stage so that I might share my experience with others. There would soon come a day when this inclination to self-analyze disappeared entirely.

I would hazard to guess that it was at this point that the first inklings of *samadhi* appeared, though it was not deep or stabilized yet. All that was just around the corner. Soon enough I would get to know the deepest forms of samadhi lama Wally apparently prized so much in his students.

In the late fall, I formally requested that Wally share the special teachings with me sometime during the winter season, but as expected, he declined. Naturally, I was still a bit bitter about his attitude and was lamenting this fact to Swami. He had come over to the barn to work on some renovations, and I was providing an extra set of hands. As usual, his presence was a welcome respite from my seclusion.

I advised Swami that I had concluded that Wally was a rather unskilled teacher. Furthermore, I felt that Wally had very little, if any, direct spiritual insight. And one more thing, I added, "Apparently Wally believes that I am not sentient."

"How's that?" Swami inquired.

"Well," I said, "Wally always says we must have *compassion for all sentient beings*. Yet he has shown me little, if any, of that lofty ideal." Then in a playful manner I added,

> Therefore, I am forced to conclude that he regards me as a non-sentient blob, and I confess I take umbrage to that. Why, I reckon that in the last hour alone I've had at least two self-aware notions…and I swear this morning…well, this morning I mighta even been on the verge of a really good idea!

Swami laughed, and then he made a suggestion,

> Oh I see…I get it. Well look… here's something for you, DJ….well…I've got a little suggestion. You might wanna check out this guy cause he's really good. He's got a weekly online radio show every Wednesday. His name is Adyashanti. Check him out. You might like him.

"Oh great," I thought to myself, "yet one more flaky Indian guru I didn't want to hear about."

But in respect I inquired, "Oh, who is that?" Swami said it was someone his partner had turned him on to. She had been following him for some years, and Swami had developed an interest in this chap as well and particularly since Osho had passed away. I knew Osho by reputation as well as through perusing a few of his written teachings, and this Indian guru struck me as being a bit dodgy. I expected this Adyashanti guy would be just as disappointing, but one never knew when it came to matters of spirituality.

I have made it a habit to at least check out every guru recommended to me if for no other reason than out of respect to the one doing the recommending. It was a good thing too, considering the outcome of my investigation.

I forgot to tune into Adyashanti's online broadcast on Wednesday. "Drat it," I thought. But having discovered that there is little that "The Tube" can't illumine, I thought I would go look there. If this guy was even somewhat known, he'd probably have some kind of online presence. Pretty much expecting to find the stereotypical bearded and turbaned, white-robed caricature of an Indian mystic, I typed a-d-y-a-s-h-a-n-t-i into the YouTube search engine.

Up popped the results, and as luck would have it, the guy was at least renowned enough to have several full pages of linked videos. I clicked on the first one expecting to be unimpressed. Immediately I thought, "Well that was unexpected. He's a pretty conservative looking white dude. And he sounds American…and he doesn't seem weird or flaky at all."

As the video played on, I could tell quickly that this chap was just a regular, unassuming, unpretentious guy. He was not looking to gain anything from his audience. I could hardly believe what my eyes were seeing. The video ended after ten minutes or so. As the screen went silent, all I kept repeating to myself was "Oh my God…oh my God," over and over again.

This encounter truly was a revelation. It was true then: Buddha did indeed exist. Of all the places to discover him, I sure never imagined he would pop up on a bloody YouTube video. I was so surprised. I had been looking for such a one for how long now? I thought it was pretty funny. I had heard it said that if you met Buddha on the road, you were to kill him…how about on social media? As it is famously said, the teacher appears when the student is ready…but from a frickin computer screen? But, why not?

I watched a few more videos and was satisfied with my initial reaction. In fact, my enthusiasm only intensified. "Well, I'll be darned," I thought. "I've waited a long time to meet you, old friend." I knew I was looking at THAT: Buddha in the flesh. I knew that the real McCoy was staring me in the face, though for the life of me I didn't have a clue yet what THAT was.

I could perceive on the one hand that this personage up on stage giving satsang was the most down-to-earth, "regular Joe" imaginable, yet something in me also recognized that this was not the case at all. *Seeing is believing* as the adage goes, but in this case sometimes *not seeing* (not comprehending what THAT was) is actually better…it's *knowing*. Undoubtedly, the button-down guy up there on stage was liberation itself. I actually started to tear up a bit as gratitude started to flood in. That was a typical response I exhibited upon beholding the Truth. My reaction was not mere idol worship nor spiritual projection. Somehow I knew I was apprehending the mystery of all mysteries, and it was a startling revelation.

Originally, I wanted to know something, anything, for myself. Now I did. I knew that Buddha nature really did exist. I once feared this spiritual business would turn out to be a bust. Now I knew without a doubt that there was an answer to the perennial question, and in this case, it went by the name of Adyashanti. If I had died then, that realization alone would have validated my quest. But as things would have it, this dying business would hold off for a bit longer. Enough time still remained to take some of Adyashanti's pointers to heart and make them my own.

> He felt that his whole life was some kind of dream and he sometimes wondered whose it was and whether they were enjoying it.
> Douglas Adams (writer)

*A Fleeting Improvised Man Awakens*

# Chapter 26

*You don't need a map to go to the truth. You are the truth! Consciousness is inherently available to us. That's it. That's the entrance way. But there's no YOU that's going through the door, because there is no you.*
    Paul Hedderman (spiritual teacher)

    One very convincing way that I could know for certain (keeping in mind nothing can be known for certain) that Adyashanti was spiritually authentic was the fact that I was already experientially familiar with many of the realizations and pointers he spoke about. At this juncture in the game, it was almost as easy for me to recognize a true spiritual master as it was for me to identify a true swordsman. When somebody speaks directly about experiences you have already had, realizations you have already attained and wisdom you have already acquired, it is impossible not to recognize a fellow traveller.

Those direct experiences not yet my own I treated as an invitation to go out and experiment with them for myself. Adya (his familiar name) never pandered to doctrine nor pushed belief systems. I can't tell you how incredibly refreshing this outlook was.

Instead, Adya was always careful to point out that spirituality was not something you cogitated over or entertained but rather something *you discovered* for yourself…in fact was something *you already were*…or from another point of view *were not*. He also projected a deep sense of compassion and stillness. A perfect role model for the heartfelt upwellings that would soon begin to arise in my own practice. I felt incredibly blessed to bump into the guy. I did at some point thank Swami for his recommendation, but I am sure he was unaware of how grateful I really was.

Doing a little research on Adya's bio, I found out that he was middle-aged, came from a blue-collar background, when younger was an endurance cyclist, attended college and had been a Zen guy for fourteen years.

Adya is not a teacher in the traditional sense of the word. At every turn, Adya made it clear that the *Truth game*, as he is fond of calling it, does not rely at all on acquiring new belief systems or knowledge. I was thrilled to no end to discover a "teacher" who was always throwing it back in our laps. He would tell us outright to "never abdicate your own authority." He encouraged us to practice radical honesty. How rare is this? Well tell me, when was the last time you heard a self-help guru or life-coach say, "My job is to work myself out of a job" and mean it? With steadfast compassion, he always attempted to empower his listeners. Bravo, I say!

Apparently, Adya had a long and frustrating career when it came to the cornerstone of the Zen tradition—namely seated silent meditation. By his own admission, he was a "failed meditator." He now invites students to practice a kind of non-meditation meditation, which sounded to me ever so much like the kind of "objectless meditation" I had naturally turned to. He was very fond of encouraging us to "let everything be exactly as it is" when we turned to meditation. As I was discovering and as Adya pointed out time and time again, letting go into the natural state means letting go of the meditator. I was not practicing stillness, but rather stillness was what I essentially was. This ideal, then, marks one of the cornerstones of Adya's pointers. To get to the bare essentials of Adya's always eloquent and very succinct teaching, I will now share what I consider to be the core message using the four cornerstones that are required to create a good spiritual foundation.

If the first cornerstone is the fact that *stillness is what I truly already am*, then the three other supporting pillars or cornerstones of Adya's teaching are as follows.

The second involves realizing how the sense of "I" is manifested through the mental construct known as *the ego*.

## Chapter 26

> To look within and not find yourself as a self
> is the beginning of finding yourself as a presence.
> Adyashanti

Adya stressed numerous times that the sense of "I" was nothing more than an assumption believed in. Self was intangible. By investigating the machinations of the ego carefully, I was left with no option but to conclude exactly the same thing. Adya pointed out how critical it was to the awakening process to understand from where and how the sense of "I" originated.

The Buddhists use the metaphor of the *house builder* to describe how the edifice of the "I" is inexorably erected by the master carpenter called ego. In order to awaken, the house must be razed to the ground. Adya's style is to repeatedly invite the seeker to fully examine the ephemeral nature of ego. Again and again I discovered through self-inquiry that the presumed self was nothing more than a self-referential mind loop.

By realizing that Truth could not be located in the realm of simulacra, it then became exceedingly clear that I was not my thoughts. That, in a nutshell, is how I went about discovering the *house builder*. Once the culprit was identified, the demolition project proceeded very swiftly.

How was it that I had so long identified with something as intangible as a shadow? I pondered this time and time again. To discover how the Magus had managed to pull off such a wondrous trick, it was simply a matter of no longer identifying with the ego, small "s" self, or the I-thought. To simplify this matter, I recall Adya saying something like:

> When in doubt don't believe your thoughts. And if that pointer confounds you again simply don't believe your thoughts and finally if you are hopelessly confused and don't know where to turn, simply don't believe your next thought.

Though that is an exceedingly simple exercise to comprehend, how many amongst us would be inspired enough to actually live life by this credo? I sure was game to try.

For me, the ability to ignore such profound spiritual wisdom and continue to live the dream of me, the lie of self, had entirely lost its allure. Like the hairworm which invades the nervous system of an unsuspecting cricket or grasshopper and eventually compels it to commit suicide by drowning, I too was by now infected with a "parasite" of sorts, a "virus," a "change agent" if you will, that similarly sought my demise, but to be clear, it wished me no personal ill will. It simply wanted me to realize there was no one present to be wished anything at all. Truth simply wanted to reveal itself to itself. This was a kind of fierce grace I had to embrace quite willingly. That ideal of realizing truth for its own sake brings me to the third cornerstone of Adya's path.

Simply put, Adya proposed a very elementary exercise that I made my own—find out what is absolutely *true*. In other words, discover what you know for certain. When I did this I came up short, really, really short. There is little in life more shocking, perhaps only surpassed by realizing no-self, than to discover that you don't know a blessed thing. Here I am talking about utilizing a kind of critical thinking technique similar to the "Socratic method." When employed to its fullest, one is invariably left aporetic. Critical analysis demonstrated to me that I knew nothing. This perplexed the hell out of me. Socrates celebrated *aporia* which he explained is a kind of wise ignorance or "knowing that you don't know, whereas the other fellow in his ignorance imagines that he does." Socrates' oft quoted paradox, "I know one thing, that is that I know nothing" sums up pretty well his propensity to be a truth teller come what may.

Socrates was fond of pointing out, or rather invited us to discover for ourselves utilizing a kind of question and answer session, just how utterly ignorant we are. In the end, his propensity for demonstrating how imbecilic humans really are (and like I said he recognized this quality in himself) proved so annoying to the authorities that he was invited to saddle up to the bar for a nice stiff shot of poison hemlock. He willingly complied with great gusto, which further pissed-off the powers that be to no end. Socrates was an exceedingly wise but equally irritating man. He was not the kind of chap you dared invite to your dinner party, at least not if you wanted everyone to remain on friendly terms.

And that is the point. We will do almost anything, which seemingly includes murdering an honest man, to uphold our right to remain in a state of complete ignorance. Here I am not referring to certain gaps or misunderstandings in our knowledge. I mean rather that you or I don't really know a blessed thing. We most assuredly don't want to admit this fact to ourselves, and this in large part explains why waking up is so rare. So for the majority, the elephant continues to remain squatting in the parlour room while they ride the misery-go-round of life. I for one had tired of that distraction and decided that the small price I had to pay, being radically honest, was well worth the cost of extraction. How then did I come to realize the "I don't know mind" of Zen Buddhist fame?

First off, to be clear, it is not an attitude or ideal I conveniently adopted, nor was it a belief system I accepted. Secondly, it didn't dawn on me all at once. The fact that I couldn't find out who or what I was, was instantly apparent. The fact that I was a total ignoramus took a little while longer to dawn.

In my experience, it seemed conceptually easier to discover that I *was nothing* than it did to admit that I *knew nothing*. How does one come to intimately know for certain that they are clueless? How does liberation begin to unfold?

The answer again comes by way of being truthful which, in turn, favours a new orientation towards beingness and a movement away from self-hood. Sometimes I find the expressions your "true-nature" and "truth-realization" a bit misleading as it implies a *someone* who attains or learns *something*. This is not the case at all. Nothing is ever added unto you in the truth game. Quite the opposite holds. Enlightenment is really the path of subtraction, the removal of self-ignorance, until nothing remains but the "null set." In other words, only Truth itself remains.

By seeing reality as it really was, not as I wished it might be, I came to see things in an entirely different light. My ego, for all intents and purposes the presumed faculty that manifested the "I-thought," the process that enabled me to have a sense of "me," was really nothing but a tool that allowed me to navigate through the imaginal realm of duality. In part, it was the sense making apparatus, and as such it did a marvellous job. But somewhere along the way, this tool naively took itself to be a corporeal entity. It imagined it was a separate self.

Everything I had ever believed in was simply not so. All the sacred cows were eventually slaughtered in the name of truth-realization. Of course, some beliefs were easily abandoned with no fanfare due to their obvious spurious nature. But this is where seekers often get it wrong, have always gotten it wrong. This process is not a matter of choosing to keep better beliefs and getting rid of the less tenable ones. The practice of finding out what is *true*, or *spiritual autolysis* as Jed McKenna calls it, relies on discounting all beliefs to discover if any truth remains.

Another crucial avenue on the path to realizing no-self, and what I perceive as the fourth cornerstone of Adya's teaching, is to understand how all beliefs were premised on a *believer* (i.e., me, who in fact did not exist). How could the following statement make sense I wondered—"I, DJ, believe so and so to be true. Yet I, DJ, am nowhere to be found." I may not have much liked the results of this kind of inquiry, but there it was—"I wasn't." That then covers the four cornerstones to liberation.

This then leaves one final part of the foundation to consider: the plaque and time capsule. These are not essential to the building's integrity like the four cornerstones are, since those blocks firmly anchor the building in space, yet for our purposes the plaque and time capsule are important since they mark the edifice's position in time.

For me, Adya's last key pointer is the one that encourages us to see how "life is but a dream" and then realize the corollary: True nature is timeless. In truth, Maya creates the illusion of time utilizing the dream state and the play of duality, but once this state of ignorance is removed, the Absolute reveals its eternal nature.

Inexorably, I came to realize that what had passed for reality in my life was nothing less than illusion, something right out of Plato's "Allegory of the Cave." Here, the ignorant prisoner is confined to a life of watching a flickering light show projected on the wall of a cave, and knowing no better, he confuses the shadow play for reality itself. I discovered that I had been in a similar situation as well.

Realizing that I had been duped was a shock, but it also came with a sense of relief. For decades I had suspected life wasn't all that it seemed to be, and now at long last I knew this to be true. At the beginning, it was quite thrilling to hear my teacher articulate this message with no reservations out in public for all to hear.

I had suspected as much, but it seemed to be something I really did not want to consider too deeply. If I had done so, I might have realized much earlier that I, too, was simulacrum. I guess that seemingly less-than-cheery proposition was what kept Maya alive all those years.

Now here was a guy who was unabashedly proclaiming that he and I and everyone else were fictional characters in a play not of our own making. If that doesn't give you pause, I don't know what would. It was quite easy for me to conceptually entertain the possibility that the world was illusory but another thing entirely to know with a hundred percent certitude that I, too, didn't actually exist. When I started to awaken from the dream state, it was like finding myself trapped in a lucid dream. Adyashanti points out that, "The greatest dream that we can have is to forget that we are dreaming."

Getting lucid in a dream is waking up to the fact that you are dreaming. But let me be clear, during lucid dreaming you may be aware that you are dreaming, but you will still be fully immersed in the dream realm. I knew this situation well as I had begun to spontaneously lucid dream some months prior to being introduced to Adya's teachings. Becoming still, finding presence, being awareness itself has a way of naturally liberating you from any dream state—nocturnal or otherwise.

When I fell asleep and began to lucid dream, I didn't have to do anything to become lucid. It happened spontaneously. I just *fell awake* in a manner of speaking. Enlightenment is no different. It's just a matter of falling awake.

I would like to make an important distinction here. One may fall totally awake from a nighttime dream, and we call that waking up in the morning. So, clearly, one awakens from a dream, one state of consciousness (nighttime sleeping), to enter another (daytime waking consciousness).

Spiritual awakening similarly has you awakening from one dream, the dream of distinction/duality/the individual, but here the analogy breaks down. In final awakening, you don't find yourself inhabiting a new realm. Reality awakens to itself, and you are no longer part of any equation. To see reality clearly, one simply comes to see the dream of me for what it is: wishful thinking, speculation, conjecture and utter fantasy. I had no idea what "I" or true-self or no-self was, but I was coming to see what I wasn't.

The Hindus talked of *neti neti*, "not this, not this," as a way to regard reality that would be likely helpful in gaining a better perspective on things as they really were. This path of subtraction or negation worked wonderfully for me as no phony ideal had to be adopted. By being completely truthful and authentic and not turning away from whatever truths were revealed, it became increasingly apparent how the illusion animated itself. Untruth came about through the mental projection of thoughts which were found to be inherently empty. By trying to discern what was true, I was always left with *neti neti*—NOT THIS, NOT THIS. DJ was eventually revealed to be a mirage.

That kind of realization was not what I had originally signed up for. I expected great wisdom to be added unto me and answers received. . I know somebody somewhere along the way promised me a great revelation or two and loads of bliss. Wasn't enlightenment portrayed as the "Great Man" realizing himself and then getting parades, accolades, laurel leaves and huge medals pinned to his chest? This demolition project was not at all what I had expected enlightenment to be about. Worse still, I no longer had the capacity to continue to deceive myself. I could no longer look the other way regarding self-ignorance. When Adya made such a preposterous statement as:

*Chapter 26*

> The difference between the dream state and enlightenment can be put down to one thought, one thought believed in...namely the thought of "I."

I knew he wasn't screwing around; no wonder few awoke. This was some really heavy shit this man was laying down. And he had such a beatific smile on his face as he destroyed you.

That is a saint for you. The good ones sit you down for a soothing hot cuppa, a buttered lemon scone and some nice pleasantries. Once you are fully relaxed, they politely offer you full headgear and a mouth piece before laying into you with a couple of stiff jabs, an uppercut and finally a hard right to your temple designed to put you out for the count. At least bruises and broken teeth are avoided as your benefactor knocks you senseless. That, again, is the mark of the compassionate guru. The best may seek your demise, but they have the good sense to consider how your corpse will appear laid out in the casket.

Invariably, you hardly ever see that sneaky one-two combo coming. Adya would eloquently and with great charm tell the assembled audience that they, in fact, didn't actually exist as they presumed, had no purpose in life and were essentially full of shit, but he always delivered the news with a joke and a smile. I surely loved him for it.

While aligning myself with the Truth wholeheartedly through true meditation, serious spiritual inquiry and aided by Adya's astute pointers, I began to experience a strange mental state. It lasted for about a month and a half.

It was marked primarily by a strong sense of incredulity and awe, tinged with great shock at times. I kept saying to myself, "This can't be happening. Not really...what is unfolding here should not be possible. How," I wondered, "could there really be such a state of affairs?

"This *waking up* business was like something straight out of the pages of a science fiction novel. It felt exactly like what befell the protagonist in *The Matrix*. "It just can't be true," I implored to no one in particular. But of course, it was undeniable. Reality, self included, was a mere illusion.

"How is this fucking possible? If people only knew."

Of course, I had no one to share these revelations with. The hermitage was deserted. There was no one who would have cared to listen even if the joint had been jam-packed. Even my spiritual buddy, Mitra, was beyond offering me comfort at this point. The fact was, from now on, I would be utterly alone. There was not a hope in hell anyone could understand my plight. I was self-immolating, and there was no one available to smother the flames. Truth be told, I would have stopped them if they had tried.

Being ever the stoic, there was naught I could do but grin and bear this terrible escapade. It took all the strength and forbearance I could muster to continue to back away from delusion. Maya truly is a seductive mistress, but I was determined to stay the course. So, I had to concede that however troubling the following revelations were, things were as they were:

"No-self is a fact. It is not something I ever suspected, but it is the case nevertheless.

"Well, I see too that the whole human race is pretty much certifiably insane, yours truly not excluded.

"My whole life is premised on a lie.

"There is no truth to be found anywhere.

"DJ is 'deluded,' or perhaps delusion itself. Is there a difference?

"The past and future don't really exist. They are an abstraction of the mind. Space, too, is a persistent illusion.

"I don't create my own thoughts through volition, nor can I control them, so obviously, I have no capacity to make choices. Free will is non-existent, though it sure appears otherwise."

My response to these kinds of realizations might run something like:

"You gotta be shittin me. I mean, that's not possible…but, yep, it sure appears to be the case when lucidity begins to dawn.

"Yep, I am not my thoughts.

"Yep, this whole enlightenment thing is really a goddamn demolition project with me in the cross hairs, and that man Adya aims to kill me.

"Yep, Yep, Yep, bloody YEP! It's all true."

Of course, I dearly loved Adya for his direct way of extolling the truth, but that didn't make those six long weeks of crisis any easier. Getting "clean and sober," or in other words becoming lucid and clear which allowed me to start to see things as they really were, sucked in the way a hangover does. But that too shall pass. Yet, there were some joyful moments during this phase as well. I'll share one memorable experience with you herein.

During an ordinary meditation period in the closing weeks of 2008, a direct and clear epiphany suddenly arose. Beyond a shadow of a doubt, in about as much time as it takes to snap your fingers in front of your face, I could see that my life was in fact a dream, that I was and had always been making the whole blasted affair up. It wasn't real. I could see this to be a fact in the clarity of the moment. It was all a dream. I laughed and I laughed and I laughed. Then the hysterics commenced.

This was the funniest realization ever. I mean, it was gut-bustingly hilarious. It was the kind of thing that has them rolling in the aisles in tears.

This was the punch line I had been eternally anticipating. It was the big reveal to the greatest cosmic joke ever told. The grand epiphany revealed itself but to whom? At that moment, I was not sure. God, was it ever hilarious. Or rather, perhaps it was "God are you ever hilarious," or maybe "I" was being the funny one here.

I remember distinctly saying to myself, "Well, DJ, old chap there you go. There you have it…you've been phoning the whole thing in all along. It seems you've never shown up for a single day's work in your entire life."

I felt a little sheepish. Like the recipient of the greatest practical joke ever engineered. Several times I thought, "Why I'll be darned. I can't believe I fell for that one." In fact, I still can't. It was truly an ingenious trick; it was brilliant in its conceptualization, genius in its delivery. Simply marvellous in the way Meister Eckhart also found it to be, "God laughs and plays," he said.

I can tell you that that kind of revelation is huge as far as awakening is concerned, but I never for an instance thought the quest was over. This disclosure was, at best, the intermission, but the "play" still had to go on. What a persistent illusion small "s" self was. My experience demonstrated that one can absolutely see through the dream state, perceive the persona as the empty mask it truly is, yet still the misery-go-round can continue unabated, leaving one nothing to do but to keep enduring the ride and hope no barf bags would be required as it continued to madly careen out of control.

> "Hey mister…mister…listen. You gotta get them youngins offa that darn contraption…its turned plumb loco…it has gone and done broke itself. Look, them kiddies is a turnin blue!"

> "Yes, frickin tell me about it, but it ain't as easy to get this piece of crap slowed down as it was to get her all fired up in the first place!"

The year was drawing to a close, and a big spiritual transformation was in the works. What was now about to play out in the ensuing couple of months marked the penultimate phase of the journey; sooner than I ever imagined, the curtain would drop for good.

> Eternity is a mere moment, just long enough for a joke.
> Hermann Hesse (writer)

# Chapter 27

*You can have the courage to climb the mountain, swim the lakes, etc. That any fool can do, but the courage to be on your own, to stand on your two solid feet, is something which cannot be given by somebody.*
    U.G. Krishnamurti (anti-guru guru)

    The Christmas season was well upon me, but I had no occasion to make merry. My routine had not varied in months. Save for the fact that I now had to jam several fat logs into the woodstove every few hours and had few, if any, TSC-related chores to do, my routine had remained unchanged.

    Regarding the hockey stick/parabolic curve analogy I previously used to indicate where I stood regarding spiritual maturation, my current position might be described now as being marked approximately a third of the way up the handle and quickly summiting. Letting go into beingness was rapidly accelerating at this juncture.

My eight hours or so of daily meditation passed more easily these days than before. An increasing sense of clarity and lucidity marked each meditation. Monkey-mind thoughts were sporadic now, meditative *efforting* was much reduced. By this point, I had entirely given up trying to analyse what was going on. Peace and lack of conceptualisation was growing ever more prevalent. What thoughts arose in the field of awareness quickly dissipated like an ice cube would vaporize if placed in a red hot ceramics kiln. Of course, I, too, was continuing to melt away. Damn you, Adyashanti.☺

At this time, Mitra gave me a care/Christmas package full of little treats. I appreciated the sentiment. I hadn't actually seen her in weeks. Eventually, the student must leave all teachers behind. Soon I would find even Adya's wise reminders no longer of much interest. I was about to abandon the canoe that had gotten me to the far shore and proceed naked and alone into the wilderness on foot.

Unlike Adam's good fortune in having a partner who could share in the misery of the fall from grace, I knew that my journey would only beget increasing degrees of isolation and loneliness. No companion would, or even could, show up to offer me solace. I was "dying," and there was nothing anyone could do about that. I had gone too far down the path to backtrack now. The "cancer" had taken hold in my marrow and was spreading fast. Resistance was futile. A certain sense of helplessness and hopelessness marked the last few days of 2008.

I had never been prone to depression. Since setting out on my spiritual journey a year ago, I had experienced various states of altered consciousness, psychological healing and novel feelings that ranged from dread to euphoria, but despair could not be counted amongst them. To my surprise, the year concluded with a bout of melancholy and funk so severe I dare say it was the first time in my life I experienced a sense of depression. Fortunately, it was not long lived.

By this point, it was clear that my ego, or the sense of egoic identification, was fast disappearing. I knew that this transformation had to be complete and permanent. This realization marked my brief foray into what I later learned some Christian mystics called *the dark night of the soul*. If you weren't a Christian but rather a Buddhist, you might refer to this state of mind as *falling into the pit of the void*.

I don't want to sound too alarmist here or give you the wrong impression. The vast majority of spiritual aspirants remain in duality for the duration and never experience this kind of wretched phenomenon. The following Bible passage from Matthew 7:13 alludes to why so few ever experience the dark night:

> Enter through the narrow gate. For wide is the gate and broad is the road that leads to destruction, and many enter through it. But small is the gate and narrow the road that leads to life, and only a few find it.

Fear not, then, if you are spiritually inclined. Odds are you might occasionally get rattled, frustrated or even suffer minor bouts of funk as you go about your seeking business, but the extreme kind of spiritual angst I am about to describe here will most likely never befall you. But if it does, then good for you.

Furthermore, in the minority that temporarily suffer this spiritual low point, the depression varies tremendously in degree from seeker to seeker. The most pronounced symptoms lasted less than a week for me and felt pretty uncomfortable but certainly not overly debilitating by the time the episode culminated on the last day of the year. Mother Teresa, on the other hand, was reputed to have suffered for some four decades. Suzanne Segal's long bout with severe depersonalization and depression, which lasted many years, is another case in point. I got off lucky with an episode that lasted about as long as it takes to subdue the typical forest fire.

Historically, we find the term *Dark Night of the Soul* first mentioned in the experiences and writings of the great Spanish, sixteenth-century poet and Christian mystic, Saint John of the Cross.

Using allegory, the *Dark Night* refers to St. John's quest to purify first his body and then finally his soul or spirit. His journey's end was marked by union with God. St. John's writings give us insight into what is at first a pretty harrowing experience but ultimately a rewarding one. From chapter nine of *Dark Night of the Soul*, we find the following description:

> How, although this night brings darkness to the spirit, it does so in order to illumine it and give it light.
>
> It now remains to be said that, although this happy night brings darkness to the spirit, it does so only to give it light in everything; and that, although it humbles it and makes it miserable, it does so only to exalt it and to raise it up; and, although it impoverishes it and empties it of all natural affection and attachment, it does so only that it may enable it to stretch forward, divinely, and thus to have fruition and experience of all things, both above and below, yet to preserve its unrestricted liberty of spirit in them all.

Compare that passage with American Buddhist teacher Shinzen Young's more clinical analysis offered here in excerpt:

> It entails an authentic and irreversible insight into Emptiness and No Self. What makes it problematic is that the person interprets it as a bad trip. Instead of being empowering and fulfilling, the way Buddhist literature claims it will be, it turns into the opposite. In a sense, it's Enlightenment's Evil Twin. In some cases it takes months or even years to fully metabolize, but in my experience the results are almost always highly positive.

For a more New Age feel, consider this passage of the subject snatched from themystic.org website:

> The dark night occurs after considerable advancement towards higher consciousness. Indeed, the dark night usually occurs like an initiation before one of these special seekers is admitted into regular relationship with higher consciousness. The dark night also occurs to those who do not seek relationship but immersion or unity in the higher consciousness. While the term dark night of the soul is used broadly, its general meaning—in the field of higher consciousness—is a lengthy and profound absence of light and hope. In the dark night you feel profoundly alone.

I don't much support the distinction immediately above regarding the "advancement of higher consciousness", for non-duality reveals this to be a construct of the mind. In Truth, there is no way to discern higher or lower anything. Similarly, "special seeker" is suspect for the same reason. I don't care for this kind of spiritual distinction making, but overall the account above seems in line with the previous two passages and my experience as well. Well then, let's get to the nitty gritty, shall we?

I will premise my experience with an inspirational maxim and something my mother used to say to us kids; the saying was born out of concern for our welfare...most particularly when we broke out the homemade slingshots or bows.

"The darkest hour is just before dawn."

And,

"You kids be careful with those arrows. It's all fun and games until someone loses an eye."

It truly is all fun and games until your "I" begins to be removed. That's when things start to get real serious real fast. When I was caught in the midst of the darkness and had no way of knowing how things would turn out, I surely never suspected that my spiritual quest was actually progressing perfectly well. In those closing days of 2008, it would have been very hard for me to imagine that "dawn's" new light, the illumined state, was right around the corner. Primarily, my experience was marked by the melancholy and sadness of a protracted farewell. It seemed like I was bidding my ego, my very self, goodbye. And that, my friends, is the most sorrowful farewell of all.

How surreal (and disturbing) is it to have to say to yourself:

So long, farewell, it was nice knowing you, old chap. We had our good times together, but it's no longer working out. It's over.

This melancholic adieu was marked by great tenderness in my heart. My ego simply didn't know any better. It certainly wasn't evil. When my spirits were at their lowest, I informed my poor forlorn ego that it was:

> ...nothing personal. In fact, you actually don't know any better. You are a mere program of sorts, the "self-code" as it were. Don't get me wrong...you were always there when things looked bleak, when no one else was around. A finer advocate and protector I couldn't ask for nor a better buddy be, but now, poor thing, you just gotta go. Farewell...(blubber, sob, blubber, sniffle, sniffle).

I really did language it pretty much that way in my mind. I was losing my best friend, and it really, really hurt.

In the first few months of meditating, I used to make deals with my ego to cool the thoughts down a bit for certain periods of time, and thankfully, it seemingly complied. I had a pretty good protector-cum-faithful friend there, but in the end I had to hang it out to dry. Although it was not a noble thing to do, it was necessary.

During my childhood, our family raised hogs for the larder. Some members of the family made the mistake of befriending the chubby porkers. Come slaughter time, we had to buckle down and get on with the nasty business at hand. That feeling was akin to what I am now trying to describe here. That is why I call this path ruthless or fierce. You can't hesitate or all will be lost. When slaughtering an animal, you must employ one quick slash of the butcher knife to the jugular. So, too, in spirituality you must use one decisive stroke to sever the head from the torso. The ego really does have to be lopped off. Graphic it may be, but that is just the way things had to proceed for me if liberation was to be assured.

And it wasn't just "I" who was being led off to the slaughter. It was all my loved ones too. Everybody was being annihilated much in the ethos Christ encouraged his disciples to adopt:

> If any man come to me, and hate not his father, and mother, and wife, and children, and brothers, and sisters, yes, and his own life also, he cannot be my disciple.
> Luke 14:26

Similarly, the *Bhagavad-Gita* has the protagonist, Arjuna, coming to terms with the fact that he must kill off his entire family in order to gain liberation. When the self disappears, so too do your brothers and sisters, relatives and parents. All loved ones will naturally fall away. All your comrades are left on the battlefield. Where's the fun in that? But wait, there's even more bad news.

All your accolades and accomplishments disappear as well. How could they remain when there is no longer anyone around to claim them? I think you can well appreciate that this is the part of the journey few spiritual traditions are keen to highlight.

Anyhow, I finished up the eulogy dedicated to my ego amidst a fair amount of tears and sobbing. The depression seemed to reach a climax, and then I got the impression as December drew to a close that the matter was resolved. I wondered if I would ring in the new year with an obituary of sorts for I felt I had well and truly resigned myself to the dustheap of history. Of course, things rarely turn out as simply as we hope. The new year was rung in with a self still relatively invigorated. Egoic identification was chugging along pretty much as it always had. Drat it!

However, I now see that my authentic inclination to sincerely drop the self, which precipitated my own dark night, really did mark a turning point. This was evident by what would transpire next. Saint John had promised light. That was about to erupt like the million candle power flood lights prisons employ to foil a jailbreak. Untruth was continuing to wilt under the scrutiny of awareness. Soon, that kind of clarity would begin to disturb me like never before.

> "This" [reality DJ] is an illusion. It's an elaborate hoax.
> Roger Ebert (film critic/writer's deathbed realization as reported by his wife)

# Chapter 28

*Fear of the unknown is what keeps everyone busily treading water.*

Jed McKenna (mythical non-dual teacher)

Using Ayahuasca to gain spiritual or psychological insight during my quest to awaken had an unforeseen but positive effect on my meditation practice. It was so marvellously efficacious at addressing negative emotional and psychological issues and traumas that none ever arose during meditation. I am led to believe by the personal testimonial of others that all kinds of disturbing mental projections may arise during various stages of meditative practice. This was not the case at all for me, and I believe, though to what degree I am not certain, that I have Ayahuasca to thank for it.

Dealing with my emotional baggage beforehand helped to foster the present situation where long, silent gaps were the norm. Along with the pronounced silence came a growing sense of lightness and joy. This was a delightful, though rather briefly lived, interlude. Soon, the joy began to be replaced by a growing sense of strange apprehension, discomfort and fear that started to really creep me out.

Subtle at first, this feeling grew ever more intense, along with the joy, as the meditation session progressed. This was the first indicator, though not pronounced yet, of what it was really like to let go into the void. A feeling of spacious awareness, clarity and luminosity slowly grew as the weeks passed by, but at the same time, so too did great unease begin to envelop me.

The joy was a nice symptom of surrender, but I quickly grew cautious of the other feeling that was arising at the same time. *Just sitting* started to feel weirder and weirder as time went by. I didn't know it then but now understand that this kind of reaction is quite common among serious aspirants as the sense of self becomes seriously eroded. A mixture of apprehension verging on dread, fear and, if severe enough, even panic can be the result of radical letting go. It was like an inky black pool of water, the void, appeared in front of me, and my aim was to dive in—but not all at once, for caution prevailed.

My strategy was to, metaphorically speaking, first just "kiss" the surface of the dark pool with the bottom of my big toe. When that proved okay, I next got a toenail into the murky depths. After more time, I finally submerged the whole toe, and so it went. Each day the waters were tested, and when nothing untoward happened, I then managed to slip a little bit further into the turbid, murky chasm of no-self the following day. But this was an excruciatingly slow affair. That is what happens when one chances upon *troubled waters*. You get disturbed. Though I found the current situation distressing, I should add that the allure of Unity, the attraction of non-separation, was always too great to ever halt my advance entirely. My feelings inclined towards the vision presented in John 5:4:

> For an Angel went down, at a certain season, into the pool and troubled the water. Whosoever then after the troubling of the water stepped in was made whole...

At least, that was how the situation appeared to be progressing. In truth, I never really entered any void, troubling or otherwise. My True nature was the void itself. What was actually transpiring was the journey to no-self. I was not going anywhere, I was simply disappearing. It was only my mind that projected an impression of stepping off into the abyss. The feeling evoked, though, was real enough and was marked primarily by a growing visceral sense of foreboding, doom and terrible dread best exemplified by a pounding chest. Soon I would become scared shitless. It was then, around the end of January, that a new pattern for my meditation routine emerged.

I would sit down to meditate, close my eyes and within two to three seconds…joy, and then after half a minute or so, great joy would be predominantly felt. As greater relaxation continued, the wonderful effects of joy began to be supplanted by trepidation. At this moment, a small light would appear in the middle of the inky blackness that my meditating mind beheld.

On first appearance, its apparent size and luminosity was that of a standard Christmas bulb. But this was no mundane lamp for it was as if there were some unseen dimmer switch that could pump thousands of additional watts of energy into this golden amber orb. It would begin to get bigger and brighter in my mind's eye until it eventually dazzled my senses with the luminosity of a solar disc. When *Sol Invictus*—"The Invincible Sun," Roman god of light—actually deigns to make an appearance right before you, bladders will be emptied quickly, I assure you. This was the most frightening apparition I had ever beheld.

Perhaps this was the same dazzling illumination that beckoned Icarus to his doom. The full effects of this luminosity would not be known for some time. I was too wary to let go into it quickly. Accompanying the light phenomenon was a horrible feeling of dread that grew in proportion to the intensity of the light.

Eventually, the dazzling darkness would overwhelm me. My heart literally constricted in outright panic. I would struggle to get my next breath until I could no longer draw one in. That point marked the end of the meditation. There were no two ways about it. I was forced to take a time out as adrenaline flooded my system due to overwhelming terror.

It felt like I was having a heart attack. This was the kind of blind panic I suspect a caged dog must feel as its abusive, enraged owner beats the hell out of it with a club. There was nothing I could do but "head for the hills" at that point. After pulling myself together, I would close my eyes again and put myself through the same dreadful ordeal all over again. Though I denied it at the time (tough guys don't let fear overwhelm them), I now admit that what I was experiencing was nothing less than a full-blown panic attack.

Though the beginning of the meditation was exceptionally pleasant, I had to end each sit after just seven minutes or so due to the debilitating anxiety. I repeated this pattern eight times an hour. In a day, I was subjected to over sixty cycles of a horror beyond all belief.

The fantasy movie *The NeverEnding Story* referred to a similar terror that marauded over the countryside instilling great fear into all who encountered it. This abomination was called "The Nothing." Whoever wrote that story really grasped the finer details of existential angst. I reckon few humans can approach something that immense and empty and not shudder in their boots.

Worst of all was the fact that there was nothing I could do to alleviate this situation. I just had to dust myself off and get back on the horse. Each time I was reduced to a quivering mass of hysteria.

At this juncture, it was clear that True meditation was the catalyst for the blind panic. What was not so evident was why it scared the shit out of me so much. For weeks I never let the golden light get too bright for I was too afraid to discover the consequences.

I had a huge problem here, so I sought out Mitra's advice. She tried to console me and offer help as best she could, but still I was too afraid to let go into the light. At the time, I wondered if the fear was caused by some buried childhood trauma and thought perhaps I should consult a hypnotherapist to resolve the issue. Of course, it had nothing to do with past traumas of any sort.

Little did I know that this anxiety was a natural consequence of the Wizard of Was going bye-bye. Wally had tried to convince me that this kind of fear was aberrant and had no place in the meditation process. "Oh no, meditation is supposed to be blissful, not unpleasant, DJ," had been Wally's "sage" pronouncement. That was terrible advice. Again…I repeat AGAIN; resisting what is, is part of the problem NOT THE BLOODY SOLUTION! Here something Alan Watts said comes to mind, "Muddy water is best cleared by leaving it alone."

For a while, I wondered what was amiss; what could I do to rectify the situation? I eventually gave up on this silly line of inquiry. Thank goodness I did for it was all going according to plan. Things were unfolding well indeed. One wonders what might have been the result of taking Wally's dreadful advice to heart. At the least, I would have wasted a lot of time and effort trying to put right what wasn't wrong in the first place. The ego often confuses discomfort for something being amiss. It ain't necessarily so.

Adya advised that fear was often a by-product of authentic awakening. Apparently Lama Wally had never come across the real thing before, so he didn't know what to make of my symptoms and simply labelled them "not good, wrong, and aberrant." In fact, it was he who was terribly misguided.

> Not till your thoughts cease all their branching here and there, not till you abandon all thoughts of seeking for something, not till your mind is motionless as wood or stone, will you be on the right road to the Gate.
> Huang Po (Zen master)

# Chapter 29

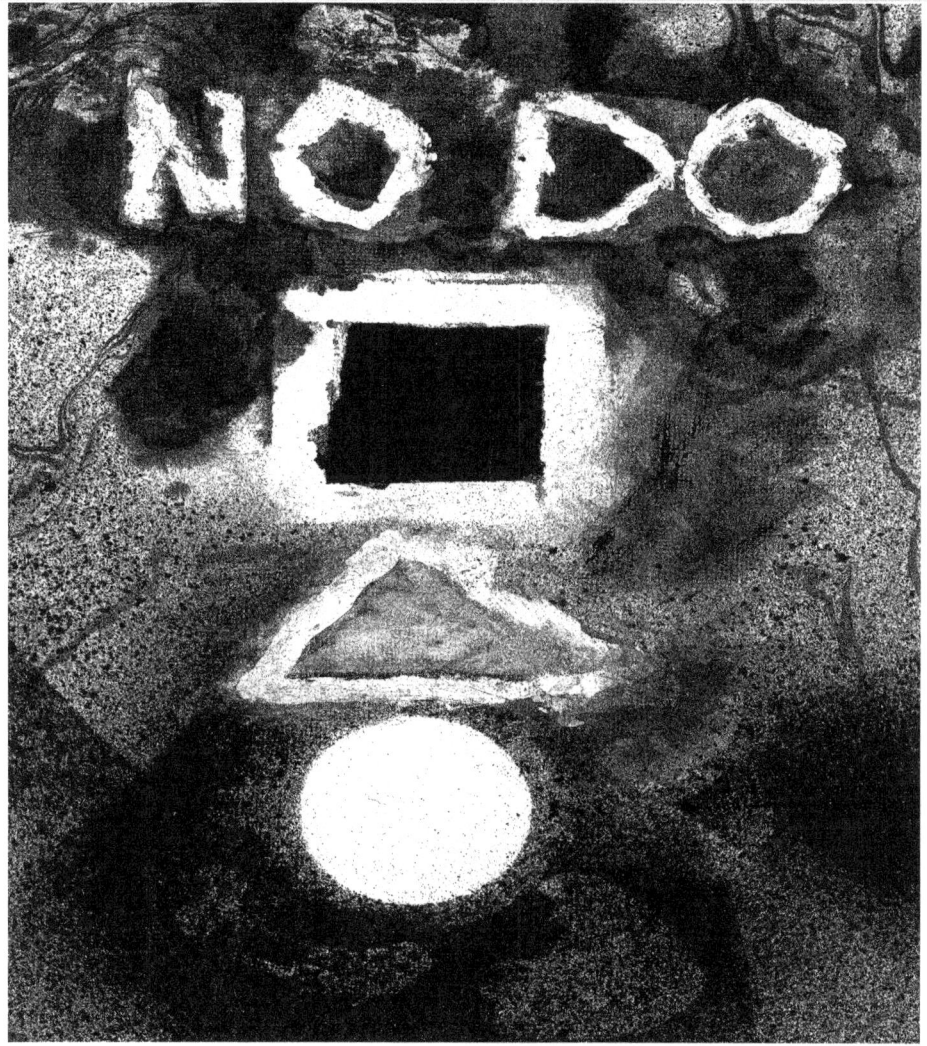

*I think it's much more interesting to live not knowing than to have answers which might be wrong. I have approximate answers and possible beliefs and different degrees of uncertainty…but I am not absolutely sure of anything…*

Richard Feynman (quantum physicist)

By the end of February, I had gotten acclimated enough to the panic attacks that I could once again begin to let go into pure beingness. There was little I could do with the terror but sit with it until it subsided enough to allow samadhi to begin.

Those foolish spiritual pundits that gave advice on how to deal with such debilitating angst might erroneously advise the seeker to go to your "happy place" or "embrace the fear with loving kindness" or "bath yourself in positive energy" or do some "rebalancing work" or "go to your inner child" or offer a myriad of other useless suggestions. The plain, simple fact was there was nothing I could do to combat or alleviate the terrifying symptoms of ego degradation save be patient and let the phase run its course. Any attempt to "do something" would have been counterproductive as it would have only forestalled the inevitable.

Besides, the kind of terror I was experiencing would have brought cold sweats to the bravest of lion tamers, a heaving stomach to the fiercest of samurai. It was just that fucking scary. I had never been in such dire distress in my entire life. Trying to face the black, velvety void of eternity upon which the blinding ethereal light embossed itself was perhaps my greatest test of all. The sooner I unconditionally surrendered to it the better. Now was not the time to draw upon the fierce stoic ethos I had mastered as a martial artist nor the will to persevere that a wilderness survival expert can draw upon. This was not the appropriate venue for a warrior or a survivalist. Now was the time to capitulate. In fact, if you consider it more closely, *NOW*, the present moment, is nothing less than pure capitulation itself. Surrender. NOW is nirvana and nirvana is cessation, and that was the only thing required presently, that and a willingness to see things as they really were.

The extreme apprehension that I felt every time silence overwhelmed me did not subside all at once, but I learned to deal with it by ignoring it as much as possible. In the way a marathon runner or cyclist pushes through the "wall" or the "bonk" simply by inexorably moving forward, I too utilized a similar strategy. I found no other solutions open to me but grinning and bearing it or embracing *the suck,* as one of my favourite survival teachers sometimes puts it, until the crisis resolved itself by its own accord.

Perhaps my ego realized that I was quite willing to suffer these relentless panic attacks day in and day out for the rest of my life. It knew I (whoever that was) had the patience, perseverance and fortitude to endure such turmoil forever, so in the end it relented and allowed me to get on with the business at hand. In the face of a hopeless situation, I had arrived at what was a sensible solution, don't you think? Do nothing.

Was there really a battle of wills going on? Who can say? I don't even know if there were really separate combatants on the field, and if there were, their identities certainly eluded me. In my final summation, the awakening game is fundamentally a great mystery to me. But at the time this tale is taking place, it sure felt like two wills were being tested. It seemed like "I" tired out the doer enough to let beingness prevail.

This new found ability to relax enough into meditation to let beingness bloom was marked in the beginning of the sit by my breathing being only slightly laboured due to a mildly constricted chest. Also my heart raced a little, but this in turn quickly gave way to the bright beacon and bliss of emptiness. This divine luminosity turned out to be the lodestar that marked my way home.

The dazzling light of spiritual illumination only began to be appreciated once I managed to cross over the Rubicon of the dark night of the soul. Surrender to the Alpha and the Omega was everything John of the Cross promised it would be and more. Indeed, this juncture marked the final stages of *samadhi*. To elaborate, I will now introduce the concept of *jhanas*.

To be clear, this kind of terminology meant nothing to me at the time. Everything was just naturally unfolding as it would. Later, I saw how my actual lived experience reflected certain spiritual markers the Hindus and Buddhists ascribe to the various *jhana* or *samadhi* states, so I offer a brief description of them below for your consideration. My experience didn't show the discrete phases or clear delineations seen below. It was more a continuum of experience than a set formula, but getting a feel for the overall jhana experience might be of interest to you.

Ex-Prince and future Buddha, Siddhartha Gautama, found two teachers who guided him during the early phases of his spiritual quest. The first teacher is reputed to have taught him the first seven *jhanas*, the other guru the eighth. Both teachers said that that was all they had to offer him. Siddhartha was not satisfied as he still wondered why suffering persisted. He left each teacher in turn and took up six years of austerity practices. This also failed to provide the answer he sought, so he next embraced the Middle Way.

On the day of his enlightenment, we are told that he sat down under the Bodhi Tree and began practicing the *jhanas* whereby he fell into deep *samadhi*. Apparently is mind then became "concentrated, purified, bright, unblemished, rid of imperfection, malleable, wieldy, steady and imperturbable." Eventually, Nirvana prevailed.

Through the sutras we find out that Buddha gave direct instructions on attaining *samadhi*, which is analogous to attaining the various *jhana* states, through what he called "right concentration." Here is what he said on the matter:

> And what is Right Concentration? Here a monk-secluded from sense desires, secluded from unwholesome states of mind enters and remains in the First Jhana which is filled with rapture and joy born of seclusion accompanied by initial and sustained attention. With the stilling of initial and sustained attention, by gaining inner tranquillity and oneness of mind, he enters and remains in the Second Jhana which is without initial and sustained attention; born of concentration, and is filled with rapture and joy. With the fading away of rapture, remaining imperturbable, mindful, and clearly aware, he enters and remains in the Third Jhana, and of him the Noble Ones declare, "Equanimous and mindful, he has a pleasurable abiding." With the the abandoning of pleasure and pain, as with the earlier disappearance of elation and distress, he enters and remains in the Fourth Jhana. This is beyond pleasure and pain; and purified by equanimity and mindfulness. This is called Right Concentration.

You might find that description a bit imponderable as did I when I first set eyes upon it. That's the thing when it comes to *samadhi*. Everyone has a hard time talking about it in anything more than a cursory manner. The Christian mystics, Hindus, Jains, Sikhs, yogis and Buddhists speak of this numinous experience in nuanced and subtle language. Though it may be difficult to articulate, there is certainly no mistaking it when it actually befalls you.

To make things even more complicated, the Buddhists outline the path of *samadhi* one way in the sutras and another in the commentaries. On the one hand, it is sometimes used as a verb as in *how one does samadhi* (i.e. the practice of concentration leading to the goal of attainment). On the other hand, it is used as a noun. Here *samadhi is a thing you attain in ever deepening degrees of realization*. Liberation or enlightenment then would be the final natural outcome of attaining the highest degree of *samadhi*. The following quote from Zen literature shows how paradoxical the situation can be:

> Zen master Tai-yung, passing by the retreat of another Zen master named Chih-huang, stopped and during his visit respectfully asked, "I am told that you frequently enter into samadhi. At the time of such entrances, does your consciousness continue or are you in a state of unconsciousness? If your consciousness continues, all sentient beings are endowed with consciousness and can enter into samadhi like yourself. If, on the other hand, you are in a state of unconsciousness, plants and rocks can enter into samadhi." Huang replied, "When I enter into a samadhi, I am not conscious of either condition." Yung said, "If you are not conscious of either condition, this is abiding in Eternal samadhi, and there can be neither entering into a samadhi nor rising out of it."

This description points to the final stage of samadhi where, like I came to intimately know for myself, the experience is no experience and not no-experience both at the same time and incomprehensibly non-dual in nature. Not much can be said about it as it defies all conceptualisation. Mercedes de Acosta says this directly in her 1960 book, *Here Lies the Heart*:

> Samadhi is a very difficult state to explain. In fact I do not think anyone has ever explained it. Doctors have tried to analyze it from a medical and physical point of view, and have failed.

Examined from the etymological perspective, the word can be broken down into its three constituent parts.

*Sam* means "to put or join together," *a* points to "endlessness" and *dhi* means "to know, to see or to witness," so altogether the meaning imparted to us is "recognizing that everything is coming together eternally," or more directly it means the actual experienceless experience of non-duality itself.

*Samadhi* is often seen as a progressive path with varying stages. It is thought to begin with a mediator who engages in one-pointed meditation and ends when that meditator disappears.

*Samadhi* inevitably culminates in the stateless state of no-mind if taken to its natural conclusion. Those who favour accolades may be drawn to figure out where they rate in the process at any given moment. I could have cared less at that point since the guy who used to consider such things important was rendered pretty much irrelevant by that point.

I might say that the prevailing movement in *samadhi* is the one away from self and towards the pure being of non-duality. It becomes impossible to distinguish between the one meditating, "me," and that which is being meditated upon. At this point, there is only emptiness standing alone in a pure field of awareness. There is no-thing and no-one to be aware of anything in particular. Time and space disappear. You disappear.

> Dying to your own attachments is a beautiful death.
> Because this death releases you into real life.
> You have to die as a seed to live as a tree.
>    Mooji (spiritual teacher)

*A Fleeting Improvised Man Awakens*

# Chapter 30

*Quantum theory thus reveals a basic oneness of the universe. It shows that we cannot decompose the world into independently existing smallest units.*

Fritjof Capra (writer)

By February, the panic attacks had released their grip on me such that complete letting go commenced. Going back to the hockey stick analogy that I have been using as a gauge to mark my spiritual progress, I was fast approaching the beginning of the taped grip area marking the very top of the handle, the pinnacle of maturation so to speak. The inferno that burned away all delusion was raging as never before.

A new phenomenon had begun to arise for me during normal daily routine. From time to time a brief interlude of awareness—the clarity begat of no-thought, of no-self—would spontaneously erupt or interject itself upon whatever might be happening. The effect was startling and wonderful, akin to how a rainbow delights us when it suddenly appears in a clear portion of an otherwise sombre, overcast sky and then much too quickly fades away again. This brief phenomenon was strikingly different from the normal mindfulness practice I was engaged in.

To be mindful now during this late stage of awakening was an eminently simple affair. If I was washing the dishes, that was all I was doing, just washing dishes, not thinking about how my meditation was going or what I might eat for dinner. Similarly, if I strolled on the beach, that was the only thing happening. It was so delightful to actually be present in the world after taking such a prolonged sabbatical (i.e., most of my life). How many decades had it been since I last spontaneously noticed the grass underfoot, heard the chirp of a bird, felt the breeze on my face, smelled the musky scent of the dank forest floor or noticed the minty flavour of my toothpaste?

Except on the rare occasion when awareness is heightened due to crisis, danger, the shock of the new or some other kind of similar excitement that jars us out of our routine, we are all pretty much oblivious to the world around us, aren't we? We take a walk in the park, get back in the car and recall little if anything of the hike, correct? Instead of engaging with reality, you might be strategizing on how to improve your relationship with your partner, lose weight, plan that next fabulous vacation, or get that big fat raise you are always dreaming of. "Existence be damned, I have a life to *think* about."

Through my quest, I discovered that I was forever trapped in the simulacra of the mind. My goal, which was becoming increasingly spontaneous, was simply to be present or more accurately to be presence itself. As the sense of "I" continued to evaporate, so, too, did the dazzling illumination and bliss of *samadhi*.

I could still make an effort and "see" the light and "feel" the bliss, so to speak, but it became less and less something I endeavoured to experience. This was the dawning of the *I don't care/know* mind. This is a key point. As the ego begins to leave centre stage, a wondrous sense of freedom, joy or even ecstasy may be perceived for a time. These kinds of intensely pleasurable feelings were entirely novel and curious to say the least. But these phenomena passed away entirely as the *samadhi* of no-self strengthened and stabilized.

After awakening, I took a look at the etymology of the word *ecstasy* to discover its roots in order that it might shed some light on this wondrous feeling *samadhi* had induced for some time. You may be interested in the results of my investigation for it addresses, once again, the concept of where the self is located, or not located, while one is in the throes of spiritual awakening. It was becoming ever more evident that self/Self was the axis mundi around which all other elements of true spirituality rotated.

*Ecstasy* is derived from the ancient Greek word *ekstasis*, which means "to be or stand outside (oneself)." Here "ek" means "out," "stasis" means "a stand." How fascinating, I thought. You *stand outside yourself* et voila—the ecstasy of the divine can't help but be revealed. There it was again—shades of the "open secret" for all to see. But you had to have the right "decoder ring" to make sense of what was being pointed to.

For one of my favourite Greek Philosophers, Plotinus, ecstasy came about when one utilized what he called *The Art of Losing Control*. He explained that you needed to *transcend your normal self* in order to become connected to spirit, God or the One/Monad. This realization came about by stepping out of self and by wider abstraction the very fabric of space. How about time? Does temporal dislocation figure into spirituality as well? Here is an interesting *Wikipedia* entry on the matter:

> ...one can be "outside of oneself" with (regards to) time. In temporalizing, each of the following: the past (the 'having-been'), the future (the 'not-yet') and the present (the 'making-present') are the 'outside of itself' of each other...Martin Heidegger who, in his *Being and Time* of 1927, argued that our being-in-the-world is usually focused toward some person, task, or the past. Telling someone to "remain in the present" could then be self-contradictory, if the present only emerged as the "outside itself" of future possibilities and past facts.

I found that entry very relevant to my own lived experience. It is quite true that when one steps outside of the self, or abandons the past and future, it leaves no one available to be in the present moment. Weird, eh? I contend that no one has ever been in the NOW, nor could they be, because there is no one present in presence.

It seems that certain luminaries throughout the ages have been telling us that if one managed to stand outside of the presumed self, ecstatic religious revelation would naturally be the result. This, then, explained the bliss I felt every time I let go of the self.

As I considered this definition further, I realized that it wasn't quite telling the whole story, for it still suggested a semblance of a self who/which remained to experience the ecstatic moment. Who was the one standing outside the self that became "connected to Spirit," as Plotinus would have it? Who is that guy, I wondered?

Maybe he was the chap experiencing the bliss. To be sure, once DJ's presumed self for all intents and purposes disappeared entirely from True meditation, I no longer perceived any sense of bliss at all. I might suggest, and Bernadette Roberts concurs, that ecstasy is where most mystics halt their journey. Why not? It feels pretty damn good. Some might say it was the most euphoric feeling they have ever experienced, but I contend it is not enlightenment. Leaving ecstasy behind, I will now move on to the related term of *enstasy* to gain further clarity on this "where is Waldo" business.

Enstasis as defined in The Concise Oxford Dictionary of World Religions reads:

Enstasy (Gk., en-stasis, 'standing into'). The experiences, or abolition of experience, arising as a consequence of those meditational, etc., techniques which withdraw the practitioner from the world, and even from awareness of the self. The word was coined in contrast to ecstasy. Examples are the jhanas.

I discovered that some yogic traditions use this concept in reference to the deeper *samadhis*. By definition and the way practitioners generally regard it, it seems that *enstasy* is described as a very similar experience to ecstasy. This is curious as these two concepts seem to be antipodes. On the experiential level, both definitions point to a displacement of self but time again is a consideration.

In the book *Meditation as a Path to God-Realization*, C. Muppathyil states, "In enstasis the idea of time ceases to exist." He also points out that with regards to objects of perception, "he knows nothing, either external, nor internal."

Exstasis and enstasis are presumed opposites, one stepping into self, the other out of self, yet both seemingly lead the aspirant to the same eventual outcome. No-self.

In truth, there is not really a "stepping" anywhere when one is deep in *samadhi*. The experienceless experience is something more akin to straddling the demarcation point between both positions. One's consciousness is neither more greatly *in* or farther *out* of "self," neither is consciousness displaced to a higher or a lower realm. In truth, this liminal kind of existence is essentially stateless and timeless. Again, dualistic terms fail here. Rather than saying that there is a movement of self "in" or "out," one might be getting a little closer to the truth to say that *samadhi* is more a case of "stasis" proper, stillness, cessation.

I also considered the idea of disstatis (not-standing) to explain the bliss of deeper *samadhi* but rejected it as it suggests someone who exists but is not taking a current position, like one in a deep sleep or a coma. That kind of experience is certainly not reminiscent of *samadhi*. For me, the concept of stasis, though still dualistic in nature, gets closest to describing one's state of being during the most pronounced *samadhi*.

In true stasis, when everything is so still that even stillness is unknown to the meditator, then the final *jhana* or last *samadhi* will have arisen. In a sense, this can only be a theoretical construct for no one is present to recognize its existence. During this terminal phase, which was about to dawn on me, at best I might say that I recognized emptiness, or more precisely emptiness recognized itself, but there is no more to say than that.

> What could I say to you that would be of value, except that perhaps you seek too much, that as a result of your seeking you cannot find.
> Hermann Hesse (writer)

# Chapter 31

*At this point the self has obviously outworn its function...We are ready to go beyond the self, beyond even its most intimate union with God, and this is where we enter yet another new life—a life best categorized, perhaps, as a life without a self.*
   Bernadette Roberts (contemporary Christian contemplative)

   That's the thing with the awakening process; it is just so darn unpredictable. I had been cautiously "dancing" around the rim of the black abyss for several weeks now, until one day I finally took the plunge and slipped into the void proper. I guess this occurrence could be forestalled only for so long.

Up until now, I had let go far enough into emptiness until trepidation got the better part of me. Then, I would flee back to selfhood just as a rat scurries away from a sinking ship in search of dry land. I felt compelled to bring myself to the brink of destruction time and time again yet was wary of losing control. How does one explain this mutual attraction and repulsion?

Actually, this symptom is a marker of the terminal stage of spiritual awakening and has been described in literature for ages. Be it Eastern Buddhist scholars or Chinese Taoist sages, Hindu adepts, Christian mystics or contemporary Western writers like Joseph Campbell, Aldous Huxley, C. S. Lewis, Rudolf Otto or Mircea Eliade, they all have made their contributions by describing this curious phenomenon of mutual repulsion and attraction.

These days the Latin phrase *mysterium tremendum et fascinans* is often employed by writers to explain the phenomenology of letting go. I have to say I was quite struck by the accuracy of this definition.

To give you a better appreciation of what I am trying to point to here, I need to introduce you to German Theologian Rudolf Otto's (1869–1937) term the "numinous," which was introduced by him in the early part of the twentieth century.

Otto coined this word from the Latin *numen* which means "command of presence" and "divine majesty." To experience the numinous often entails a feeling of shock and awe when in the presence of God or some power greater than yourself. Depending on the situation or the experiencer's present demeanour, the shock could give way to revulsion or attraction. It is also important to understand that these feelings are evoked through direct spiritual experience of the numinous itself. Apprehending the numen, much like seeing a UFO or bumping into a bear, is such an immediate and evocative experience that it can't be mistaken for anything else.

The expression *mysterium tremendum* is commonly attributed to Otto these days as a basic concept in the phenomenology of the numinous experience, though in fact it seems he never actually used the term. The German phrase *schauervolles Geheimnis*, "terrible mystery," is what he actually favoured. The oft quoted Latin misattribution seems appropriate enough to me when attempting to explain the effects the numinous experience may have on us.

From "mysterium" we get the idea of "wholly other," which is quite outside one's normal paradigm. By adding "tremendum," the sense is further refined to a mystery beyond all mysteries that evokes in the experiencer feelings of repulsion, awfulness, dread, ruthlessness, absolute unapproachability, the fear of God, panic and even terror.

I once experienced a sailing accident, a full capsize which caused me to abandon ship and frantically swim for dry land. One leg was injured, only one arm was serviceable and my life vest was faulty. The level of fear engendered by the possibility of drowning was not dissimilar to my first apprehension of the numen. Escape often seems the only viable option. Sometimes though, the opposite inclination may arise and simple stupor instead may be the coping strategy.

Since the *mysterium tremendum* is a result of coming into contact with the radically "Other" (i.e., is unlike anything we have encountered or ever will encounter), it can arouse a mental state of insensibility, a blank, unresponsive wonder and astonishment that strikes us dumb with amazement absolute. To be less pedantic about it, I might describe my first foray into the numinous as an incredulous "Holy shit."

C.S. Lewis in his book *The Problem of Pain* offers the following evocative description in his attempts to give his readers a feel for the numinous experience:

> Suppose you were told there was a tiger in the next room: you would know that you were in danger and would probably feel fear. But if you were told 'There is a ghost in the next room', and believed it, you would feel, indeed, what is often called fear, but of a different kind. It would not be based on the knowledge of danger, for no one is primarily afraid of what a ghost may do to him, but of the mere fact that it is a ghost. It is 'uncanny' rather than dangerous, and the special kind of fear it excites may be called Dread. With the Uncanny one has reached the fringes of the Numinous. Now suppose that you were told simply 'There is a mighty spirit in the room', and believed it. Your feelings would then be even less like the mere fear of danger but the disturbance would be profound. You would feel wonder and a certain shrinking—a sense of inadequacy to cope with such a visitant of prostration before it—an emotion which might be expressed in Shakespeare's words 'Under it my genius is rebuked'. This feeling may be described as awe, and the object which excites it as the Numinous.

The *mysterium tremendum* is also described in *The Doors of Perception* by Aldous Huxley in a similar fashion:

> The literature of religious experience abounds in references to the pains and terrors overwhelming those who have come, too suddenly, face to face with some manifestation of the *mysterium tremendum*. In theological language, this fear is due to the in-compatibility between man's egotism and the divine purity, between man's self-aggravated separateness and the infinity of God.
>
> Via the *mysterium tremendum*, you realize the ineffable is far far beyond—unreachable and defies description. God is felt to be a dreadful and fearful entity in whose omnipotent presence one has no agency. A sense of separation or alienation may overwhelm one if this part of the numinous holds dominance. If you stop there, you either become an atheist, an agnostic, or a loyal but distant follower. But fortunately the *mysterium tremendum* is but half the story...

A friend of mine once took an exceptionally powerful entheogen that catapulted him into the realm of the numinous. Upon his returning I inquired, "How was the trip?" Whereupon, with eyes still full of amazement, he replied, "I just got fucked by the universe." Further elaboration on his part revealed his experience encompassed both sides of the numinous experience for while he was repulsed, at the same time he was attracted.

This attraction is spoken of as the *mysterium fascinans*. It marks the alluring and fascinating side of the numinous experience. Those kinds of feelings are opposite to the *tremendums* and include feelings of tenderness, sweetness, reverence, potent charm, succour, vitality and attractiveness.

As the *tremendums* and *fascinans* often appear concurrently, this episode could be described as leading one to an impasse. We are both drawn away from and attracted forward into a kind of liminal space where, paradoxically, we feel we are in a totally unknown territory yet sense a familiarity akin to being at home.

As such, the following feelings which also arise during contact with the Godhead could be perceived as either positive or negative, depending on how the person reacts. These other responses include a feeling of the stark sense of presence, an "overpoweringness," majesty, stark power and might, exaltation, a sense of one's own inconsequentiality in contrast to a Divine power, energy, urgency, will, vitality, insignificance, emptiness, and awe (generally positive feeling though if extreme may become overwhelming and awful). That, then, will have to suffice as an introduction to my own numinous experience which was presently about to unfold.

The following account is my most intense brush with the numen up to that point. It transpired as the snow began to melt and as 2009 was transitioning into spring. I mark it as the first occasion when I wholeheartedly entered the void with no reservations whatsoever. This kind of experience can't be mistaken for anything else but radical letting go and the journey into no-mind. When it occurs, it changes everything in the same way a family is forever marked by the birth of a newborn or similarly the death of a loved one.

It indelibly alters the way one identifies with self, other and existence in general. At this point, I was one footfall away from enlightenment, even closer. In truth, not even a whisker's breadth separated me from true nature. It always was closer than close. I just failed to recognize this fact as I presume you also do presently. This overwhelming episode marked as close as I could get to the terminal stage of the journey, the final revelation, without the whole thing collapsing in on itself and coming to a grinding halt.

Though my inclination to be authentic was about to pay big dividends, enlightenment's final guise would remain elusive for several more months to come. I was now about to enter the costume ball, be introduced to the Magus and yet still find his true identity obscured behind a mask. Soon though, in fact much sooner than I ever imagined, the final reveal would occur. The vizard would drop, and at that point I would be astonished to find none other than myself. But all this was still several months in the future. What I am about to describe now is how I came to perfect *The Art of Losing Control*.

I was about to retire for the evening. It was the end of another long day of meditation, and I was looking forward to the sweet respite only sleep could bring. I was still meditating some eight hours a day. The sessions were always marked by luminosity, great freedom, a lively sense of awareness, and joy. The golden light would still make its appearance, but this phenomenon was of no interest now—not much found in meditation was. A certain growing sense of lightness-of-being pervaded all. This sense of lucidity and spacious awareness was always most evident during the final meditation of the day. I reckon this was because at this late hour my ego was very fatigued and my defenses were at their lowest.

To be clearer, though at this point self-will was greatly weakened, still there was a sense of subtle resistance to what was unfolding. The demolition project had neared its completion but certainly some semblance of an "I" still existed as does a weakened form of the polio virus still persist in a modern vaccine. When not in meditation or being mindful, my thoughts still spontaneously projected to the past and future if left to their own devices. This is how the ego imagined itself into existence, and it was still doing a pretty damn fine job of it. Of course, throughout the day brief interludes of clarity interjected with increasing frequency. These moments were more wonderful than ever and less jarring since they were becoming much more commonplace. So it was upon this backdrop that the following incident transpired.

The void now opened up with the invitation to jump in just like it had been doing for some weeks now, but I was holding back due to fear and trepidation, if nothing else. I hadn't yet dared to completely let go. For some days, I had been cautiously circling around the "rim" as one would a dangerous volcano caldera. The unfathomable blackness beckoned me to enter, but I still resisted the urge to merge. I got ever nearer though, which is when a really weird feeling would start to overwhelm me.

That was the pattern then. Inexorably, a force attracted me ever closer to completely surrendering into the unfathomable, and then another opposing force would cause me to rein myself back in at the last moment. However, this evening things would be different.

Finally, metaphorically speaking that is, something in me emboldened itself enough to allow at least half of my "body" to slip into the deep before I pulled out of the *troubled waters*. This was huge since up until now it had been no more than a dangling lower leg sunk into the void for the briefest of moments. This occasion was precedent setting.

As a consequence, a very stark and weird feeling was registered, but it was not so unsettling or shocking as to terminate the enterprise. After a moment of screwing up my courage once more, I again repeated the experiment to no ill effects. This time, some innate knowing registered a certain familiarity with this terrain. It was a strange land but seemingly not entirely unknown. I recall a similar brief encounter with it once or twice during various plant-medicine sessions. Additionally, a similar feeling was registered on the occasion when I "threw in the towel" for a moment and the struckless sound of *anahata nada* piped up. What transpired next, though, took me by great surprise as the experience about to unfold would be much more intense than those just mentioned.

I guess on this evening "third times the charm" as they say, and indeed this time I finally bloody well went for broke and bet the whole farm. To be precise, I just let go completely with no reservations whatsoever.

HOLY FUCK!

A force or presence so unimaginably huge overwhelmed my entire being such that it felt like a spiritual tsunami had knocked me over. There was no hope for survival on this occasion for I was now intentionally wearing no life preserver. This experience was much too primal and immediate for me to conceive, never mind cope with, if in fact there was anyone now present to deal with anything at all...which there bloody well wasn't! An experience akin to no-self had just broken out.

Astonishment prevailed. At the same time, an unbearable electric current, or rather perhaps it was concentrated two-hundred-proof high-test bliss, proceeded to course through the body-mind complex like a junkie on an overdose of the really good stuff. It was quite incapacitating. It felt ever so much like sexual climax which registered at least a nine or ten on the old *orgasmatron scale* (see previous book for definition and discussion).

Once upon a time, I had relished a lesser moment of bliss induced by an entheogen. That pleasure was perhaps on the order of three or four times what I normally experienced during climax. That kind of experience I could enjoy/endure for some minutes, but this new level was simply unbearable. As Alan Watts once pointed out, the human nervous system simply can't cope with such extreme levels of pleasure. It's like overloading the system so much that the wires begin to fry. I quite quickly had to bail. The experience ended.

There was an inclination to continue on with the movement into unity, to totally surrender into the Absolute, as it were. Yet the extreme energy, amazement and shock and awe of the mysterium tremendums was too intense to endure this time around. The experience could not be sustained by a time-bound, frail mortal such as I.

I guess from outward appearance, the experience lasted about as long as it takes to inhale and release several times in a row. From the point of view of a knowingness that transcends the mind entirely, it actually was of sufficient duration, for how does one accurately count the measure of a moment out of time to impart one important piece of wisdom? I now knew beyond any doubt that nothing was as it appeared. Previously, I described the occasion that arose that directly showed me that I had been dreaming myself into existence, but this epiphany was more radical still.

To learn that all was illusion, I discovered *what I wasn't*. Now I learned what *I was*, or more exactly still, I became what I truly was. This is the kind of revelation you receive when you get a foretaste of what it is like to cease to exist.

It was now irrefutably recognized that something existed beyond, or outside, of time and space, a profundity extraordinaire. This void was incomprehensibly huge. A vastness so expansive, so all pervasive, you couldn't help but tremble in its presence. I didn't know what it was, but it was clear THAT it was, and it seemed that, if only for a moment, I was not separate from THAT.

*Tat tvam asi*—thou art That. The *Upanishads* speak of Tat/Brahman, the True Self, the transcendent reality beyond the beyond, in the same manner as the THAT which I now recognized directly. Half of this equation then was realized as I sat there "frying" in the electric chair. Yes, THAT indeed exists.

*Chapter 31*

But of course, the quest was not yet quite over. I wanted the whole truth and nothing but. This revelation, as far as awakening goes, was merely another appetizer or perhaps the first plate in a multi-course feast. The rest of this tale then chronicles how I stumbled across the realization of the second part of the formula THAT=thou. THAT had been discerned though it was little more than a sideways glance at this point. How about "thou"? Soon "True Self" would be revealed in all its eternal glory, and with that, the quest would come to a close.

> If you gaze for long into the abyss, the abyss also gazes into you.
> Friedrich Nietzsche (writer)

# Chapter 32

*Let go of the battle. Breathe quietly and let it be. Let your body relax and your heart soften. Open to whatever you experience without fighting.*
  Jack Kornfield (Buddhist teacher)

The "orgasmic" *unbearable lightness of being* that I described in the last chapter left me spent in the way sexual release does. I wondered if this feeling was a physiological artifact somehow related to human neurology. Though of no real consequence to the awakening process, still, I was curious enough about this phenomenon to do a little research into the field of human sexuality and brain morphology. What did neuroscience understand about the orgasm, and could it in some way help explain my curious reaction to extreme letting go? I found the results of this inquiry to be quite fascinating.

"First contact," though brief, felt ever so much like floating on a boundless silent Sargasso Sea of pure energized bliss. The French term for orgasm immediately came to mind as I considered this phenomenon more deeply.

I found it quite remarkable that the French expression for orgasm, *la petite mort*, "the small death" so well encapsulates the feeling of peace, stillness, detached awareness and transcendence evoked immediately after both sexual release and the kind of letting go I just experienced. For what is radical disintegration of the ego other than a kind of death…the death of small "s" self. This may help explain why the body produced the same physiological response to both the *small death* of orgasm and the disintegration of ego.

Spirituality and sexual practices have a long-standing relationship. Many sects favour abstinence or chastity. On the other hand, there are those that utilize Kundalini/tantric practices or sexual yoga (favoured by certain Tibetan Buddhists sects) or more contemporary movements like the American *OneTaste* franchise that promulgates *orgasmic meditation* as a means to spiritual wakefulness. Guru Osho has said on the matter, "The experience of orgasm itself is always nonsexual. Even though you have achieved it through sex, it itself has no sexuality in it. And my own understanding is that meditation has grown out of the experience of orgasm." Osho here seemingly identifies the similarity between the beingness of letting go or the stillness of no-self and the momentary gap in consciousness orgasm induces. So let me now turn to science and let it weigh in on the matter as well.

It was apparent from the 2011 *Scientific American* article entitled "The Neurobiology of Bliss" that brain research had made some tentative forays into this area, and the data suggested that the sensed feeling of orgasmic release and the bliss of spiritually letting go were related.

The article postulated that recent brain scan research has shown that the state of bliss, orgasm, and deep meditation have three similar qualities related to self that undergo a significant shift from the norm when these states are being expressed. The following qualities are found to be radically diminished.

- sense of self awareness
- body perceptions
- ability to sense pain

Bliss, orgasm and deep meditation lead to a momentary extreme slowing or even shutting down of the internal monologue. In these moments of ego eradication, you are no longer present, and thus joy and bliss can abound. One study even located a centre in the brain that actually shuts down when letting go commences.

Janniko R. Georgiadis, a neuroscientist at the University of Groningen, co-authored a brain scan study which found out how certain regions in the front of the brain cease operation during orgasm, especially one just behind the left eyeball called the *lateral orbitofrontal cortex*. Speaking directly to the matter he said:

> Shutdowns in the brain's prefrontal cortex appears crucial. It's the seat of reason and behavioural control. But when you have an orgasm, you *lose control*.

"You lose control"—Bingo! Plotinus' *The Art of Losing Control* immediately comes to mind once more. So there you have it. There was indeed a scientific correlate between the bliss of orgasm and letting go, and it seemed, at least in part, to have to do with throwing a monkey wrench into a specific centre of the left hemisphere. The finding that the left hemisphere is crucial in moderating the bliss of no-self is further supported by the experience of neuroanatomist and author Jill Bolte Taylor.

In Taylor's award winning, and highly inspirational book, *My Stroke of Insight*, Taylor chronicles her brush with death due to a massive stroke in the left hemisphere of her brain. I found the details of the effects of suffering a debilitating stroke to be uncanny in the way it portrayed an experience very akin to an episode of terminal spiritual awakening.

Taylor postulated that as her left hemisphere shut down, the person she took herself to be was entirely eradicated and this, in turn, left her with a profound blissful sense of no-self. I was really struck by how similar her description of brain quiescence due to trauma was to my own experience of spiritually letting go, right down to the particular way she spoke of an *energetic arising*. Here I quote her, "I felt as if I was an electrical being; an apparition of energy." Taylor's words are an entirely accurate description of what I felt when I first apprehended the void.

Furthermore, the following passage pretty much left me speechless as it so well described the journey from self into the stillness of the abyss, yet what is being described here was not a product of spiritual practice at all but simply an artifact of a failing brain:

> ...the energy of my spirit seemed to flow like a great whale gliding through a sea of silent euphoria. Finer than the finest of pleasures we can experience as physical beings, this absence of physical boundary was one of glorious bliss. As my consciousness dwelled in a flow of sweet tranquility, it was obvious to me that I would never be able to squeeze the enormousness of my spirit back inside this tiny cellular matrix.

This certainly portrays the movement from egoic self into oneness or unity. The fact that it was facilitated by brain injury is quite astounding to me. Taylor further elaborated on the destruction of her ego with:

> I existed in some remote space that seemed to be far away from my normal information processing, and it was clear that the "I" whom I had grown up to be had not survived this neurological catastrophe. I understood that Dr. Jill Bolte Taylor died that morning, and yet, with that said, who was left?

Who was left indeed? There's that perennial question again. Bernadette Roberts, contemporary Christian mystic and author of several books on the no-self experience, asked precisely the same thing of herself when she posed the following question, "When the self falls away, what remains?" By way of answer, Meister Eckhart offers an enigmatic clue with, "Only the hand that erases can write the true thing." Anyhow, eventually Taylor was able to formulate an answer of sorts to that question, and it could have just as easily emanated from the lips of anyone who has ever spiritually awoken.

For several years after her stroke while Taylor recovered from the tabula rasa of not-self, she existed in, or more exactly as, limbo itself. Utter stillness and silence prevailed where she was simply a "fluid," as she describes it, at one with all that was. No longer able to draw upon her mind to create distinctions, she realized reality was *One* or "just one big indivisible seamless mass of everythingness" as I would be inclined to put it.

I found Taylor's testimony to be quite amazing in its capacity to reflect my own realizations. She says that her shift in perspective—her *stroke of insight* as she refers to it, which by the way allowed her to continue to abide in peace even after she made a full recovery—was purely a matter of brain damage. When her left hemisphere packed it in, it left only the expansive bliss the right hemisphere could provide.

For a time, I wondered if spiritual enlightenment was similarly simply a matter of modifying the way the brain was wired. Taylor is adamant that this is the case. How does she know this for certain, I wondered? Is enlightenment manifested from within, from without or neither…or perhaps even both. That is a rather difficult thing to deduce, and I'll leave it at that for now.

I don't know for certain if brain pathology has anything to do with awakening, and it doesn't matter if I ever find out. Liberation itself is the goal. I suggest Taylor (and Buddha as well) might say that the take-home lesson here is that peace and freedom are everyone's birthright. All we need do is learn to reorient ourselves in that direction, as she herself has continued to do even after her recovery period. My own brief foray into the "expanse" made me more determined than ever to let go into the pure nothingness of being.

> I am nothing but the empty net which has gone on ahead of human eyes, dead in those darknesses…and in my net, during the night, I woke up naked, the only thing caught, a fish trapped inside the wind.
> Pablo Neruda (poet)

# Chapter 33

*A human being has so many skins inside, covering the depths of the heart...We know so many things, but we don't know ourselves! Go into your own ground and learn to know yourself there...The eye through which I see God is the same eye through which God sees me.*
   Meister Eckhart (Christian mystic and writer)

   Christian mystic Meister Eckhart has a perspicacious way with words when it comes to his poetic descriptions of the awakened life. Consider the following, for example:

> Up then noble soul.
> Put on thy jumping shoes which are intuition and love and overleap thy worship of thy mental powers, overleap thy understanding and spring into the heart of God, into his hiddenness where thou art hidden from all creatures.

I find delight in that description, and it assures me that that guy was speaking from direct spiritual experience. "Jumping shoes" indeed...what a wonderful turn of phrase to employ when pointing out the limiting nature of the conceptual realm. Let it serve then as the perfect metaphor for the final phase of my journey. This idea of the necessity to emasculate the cynical intellect or disempower the egoic centre is critical if Spirit is ever to be realized. And this Eckhart further points out must be done through the faculties of love, intuition and faith, which not coincidentally was what was precisely occurring in my spiritual endeavours during the last few months I spent on "death row."

In my true meditation of "no-mediation," my contorted fists of anxiety for the first time relaxed fully into unclenched hands ready to embrace the Divine whenever the opportunity arose. Taking that "great leap forward" into the unfathomable had changed everything.

The morning after my first foray into the void, as I sat down for the opening meditation of the day, I immediately fell into emptiness with no distress at all. It was marvellous. What had all that muss and fuss over so many months been about, I wondered?

Dropping into the pure beingness of the Divine now became as pleasant as Eckhart described. In meditation, I had finally acquired the faculty to slip on my very own pair of jumping shoes and within a second or two leap into the undivided, unbounded and unmanifested state of pure beingness any time I pleased. All I had to do was put my mind to it, or rather not put my mind to anything nor anywhere at all, and there it was not—absolute emptiness.

I discovered, much to my surprise, that there was in fact a small cadre of historical Christian contemplatives who really knew a thing or two about Christ consciousness back in the day. More astonishing still was the fact that there were several contemporary ones as well. I realized that the *open secret* was not as obscure and hidden as I might have first imagined. In fact, I discovered accounts of spiritual awakening that ran throughout many traditions. The Truth was there for anyone to see if they so desired. Most don't as there is simply little interest. Yes, enlightenment is a rare occurrence, but it is not a special thing only the worthy few can attain. Consider how the prehistoric coelacanth fish first came to light, and it may serve as a good analogy to what is being pointed to here.

The coelacanth was once considered extinct, and its existence was only known from the fossil record. Amazingly, it was chanced upon in a fisherman's net early last century. The scientific establishment was really keen to procure another. Great rewards were offered. A British scientist spent many fruitless years trying to secure another specimen until some backward, remote island natives caught wind of this scientist's quest. To his great delight, they rewarded him with many more specimens. The problem in the beginning was the fact that this scientist was an academic, not a fisherman. He knew neither WHERE nor HOW to look. The coelacanth had been staring him in the face all along. He just lacked the education, tools and wherewithal to "discover" something that was plainly there for all to see.

When the ego finds out that there is nothing in awakening for it, that there are no "keepers" so to speak, it chucks its few awakening experiences back into the murky depths and moves on. Perpetual seeking then is one powerful method Maya employs to maintain the appearance of the dream state. St. John of the Cross spells out precisely how the spiritual aspirant must proceed if closure is ever to be realized:

> To reach satisfaction in all, desire satisfaction in nothing. To come to possess all…you must go by a way in which you possess not. To come to what you are not, you must go by a way in which you are not.

Christ tells his disciples essentially the same thing when he says that all they have to do is give up *everything* to become his disciple, and St. John positively concurs. This going by the "way in which you are not and have not" is the price one must pay to enter *the kingdom of heaven,* so to speak. But this Kingdom is a whole lot more, and less, than most Christians imagine it to be.

So how is this facilitated? How does one actually go by a way in which you are not? This pointing seems counter-intuitive at best and impossible to appreciate at worst.

Well, for me it involved finding the last piece of the puzzle which was the practice Hindus call *bhakti*, or devotion to the Divine. I might speak of it as a heart-centered inclination as opposed to realization that arises through the conceptual mind. In other words, I am speaking here of a transcendence of the mental realm via the non-conceptual faculty of love and devotion. David Carse, author on non-duality, feels that it is essential:

> Despite traditions to the contrary, there simply cannot be true jhana without true bhakti, there cannot be the ultimate understanding without the ultimate surrender. Certain personalities will try to avoid one or the other under the guise of some higher wisdom, but always at the cost of wholeness.

This movement arose quite spontaneously in me. No one advised such a practice, and if they had done so, I wonder how authentic it could have been. How can the heart open other than through its own tenderness? Here I again turn to Meister Eckhart for some clarity:

> This identity out of the One, into the One, and with the One [exstasis, enstasis, and stasis—DJ] is the source and fountainhead breaking forth of glowing love.

Rumi, the Persian mystic and poet adds, "The astrolabe of the mysteries of God is love." Truly love was the final sign post I needed to chance upon in order to come to fully embrace the beloved.

Meditation became my favourite thing to do. My heart felt like it would burst due to the upwelling of love that arose within it. That sentiment isn't entirely metaphorical. There was actually a felt sense in my cardiac region that kinesthetically oozed passion. The heart centre literally beamed and glowed with love. The feeling was sublime. The ancient Greeks coined the term *agape* to describe the highest form of love, a kind of unconditioned passion stripped of self-interest. This is what I am alluding to here.

Meditation now engendered extreme feelings of love and tenderness that increased as the intensity of the golden light also strengthened until in less than a minute's duration, the growing crescendo peaked, and in a flash everything vanished. An hour later, something made me stir, and I would be surprised to see the session was over. Going back to the old hockey stick metaphor for one last time, the place on the stick which would now mark my point in the journey would certainly be on the upper taped handle area, fast approaching the final end knob. Soon, there would be no wiggle room left to speak of.

Before the meditative experience swept me away entirely into the oblivion of *samadhi*, I repeatedly noted a strong sense of clarity and spacious awareness. There was also this odd sensation which felt a bit like being on pins and needles or being subjected to a low amperage electric DC current which made my body slightly "tingle." If I elected to open my eyes at this point just before I disappeared into eternity, the scene appeared essentially monochromatic, low resolution/definition and rather two dimensional. The scene was reminiscent of how a poorly tuned, fuzzy TV picture would appear or else how a falling snow vista might look as flakes tumbled lazily downward. The view was more one of dancing specks than a concrete three-dimensional reality.

Oddly enough, with eyes fully closed, there was a sense of illumination that was set apart from the dazzling amber light display I beheld in my mind's eye. Like *anahata nada*, this sensed "illumination" had no source. Somehow things felt a whole lot less murky, but I had no idea why. The feeling of spaciousness was the same. I never knew what to make out of the sensed impression of an immense spaciousness, or a non-containability, that had no cause. Humans have no way to define or relate to such non-dual arisings.

Every time I sat down I was always struck by the enormity of it all. Realizing that Reality is the formless and boundless ground of being can be disturbing if the mind turns in that direction. Fortunately, mine didn't, for I was no longer moved to consider the immensity of it all. I was actually engaged in becoming it. So much so that one day, just after I had arisen and eaten breakfast, stillness actually broke through spontaneously into normal mundane reality just as I finished up my last sip of morning tea. This occasion turned out to be quite a shocker for it took me totally unaware.

This experience was reminiscent of my Ayahuasca induced *hohlraum* episode. Stillness now prevailed with no thoughts arising at all. I just sat alone in complete silence. The first twenty or so minutes were kind of perplexing but not disagreeable, though as the minutes continued to roll on the more perturbed and anxious I became. My mind finally chimed in with a "You can't live like this…with no thoughts arising…you will be bored!" Soon thereafter, I started to try to conjure up a thought…any thought…but it was all to no avail. I literally could not recall anything from my past or project to a supposed future. It was getting all too weird for me. After about an hour of utter silence, I began to lose it. The profound quietude had become so disconcerting that I was bordering on a panic attack. I began to wonder if I was going mad. In the growing discomfort, I debated whether I should call Mitra or not. If I did, it would have been a precedent. Moreover, I imagined I would have appeared to be weak, so I preferred not to. I started to pace around the room in a state of increasing agitation. I actually picked up the phone a couple of times, but in the end I resisted the urge to call for help. Finally, I decided to try to meditate. As soon as I got seated on my meditation chair and closed my eyes, a thought of the past welled up. Boy was I ever relieved. With that, the phone rang. Incredibly, it was Mitra. She had never rung me before. She asked me what was wrong for somehow she had sensed my growing distress. I had long held out the possibility of psychic abilities. This highly charged incident proved to my satisfaction that so called "supernatural powers" could on occasion come into play. I was flabbergasted that Mitra had rung. How had she known…? I told her all was well and hung up the phone. My mind was now back to functioning as it always had. This kind of incident never repeated itself. Of course, enlightenment did finally occur one day soon, but it differed substantially from this particular interlude of stillness. This episode had some "self" present. The paradigm shift about to unfold would not.

As my formal True meditation sessions continued, the deepest state of samadhi prevented any conceptualizations at all from arising. Eventually, I entered a state as imperturbable as a flea sitting on the back of an elephant. Actually, except for the fact that this *samadhi* arose and fell away again, I wouldn't even call it a state. I have no words to describe the ground of being as it rests entirely outside the bounds of duality itself.

The heart-centred openness that was blooming when I dropped into the silence of meditation also spontaneously began to arise during daily routine. The world was appearing ever more marvellous. At times, I felt like giving a congratulatory big round of applause to the whole darn thing with a "Good for you. Excellently played, old boy. You've done well," and a slap on the back thrown in for good measure. As I no longer paid much heed to my critical nay-saying ego, reality seemed to be cast in a whole new light.

What kind of light? Well, during my filmmaking days when I was shooting outdoors, I sometimes aimed to begin an hour or so before sunset. The scene was bathed in a cheery, warm amber glow. In cinematographic parlance it's called the *magic hour*. So here's the thing, somehow I had failed to recognize that this was how reality appeared all the time if my mind wasn't informing me otherwise.

I began to seek out experiences that were less likely to cause me to identify with the egoic mind and instead move me ever nearer to the realm of heart-centred agape. Rumi's ecstatic poems of his love for the Divine were inspirational in this regard as were the writings of Kabir, but even better were the mundane things life had to offer that previously I had somehow overlooked.

A pasture field festooned with numerous decades-old weathered and greying stumps left to naturally decay in situ like a field full of giant truncated mushrooms was a marvellous sight to behold. Similarly, a frog jumping into the pond, a termite mound, shellfish stubbornly clinging to beach rocks and a long abandoned car incongruously shoved deep into the forest, all evoked a sense of mystery and wonder.

My oh my, such a shame it was to have been missing out on heart-centred, tender awareness for so long. Sometimes I whimpered, at others I balled from the depths of my being. Beholding such beauty would even have had the great Zeus down on his knees, I reckon.

You might well imagine that the utter solitude had finally driven me bonkers... hopelessly mad, but I assure you quite the opposite was true. I wasn't being driven away from my senses but rather coming back to them. I assure you that the mundane is quite extraord-inary when viewed from a new, invigorated perspective. I spoke in my first book about *Cezanne's carrot*. These experiences I speak of here are precisely what the old dab hand was going on about. A revolution clearly was in the works when things were perceived anew!

I utilized online video, mostly YouTube, to further encourage my heart to open. I watched snippets featuring comedians from the past like Groucho Marx, Jonathan Winters, Frank Gorshin, or the *Monty Python* crew, for example, or silly shows like the old *Carol Burnett Show*, *Laugh-in* or that preposterous masterpiece, *Get Smart*. These playfully silly dalliances all worked wonderfully well to inspire an awakening of the heart. Laughter truly is the best medicine. It seems that the Chan patriarchs of old were often a merry lot if the Chinese accounts of these zany Zen masters are to be believed. Take Tang dynasty master Huang Po for instance:

> As for sitting, sitting is something that should include fits of ecstatic laughter-brayings that make you slump to the ground clutching your belly. And when you struggle to your feet after the first spasm passes, it should send you kneeling to the earth in yet further contortions of joy.

Another who famously embraced the positive effects of humour was writer Norman Cousins. In the 1970s, he was suffering from a life threatening illness, and he cured (cheered) himself to good health using laughter therapy.

Let's face it, when you are laughing, there is no room for worries and tears, is there? But it wasn't just comedies I turned to.

I also enjoyed snippets of serial TV from the '60s and '70s. I favoured the quiet composure of *Kung Fu's* protagonist Caine and the ribald wit of Hawkeye from the *Mash* series. The original *Star Trek* franchise was powerful as well. I watched the conclusion of Alastair Sim's version of *A Christmas Carol* numerous times. The last ten minutes or so never failed to open the emotional floodgates. No less inspiring was the power music had over me.

*Chapter 33*

Music held a special place in my heart. In fact, it has been a lifelong companion and muse. For spiritual purposes, I found the trance/dream subgenre of techno music to be particularly glorious. Certain ethereal new-age type composers such as old school Kitaro, Enya or Vangelis could also be inspirational, as well as more contemporary artists like Deep Forest, Enigma or Imogen Heap. A common thread running throughout all of these musical stylings was a heavy emphasis on the synthesiser. Listening to these artists and others would invariably induce a rapturous breakdown, or break-out, from the dream of me.

Appreciation for visual arts and music stems directly from the realm of the senses, not from the conceptual mind. Similarly, true spiritual revelation must eventually come to include an awakening of the heart which arises through inspirations of a non-noumenal (noumena are objects that can only arise in thought) nature.

Above I made reference to a "rapturous break." Let me explain further. Rapture is derived from the Latin "raptus" which means "a carrying off." The feeling of euphoria, delight, enchantment, bliss and ecstasy again finds its roots in the fact that one moves away from the egoic centre. One is *carried away* or no longer present. To this end, I employed music as an enlightenment tool to free myself from the grips of "me." Electronica was liberation technology plain and simple. I will elaborate further on this topic in the next chapter.

> In order to maintain an untenable position, you have to be actively ignorant...Keep your facts, I'm going with the truth.
> Stephen Colbert (comedian and writer)

*A Fleeting Improvised Man Awakens*

# Chapter 34

*It's a cover up, it was a cover up operation all along*
*Honing in, I'm honing in on the heart of it all*
*Toughen up, I've got to toughen up*
*Coz I'm breaking it all apart*
*What's at the heart*
*What's at the heart of it all?*
*Who am I now? Who am I now?*
    Imogen Heap (musician)

> Music has charms to sooth a savage breast
> To soften rocks, to bend a knotted oak.
> *The Mourning Bride* William Congreve (1697)

I don't think I can extol the power of trance music enough when it came to opening the heart centre in my own practice. Of course, I can only relate my own experience here. Your mileage may vary.

I found that there is only one thing more stubbornly unyielding than the Great Pyramid of Cheops, and that is the cynical ego. Yet as Congreve states in the previous passage, music may "soften" a rock as it so, too, may melt a recalcitrant heart.

"Softening" was instrumental in addressing the last vestiges of resistance in my psyche. Perhaps this was why Adya spoke of awakening first in the head and then later in the heart. That is how it worked for me. I understand not everyone resonates with the healing power of music. If it doesn't float your boat, then seek out your own bliss. Maybe it is dub poetry, cycling, painting, throwing a clay pot, gardening or hoisting yourself to the top of a mountain. Apparently for Rumi it was dance:

> Dance, when you're broken open. Dance, if you've torn the bandage off. Dance in the middle of the fighting. Dance in your blood. Dance when you're perfectly free.

Does that "eccentric" Rumi seem a bit extreme? Well, apparently even the staid and somewhat bitter existentialist Nietzsche got it, "And those who were seen dancing were thought to be insane by those who could not hear the music."

The famous author and neurologist, Oliver Sacks, cannot recommend enough the transformational power of music. Many may know of his book, and the subsequent movie, entitled *Awakenings* in which we discovered how the drug L-Dopa was used to bring patients out of their trance state. Less well known was the non-pharmaceutical method he employed, namely, music therapy.

The therapeutic power of music in alleviating the symptoms of *sleepy sickness* was nothing short of miraculous. Other than the drug L-Dopa, this was the only other efficacious treatment that could stir the catatonic patients from their stupor. These poor souls were so enfeebled that they were unable to even raise themselves off their wheelchairs. However, once exposed to music, Sacks reports that they could sing and dance and became "completely alive." This stunned Sacks, and he called it an "absolute revelation." He says, and I quote, "They were liberated by music. They were freed by music." Similarly, I can report that music has the power to spiritually awaken one lost in the trance state of "me." It seems that Sacks would agree with my appraisal of music as being nothing less than "liberation technology." Good old Taoist sage and revered teacher Lao Tzu has a strong positive opinion of it as well, "Music in the soul can be heard by the universe."

That seems to be pretty high praise indeed. I might tweak that statement a bit in the name of even further clarity and say that I found music in the soul to be none other than the universe itself. Lao Tzu is considered one of the most revered sages of all time, but let's consider an even higher authority. Why not let the Gods weigh in on the matter?

If we consider Apollo, Greek God of the Sun, light, truth and music, he seems to have found music enchanting beyond compare. Story has it that this conductor of the choir of muses was so charmed by music that he often forgot to be angry. So apparently, even Gods find the power of music to be enthralling, soothing and liberating. I think it no coincidence that the ancient Greeks chose to personify through the visage of the great Apollo the qualities of light, truth, and also music. Inviting all of these qualities into my life certainly fostered a favourable environment for the numen to eventually reveal itself. Experientially, I found certain styles of electronic music more than capable of moving attention away from ego, or in other words facilitating a letting go into the Light and Truth of Being such that great euphoria, love and tenderness erupted from the depths of my soul.

Frankly, I had never experienced such heartfelt passion and joy in my life as when I closed my eyes and got very still and then listened to one of my favourite music pieces. So you might well wonder, "But aren't you waxing fond about that lifeless, soulless, raucous, synthesiser-based electronic techno crap? Isn't that a pretty cold, mechanical and artificial medium to employ in a heart-centred way? Where's the Spirit in that? Isn't that antithetical to what we are talking about here?" No, not at all. That is, the multitudes and I find that not to be so. To appreciate why this is the case, you only have to consider the following definition from *The Urban Dictionary* which reads in part as, "Trance is fundamentally a euphoric electronic dance music genre whose progenitor is classical music, house and techno." I find this genre to be one of the preeminently uplifting, beautiful and spiritually relevant genres of music available to us today.

Due to stylistic similarities, trance and classical music compositions can be converted from one to the other quite easily. The *breakdown* (the softer, more emotional, gentler part immediately following the song's climatic build-up) is often considered to be the heart of a trance track. It is especially powerful if it derives from one of the more euphoric genres, such as *chillout* or *dream*, which I find emotionally charged and uplifting. It can either overcome the listener with joy or make them spontaneously burst into tears. I certainly experienced both feelings regularly while letting go into the melody through silent sitting and sometimes even enjoyed both feelings simultaneously.

A website devoted to spirit, science, and metaphysics has a collection of recommended artists under the banner, *Spiritually Inspired Conscious DJs & Producers You Should Be Listening To*. Here is a sampling from the site to help give you a better appreciation of the genre.

- **Lulacruza** is powerful medicine music with a modern electronic twist from South America. The duo blends female vocals with amazing sounds captured from nature. It is music of the heart.

- **Phutureprimitive's** music is best described as dripping wet love drops of nasty mind melting sonic bliss. I'll leave you to figure out what this means, but I'll tell ya, he brings a great conscious vibe to heavy and sincere dance music.

- **Kalya Scintilla** is a very talented DJ, with deep spiritual roots. He loves to bring his spirituality out to the open and share with everyone during his live disk jockey sets. His music is a mystery school in itself.

- **Love and Light,** as the name implies, shows these guys to be super sweet and they always make sure to let everyone know they are there for love! They make sure to emphasize the fun side of love, often bringing heavy and groovy beats to make you feel at home.

Techno was born during the early 1980s. It's been suggested that the genre's label arose due to its association or philosophical identification with the so-called techno rebels born out of those times. This perceived societal movement was a direct reaction to the disempowering and alienating effects of our modern technological age. A *Wikipedia* writer suggests "techno music is an expression of technological spirituality."

In practice, it cannot be denied that many free spirits find solace and spiritual comfort when immersed in certain styles of synthesiser music. One only has to understand its importance at the annual almost seventy-thousand strong Burning Man festival to get an idea of what I mean. For many Burners, as they are colloquially called, it is an integral part of their spiritual experience. On a more intimate level, I grabbed a few testimonials off the web to give you the flavour of how this music is regarded by the spiritually inclined, techno rebels of the new millennia.

Here is an excerpt from a blog entry:

> I'LL ADMIT: I never really "got" electronic music until my first visit to the Burning Man Festival in 2009.
> ...(until then) I'd been pursuing my own spiritual path through Eastern traditions such as Buddhism and Yoga. It took the experience (of the festival) to invoke transcendence, a deep inner-knowing that I've been able to cultivate in the years since, and has informed my own pursuit of art, activism, spirituality, and community.

And from "The spiritual aspect of rave culture" by Nicholas Saunders, *The Guardian*, July 25, 1995:

*Chapter 34*

Last year I took a seventy-year-old Zen monk to a rave party. He was curious enough to overcome his dislike of the music until his face lit up with a revelation. "This is meditation!" he shouted above the noise. Later, he explained that the walking meditation he taught involved being fully aware "in the moment" without any internal dialogue separating actions from intentions, and that the same definition applied to the dancers all around him.

The following is a reactionary Christian blog which is critical of the genre. I find it laughably ignorant:

> You are very wise to heed both the warnings of the priest and your own inner "alarm bells" (i.e., tiny tingly [sic] wierd feelings).
> …Techno trance is also entering the Christian music genre. This is concerning because this type of music encourages the emptying of the mind and subsequent altered states, leaving young listeners who are hungry for spiritual "experiences" vulnerable to whatever mischief the devil wants to work while they are otherwise "asleep"…Music is definitely being used by the powers of darkness as a conduit into the lives of the unsuspecting…While I'm sure there are many kinds of techno trance music that are not associated with the occult, the fact that it has as its goal the induction of trance-like states is worrisome. For this reason, my advice is to heed the priest's warning as well as your own instincts and stay away from this music.

It's been a long-held belief of mine that when the more radical and ignorant elements of Christendom dissuade you from trying something, or outright ban it, it is probably something of great merit. The "emptying of mind," "altered state of consciousness," and "tingly weird feeling" this blogger advises her readers to avoid are in reality simply several of the more positive symptoms that spiritual maturation and direct union with the Divine can foster.

The writer claims that techno can induce a trance-like state. My experience is quite the opposite. It is one of the few tools available to us that can actually extract you for a period of time from the dream of me. Similarly, she is misguiding us when she claims trance music can put you to sleep. Actually, it may help you awaken. From the egoic viewpoint, of course, this must be avoided at all costs. It's like what Richard Bach said, "What the caterpillar calls the end of the world the master calls a butterfly."

What this Christian woman calls an "evil trance" I recognize to be waking up to reality itself. One way of describing enlightenment is to say it is akin to awakening from the narrative of me or the trance state, so in this regard, trance music is actually *anti-trance* music. This position has been forwarded by several filmmakers and writers alike.

I enjoyed reading papers such as "Trance Music and Altered States of Consciousness: An Analysis of Trance and House Music as a Transcendental Force" by Jamil Karim, for example.

Here Karim employs a cross-cultural comparison of the early archaic use of ritualistic or shamanistic music vis-a-vis electronica and its capacity to evoke a similar altered state of consciousness. This state, Karim carefully points out, lies directly in the realm of the spiritual. Another excellent paper is "Neotrance and the Psychedelic Festival" by Graham St. John. This lengthy paper explores the religio-spiritual characteristics of trance music.

For an even more comprehensive exploration, I found several books are available on the subject such as *Dancing in the Streets: A History of Collective Joy*, by Barbara Ehrenreich and Robin Sylvan's exhaustive treatise entitled *Trance Formation: The Spiritual and Religious Dimensions of Global Rave Culture*.

In the book, Sylvan makes the point that when it comes to mass gatherings infused with music and dance and the ecstatic feeling this combination engenders, everything that is old is new again. He feels that fundamentally nothing has changed between the archaic spiritual forms of tribal dance and its technological, reimagined, modern version. He stresses how techno dance parties have reinvigorated the old, tired and worn out rituals most organized religions still try to foist onto their believers. Electronic music, he asserts, accesses the same circuits hard wired for religious experience that the ancients relied upon for their transcendence. Yet, it does so in a way uniquely suited to twenty-first century sensibilities.

A great companion to this book is the documentary film *Electronic Awakening*. The film describes the relationship between music and consciousness, metaphysics and mythology as well as the experience of the Divine as revealed through modern dance culture. Rave parties and electronic dance music is reported by numerous participants to be a spiritually transforming event.

To close, I am certainly not saying you have to go to a rave party if you seek transcendence. I know many people have little affinity for music. But if music is something that has always been near and dear to your heart and moved you in ways that you can't explain, why not get very still and quiet or alternatively spring to your feet and sway to the beat while listening to Robert Miles classic song "Children." It is considered to be one of the first trance compositions ever written. The results may surprise you.

You may already have a favourite genre or artist that moves you like no other, for example, you may appreciate Kirtan, the chanting music of devotional yoga; Sama, the spiritual music of the Sufis; Christian liturgical music; or great classic composers like Bach, Beethoven or Mozart. If so, then of course employ that instead. It's not important what you listen to but "how." Fundamentally, the point is not to "listen" to it at all but rather be the music/sound. Come to discover that the listener and the listened are not different. If you find yourself no longer present, then you have certainly caught my drift, for you will be "doing" nothing at all. And that, my friends, is the *sound of silence*, the sweetest hymn of them all.

> It is not the pursuit of greater and greater states of happiness and bliss that leads to enlightenment, but the yearning for Reality and the rabid dissatisfaction with living anything less than a fully authentic life.
>
> Adyashanti (spiritual teacher)

# Chapter 35

*Out beyond ideas of wrongdoing and rightdoing,
there is a field. I'll meet you there.
When the soul lies down in that grass,
the world is too full to talk about.
Ideas, language, even the phrase "each other" doesn't make any sense.*
    Rumi (mystic)

    The snow by now had long ago melted as winter gave way to spring. What a joy to sit basking in the warmth of the south-facing windows that overlooked the pond and find it once again filled with clear spring run-off. Deer came to drink from its refreshing depths, ducks to frolic about. The orchard and meadows were once again verdant. And perhaps most terrific of all, I no longer had to freeze my ass off when attending to a call of nature. The world seemed such a jolly place to be in now that the edifice of me was pretty much torn down. The demolition project had gone well. All the heavy machinery, the crane, the foreman's shack, most of the crew and the food truck had moved on. All that remained was for the skeleton crew to complete the final mopping up process.

My mindfulness practice by now had become exceedingly uncontrived and natural. I had come to discover that staying present was no more complicated than simply reconditioning the mind to pay attention. The *Death of a Salesman* had it so right, "Attention, attention must be paid!" True awareness is to find yourself no longer being mindlessly sucked into the virtual reality of the past or the future at every moment.

It was abundantly clear that the only way I could get to the bottom of this awakening thing was to discover what I wasn't. The corollary had proven impossible. There was no way to affirm anything except perhaps to know that I did not exist in the way that I had previously imagined. So the quest continued to be like playing a losing game of The Hangman's Noose, wherein I found out what letters the word didn't contain until I finally ran out of options and consequently lost the game when the "man" was hung. The only difference is that in the "truth game," you actually win the whole shebang when the noose finally tightens firmly around your own neck. Graphic, but quite true, I assure you.

When I speak of "running out of options" I mean engaging in a futile search to locate the thing you take yourself to be. As I keep reiterating, small "s" self could not be located anywhere. I tried to find something that I could affirm about "me," something I could hang my hat on and say was just so, but I could not. The Bible, in a similar manner, speaks about this inability to assume any position in the passage from Mathew 8:20 which reads as follows, "The foxes have their holes, and the birds of the air have their nests. But the son of man has nowhere to lay his head." I could see that everything was in flux and relativity. So there was not much to do except continue to relax and let go into the enormity of it all. I was like a caged bird whose cruel master plays a terrible trick on it. Each day, the bird's keeper removes a centimeter of its perch. Sooner or later that little feller is gonna be left with very little wiggle room and shortly thereafter, BAM—*birdy go boom*. I was enthusiastically prepared for that inevitability, but frankly I never imagined it would actually befall me.

This whole enlightenment thing still seemed pretty remote and inaccessible. That was the problem. I still imagined it to be somewhere off in the distance at a future time and place. Of course, I had heard that this was not so and that the Absolute was closer than close, that it in fact was right here and now; yet my mind struggled with this proposition.

Of course it did. Awakening had nothing to do with what I thought. As I have gone to great lengths to point out time and time again, it lies entirely outside the realm of the noumenal as well as the phenomenal. To the mind, enlightenment will always be an abstract concept *somewhere over the rainbow*. That is until it isn't. Awakening will remain something to be perpetually envisioned and always regarded to occur only at some future date until something recognizes the fallacy of this thesis.

## Chapter 35

My best strategy remained the one based on deconstruction. I endeavoured to find out what I truly was by revealing to myself WHAT I WAS NOT. If you are an authentic awakenist, then I encourage you to investigate what is untrue. You may find that this tact can work a miracle. When you exhaust this course of inquiry, you will be astonished by what is revealed.

What I am pointing to here is so radically different from what we normally value that it lays in fact on an entirely different playing field. It has nothing to do with what you "know" and everything to do with what you "know not"...or what "you are."

I discovered that "I," the sense of being a "me," was based on an assumption or premise that didn't pan out upon scrutiny. I knew nothing with a hundred percent surety. I didn't know, for example, if Hitler was truly the Devil incarnate, Mother Teresa a compassionate benevolent saint beyond compare or even if the earth was round. To be clear, I am not saying that the earth is not round, merely that I don't know this by direct experience for I have never travelled in space. I kept trying to find the truth, but I couldn't. The Truth of being was an even more slippery feller.

Further, I wondered how anything could be true when it was premised on a "knower" that seemingly had no objective qualities and could not be located anywhere. How, I wondered, could I seriously entertain the possibility of knowing anything when the guy that claimed to be beyond ignorance simply did not exist? There was no getting around this impasse. So it all seemed pretty hopeless at this point—helpless and hopeless. This state of affairs simply was as it was. I had no wish for it to be otherwise. In retrospect, I can now see how fortunate I was during those last days. Things were progressing perfectly.

Meditation too was simply as it was. A few months back, it had been a highly pleasurable endeavour. I can see how many could get addicted to this marvellous state of bliss. But spiritual maturation continued to progress. There was now so little bliss or joy available that it wasn't worth mentioning simply because there was now so little of me in the picture to care.

I closed my eyes; immense joy upwelled for several moments, and then in a fashion similar to how a stage magician carries out his most masterful trick...*presto*...*chan*go...the audience gives a little gasp and...the pretty lady has somehow disappeared right before its eyes. Like that dumbfounded audience, I too have no idea how this disappearing act was actually pulled off. I can't precisely tell you how self disappears. The mechanics of it are vague. However, that the self dropped away, time and time again, was irrefutable.

The mysterious nature of the *samadhi of no-self* was evident in my inability to objectify reality. When I tried to bring into focus what was happening, I was once again stuck in the conceptual realm of mind which clearly was not the *samadhi* experience of *no experience*. I could not have my cake and eat it too.

I could either be an "I" and try to imagine what this "not-I" experience must be like or let go into the expanse and be non-duality itself. That is the non-conceptual realmless realm where nary an "I" or "not-I" existed or didn't exist. Have I confused you yet? I sure hope so.

As I keep repeating, this stateless state of affairless affairs is so radically different that it defies any attempt to describe it. Of course, the chance to abide as pure beingness was sublime and always welcomed. I would have been well pleased to continue in this vein for the rest of my life. Meditation was now my passion. I loved it above any other endeavour because it was no endeavour at all. It was simply abiding as true nature.

With irony and great amazement, I was about to discover that I had already and always been True-self inside or out of meditation. It was about time to put the quest to bed for good, shuffle off the stage and retire or to discover that both sides of the equation we considered previously, That=thou, are actually one and the same—both null sets.

$$\{\} = \{\}$$

> We cannot storm the gates of heaven. Instead we must allow ourselves to become more and more disarmed. Then the pure consciousness of being becomes brighter and brighter, and we realize who we are. This brightness is what we are.
> Adyashanti

# Chapter 36

*Lift the veil that obscures the heart and there you will find what you are looking for.*
  Kabir (mystic)

Well I'll be darned if grace didn't finally strike. I guess enough wiggle room had finally been removed from the perch that the "little birdy" could no longer avoid its kamikaze death plunge into oblivion. At least it would appear that way from the viewpoint of normal reality. In truth, just as St. Francis said, "What we are looking for is what is looking," so I must stress that ultimately none of this seeking business is necessary…yet it *appeared* to happen in my case. So in the spirit of completing this truthful fable, let's continue. It'll be worth a few more giggles I assure you, if nothing else.

It was a mid-May afternoon just like any other spring day. I clearly recall the vibrant blue sky and cheery meadow-scented breeze that wafted through the wide-open door of my room. It was just about time to plant the spring garden with the main summer vegetable crop. These days, True meditation still occupied most of my attention, though I persisted in surfing the net in search of spiritually edifying material when the time allowed.

To that end, I was reviewing some rather short but relevant spiritual videos hosted by American Truthist Michael Kavanagh. He had written a book entitled *The Awareness Method,* and though I had yet to read it, I found his YouTube channel inspirational. He was a good teacher and quite probably awake in my estimation. He hadn't produced many clips yet, perhaps twelve or so, but I had watched those several times each. His discourse stressed awareness and mindfulness. He was a fairly young man, very confident in his outlook and seemingly in love with life. Above all else, I took him to be an honest kind of guy in the same way I regarded Adya. That afternoon, for no particular reason, I decided to once again take a little break and watch a few of Kavanagh's videos.

I no longer recall the first one I viewed, but the second is forever indelibly marked in my memory. It had three "movements" or themes, so to speak. The first part of the three entailed an invitation to awaken here and now. As I said, Michael always struck me as a sincere, well-meaning man seemingly uninterested in resorting to sensationalism or hyperbole to get his point across. His presentations were always pragmatic and matter of fact.

Oddly enough, this was the first spiritual video I had ever encountered that featured a teacher personally extolling us to awaken in a direct fashion. So that invitation was what unfolded in the first part of my description below.

Then the middle bit that followed was, more or less, something I call spiritual "blah blah." This lasted for a minute or perhaps a little longer (alas I am not certain for Michael's videos are no longer available). The final section of Kavanagh's video was another direct invitation of sorts. This time he asked us to look and see reality for what it truly was. In other words, he suggested we *be here now*. Further, he pointed out that this was an eminently easy thing to accomplish.

Kavanagh was, in a metaphorical manner, doing an old Zen trick whereby the master banged his dharma staff on the floor time and time again and shouted, "Just this…look see…Just this!"

Though perhaps I should clarify and say it was more of an invitation to the viewers to just look for themselves and see what was already right in front of their noses. With the best of humour and compassion a wisdom master can summon, Kavanagh kept repeating it was "nothing special." "Here it is," he told us, "just this." Again he repeated, "It's already here" and then added with an even more beatific smile, and I'm paraphrasing a bit since I can't review the video for the reason I explained, "It's just this simple moment, just this folks." And with that final revelation…get ready for it…now here is the shocker…THE BIG REVEAL…the moment everybody has been waiting for…NOTHING…nothing at all special happened to me. The video ended and that was that. Sorry to get your hopes up guys and gals.

Just like on all the other occasions that I had watched one of his videos, Michael Kavanagh failed to inspire any great transformation in me or deliver the goods. But that was to be expected. I had watched a myriad of videos produced by many authors, and the results were always the same. I was still Truth unrealized. Boo-hoo.☹

Compulsively, I kept watching these videos, and still nothing changed. I kept the faith and always held out hope that the next one would inspire some miraculous epiphany or transformation. That seems to be the lot of a seeker. As I mentioned previously, "Always becoming, never became." So, of course, what transpired next took me completely by surprise.

My mind said something to the effect of "Hey, DJ, why don't you watch that darn video again?" I remember some part of me smirked in response, probably egoic projection, and said, "Sure, why not? Sure, I'll go ahead and watch that lame drivel all over again. Who cares?"

I gather that it was at that moment that the ego softened a bit. It seems that its hold on selfhood relaxed enough so that what transpired next took it totally unawares. I reloaded the clip I had just viewed and hit play again.

Of course, it simply featured precisely the same material I had just watched. When I got past the spiritual blah blah portion and moved on into the conclusion, something caught my attention. Michael's broad smile seemed to be beaming and more animated than ever. Immediately I sensed an intimacy and immediacy to what was unfolding that had not been present the first time around. It no longer felt like dear old Michael was projecting himself from a two-dimensional computer screen which was separate from me, rather it started to feel ever more like he was in the same room with me; furthermore, the gulf between us was shrinking moment by moment. I felt a sense of tremendous love and compassion begin to well up. It was like an old friend was inviting me to take note of something quite extraordinary and irresistibly wonderful. More amazing still, it became apparent that I didn't have to do anything to accomplish this.

For lack of a better word, I will say that "he" (for who or what this "Michael" character really was, was at this moment becoming harder and harder to ascertain) was becoming progressively less distinct as the seconds ticked by (or perhaps it was "I" that was becoming less apparent). "He" was telling me it was JUST THIS. It felt for all the world like he was addressing me directly. His spirit connected to mine, my spirit to his. He beside me. Me next to him. A certain sense of very palpable familiarity quickly grew.

"This is all it is old buddy DJ, all it's ever been. Come on…cut the crap…you know better. Just look and see," came the increasingly comprehensible message. And there was such mirth and good humour about it that it felt like the whole universe was smiling along with the both of us, or maybe there was only a single grin devoid of any self at all, like the Cheshire cat that disappeared in *Alice in Wonderland* only to leave behind his solitary smile.

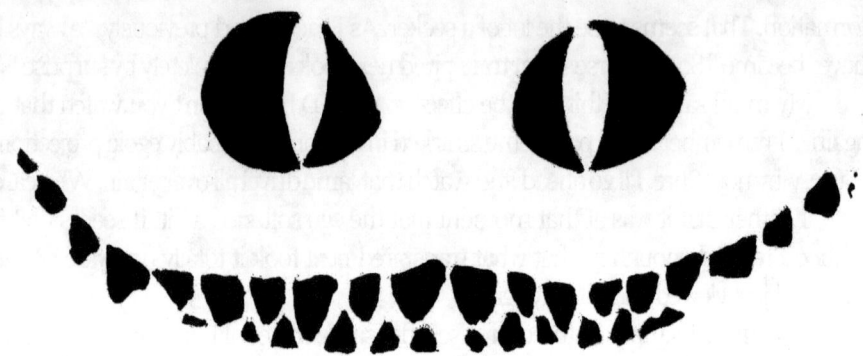

There was a settling back and into *something*...or was it rather *no-thing*? Resistance then completely vanished as did the distinction between Kavanagh and myself. I might go so far as to say Spirit was now addressing itself directly, which seems like a fantastically absurd proposition to make…yet, I will stand by it. This moment was wondrous beyond words. The final resolution that only grace begets had occurred.

There was now a completely unobscured seeing. JUST THIS. Something momentarily forgotten was now being recollected. JUST THIS. This direct knowing was not something being shared between two (and as I presently tap out these words on the Word processor, I am moved to weep once again at this profound recollection).

Spirit was *now* revealing something to itself. No, that is not quite right. Spirit was the *NOW*, and the numinous NOW revelled in its own consciousness, the aware eternal moment.

## Chapter 36

The Monad, The ALL, God if you will, seemingly for the first time ever (for this kind of revelation I suspect always feels as if it is freshly minted and discovered for the very first time) caught its own reflection in the mirror of consciousness. This is nothing less than the reflecting pool of existence itself. And what was recognized was good. This moment out of time did not mark original sin but rather original revelation, that is the falling out of duality back into *primordial peace* (which by the way in Sanskrit is spelled *adya shanti*).

In that moment, there was no longer a DJ, an M. Kavanagh, a world, nor even Spirit itself. The seeker, the sought and seeking all simply vanished as if never having existed in the first place. All of manifest reality disappeared as well. The recognition of true nature was instantaneous and complete. This was nirvana which literally means "cessation." Zen master Foyan's *instant Zen* had been realized!

Time and space imploded. Absolute peace and emptiness prevailed. From a relative point of view, some minutes must have elapsed, though I was not aware of this for I was not. That is non-duality for you. I didn't have a past life review or receive a download of information as my teacher reports. I simply became truth realized. This was an exceedingly simple, direct knowing that I could never have imagined in a million life times for it transcended imagination altogether. When the senses finally got switched back on, the DJ character never quite made it back in one piece or at least not in its former self-identified persona.

For all intents and purposes this was the moment when the story of DJ ceased. He had gone out on a spiritual quest and never made it back. All of the previous spiritual hullabaloo now no longer made any sense since there was no longer any relevant questions that needed to be asked nor answers that needed to be received. The narrative of "me" had essentially concluded. DJ was now mortally wounded and holding on only by the thinnest of gossamer threads. Quite soon, that locus would be severed for good. Certainly any further seeking was impossible. With seeking no longer an option, so too the seeker was rendered immaterial.

When the senses came back online, it still felt like the ineffable was regarding itself and marvelling at its splendour. The immediate feeling was glee and immense love. An unconditional agape, a love completely devoid of self and so unwavering in its tender regard for all things that nothing escaped its loving gaze; it enveloped everything. This kind of all-pervasive compassion was far outside the realm of normal purview. In fact, I had never felt anything like it before. I was almost incapacitated by this heartfelt love for all of existence. I might say mankind is not built to experience such strong, unwavering, tender-hearted emotion, but fortunately there was little "man" left in the equation, so all was going exceedingly well.

Next thing I knew, I was bowing to Spirit or more exactly Spirit was bowing to itself in recognition and gratitude. This conditioned inclination was quite natural since I had lived so many years in Asia, and in this instance it took the form of me bowing to myself, who now once more appeared in the guise of Michael on the video screen. And I'll be darned if Michael didn't literally bow back to "me." I'm not kidding. As soon as I did a deep formal bow towards the screen, Michael appeared to instantly reciprocate in kind.

Later, upon reflection, I thought this to be quite miraculous. I know what I saw. Buddha bowed to itself. How could a screen character know I was bowing to it and return in kind, I wondered? I decided to review the video footage. I found out Michael had moved in to turn the camera off and thus lowered his head in sync with my bow at precisely the right moment so as to give the impression it was a sign of mutual respect. That then could be the "rational" way of explaining the mystery, but I know better. Something was exchanged in that moment, and it had nothing to do with YouTube and video angles or bending down to turn off a camera. The One revealed itself to itself and was overjoyed. That could not be denied.

> I may not have gone where I intended to go, but I think I have ended up where I intended to be.
> Douglas Adams (writer)

# Chapter 37

*So I will show another me. Today I don't need a replacement. I'll tell them what the smile on my face meant. My heart going boom, boom, boom, hey, I said, you can keep my things they've come to take me home.*

   Peter Gabriel (musician)

    I AM. No more than this. Just—I AM, the eternal glancing backwards at itself and smiling.

    Or, as Dr. Seuss put it, "You are you. Now isn't that pleasant?"

    Then as if by some unseen umbilicus, the navel of the world, the axis mundi, beckoned me back into duality. The parachute billows behind the capsule and then with a thump—

*splashdown*. I am back. Or at least some slight semblance of me has returned. Quick systems check. Yep, all systems are a go; all senses are back online.

First impression. What an amazing, ephemeral and ultimately incomprehensible thing existence is. This capacity to objectify…how astonishing! How unreal.

The conceptual faculty returned with an exuberant, "Holy shit!" Followed by a pause and then a decisive "How fucking amazing." I turned away from the computer monitor to take in the whole room…or rather was it the entire cosmos? I'm afraid no one was presently available to make that call.

There was such a huge sense of recognition. "No doubt about it. This is it," I remember thinking, or maybe I never actually cognized that. Maybe there was just a sense of recognition sans the mind chatter…I don't recall well enough now to make that distinction.

But I do remember one of the very first thoughts that arose right after "re-entry" which was loud, clear and filled with incredulity:

> But this…but this new way of being is just like how my meditation has been over the course of the last few months. This IS meditation. Now it's somehow just been brought out into the ordinary world.

How unexpected to discover that enlightenment was just TRUE meditation, was just EXISTENCE itself. I remember I went on to note:

> If only I had had a real teacher handy to personally guide me along the path, then surely he/she would have pointed this simple, blatantly obvious fact out to me a long time ago. What a pity. Such guidance sure could have saved me some time. Oh well…c'est la vie.

Apparently, other seekers who awaken arrive at a similar conclusion and are equally struck by how uncomplicated, uncontrived and blatantly apparent this *no-thing/true nature* is. I have heard tell that these newly awakened beings also lament the fact that nobody pointed out the obvious to them sooner. But of course, this is an erroneous conclusion. Nobody can point out to you what you already are. Only through the mysterious faculty I call grace does Reality ever become apparent.

There is no way to impart to you or relay the feelings of how fantastic and liberating it was to have the story of DJ come to a close. It was precisely as my teacher had maintained: an immense burden was indeed lifted off my shoulders, one that I had never even suspected existed. Suddenly, there was now an intense lightness of being like I had never experienced before. You may recall the mythological story of the Greek king Sisyphus condemned to eternally roll a huge boulder uphill as a form of punishment. I was shocked to learn that I had been carrying around a similarly crippling burden strapped to my back all along. Unlike that poor wretch though, I had suddenly become unencumbered. How liberating! I wasn't merely free now; I had become freedom itself.

Joy and happiness abounded. Everything was smiling at itself. Reality had become one great big "YES!" This was the true "love-in" John Lennon once upon a time sought. I felt just like I imagined Scrooge must have when he "awoke" from his dream of being a miserly old curmudgeon.

Just as Ebenezer exclaimed, I too was as "giddy as a schoolgirl." I could scarcely contain myself. As the recognition continued to sweep through me, I giggled in amazement. It was irrefutable. I was not the story I had taken myself to be. I was not an object in the field of awareness but rather *subject as awareness itself*. Adya had promised and delivered. This truly was the "end of my world as I knew it." Good riddance.

Waves of déjà vu began to overwhelm me. I think that everyone can relate to the typical feeling of déjà vu which is the experience of having the absolute certainty that the present incident unfolding before you has already occurred. This experience however was not exactly like the typical fleeting moment of recognition we all have, no, not at all. These recurrent déjà vu experiences kept piling on one after the other. Amazingly, they lasted several seconds each. A typhoon of familiarity was bowling me over. This feeling was extremely intense and strange, to say the least. Something was immediate and just so darn familiar.

Or maybe something was recognizing itself as if reality itself or all of existence was apprehending its visage once more after enduring a span measured to be eternal and then in recognition…gasped in amazement. The "newness" of the moment seemed intimately familiar, yet I knew not how. This familiarity and intimacy gave rise to the impression of a sense of a homecoming of sorts. It's like arriving back to your little cottage in the woods after going on a long, arduous and unexpected journey. For a moment, you had forgotten how the old place looked, but now that you have a soothing cup of chamomile tea in hand, are sunk deeply back into your favourite overstuffed easy chair and find your cherished tartan mackintosh once more draped over your lap, you find the world has again been set right. How glorious to be home. "That was a job well done," you pause to reflect as you kick back on the recliner. Then you are awash in the fragrance of your beloved once again and relax deeply into the familiar embrace of the Divine…ahhhhh…

I'm being quite literal here. This shock of recognition and relief caused a moment of deep, deep sobbing which reverberated throughout eternity. The release seemed complete and utterly fulfilling. Yet my ego would not, could not, settle for just this quiet interlude yet.

Instead, my mind set about trying to figure out what was instilling these novel feelings. The seat of rationality seemed compelled to categorize them. Figure them out. I remember clearly thinking that since this sense of familiarity was so overwhelming, surely then all I had to do was access a past memory that would recall it from a previous occasion. Plainly put, my mind was once again compelled to try to objectify reality in order to make sense out of it.

The thought arose:

Somehow this intense sense of intimate "knowingness" and familiarity must already be known to me. Otherwise, I would not be having these weird déjà vu experiences. It must be stemming from my childhood. If I go back far enough in time, I should be able to recollect it. Then all of this will become clear.

So, of course, since the tyrant always got what he wanted (certainly this was his last hoorah) that is precisely what I attempted to do. In between the bouts of déjà vu and a constant stream of unconditional love, I tried, and failed, to locate the source of the déjà vu.

To try to recollect this feeling was like rifling through every drawer in a huge filing cabinet in a desperate bid to find the one memo that didn't exist. Compulsively, my mind kept insisting the answer was not far off and could be found if I just went back far enough in time. But it was a futile search. For beingness is not locatable in time or space. Non-duality is not "findable."

After a good five minutes or so of this futile endeavour, my mind grew weary of the enterprise and gave up. Rather than try to find the roots of the experience in time, it now altered its approach and began to look for an answer in space.

"Yeah," I said with growing confidence, "yes, I know this...(pause scratching head)...(more reflection)...yes, indeedy, I do, I DO know this," then more reflection. Subsequently, uncertainty followed again by "I do know this" only to have this notion be replaced by another. "No, that is not it, now I get it...not *I know this* but rather *I AM this*."

But again this notion proved unsatisfactory. After more contemplation, further reflection and several more pauses, I landed next on "Hey wait a minute, it doesn't concern a *this* but a *YOU*. Yeah, that is it, not I know this but rather I know you." But once again, that conclusion failed to satisfy. It was resolved with, "It's not I know you, but rather *I am YOU*."

And that was that. My mind was finally satisfied enough to shut the hell up. Though, to be clear, that final thought is not quite it either for it is neither a "this" nor a "that," a "you" nor a "not you" nor even a "me" nor a "not me." Anyhow, my mind went silent...or rather the ground of being just was and as such the déjà vu petered out, leaving...???

NOW, as I arose from my chair, there was simply a sense of wonder, awe and gratitude for the present moment. "I decided," though to be clearer I might say a decision simply arose bereft of any decider whatsoever, to leave the confines of my room and head out into the orchard in order to just "be" with everything. Here duality fell away completely. In truth, I was not heading out anywhere, for the orchard, along with all objective existence, had entirely vanished!

Out of convention and due to the dualistic constraints relativistic reality imposes, I am left with no alternative but to use personal pronouns like, "I," "me" and "mine" when describing the following account. Yet keep in mind that they are merely mental constructs not applicable to the unfolding reminiscence at all.

I opened the orchard gate and headed out into a primordial realm of timeless and spaceless beauty and wonder. Now I refute what I have just said. In point of fact, at that moment there was neither "into" nor "out of," nor "going" nor "coming," nor "beauty" nor any other concept a separate "I" could ascribe to anything in a relativistic dualistic manner. Once again words fail, but I will now continue to employ them to give you the flavour of what was not happening. Since nothing was happening and as there was also presently no doer, my mind remained as still as water chilled to absolute zero.

The world had turned inside out. The foreground, which had always been the point of interest, receded and now became as if transparent, leaving only the background, or in other words all of reality, to be brought into focus simultaneously. This is a most peculiar way of being since it is impossible to focus on everything all at once. Reality had become an indivisible seamless mass of everythingness. The instinct now was to no longer engage in distinction making. While objectification had been the norm, it was now replaced by the knowing that everything was, in fact, the grand subject. There was just "I" everywhere I looked or looked not.

I will again point out that while the following description gives the "flavour" of what was unfolding, don't confuse it for the thing itself. What was happening/not happening was not conceptually realized at that time. It was more like the flow of *no-mind* just *was*. My mind was truly lost then, so there was no inclination to cognize anything.

Intense feelings were being registered, but they were being felt by no one in particular. And what feelings they were! As I already mentioned, an acute sense of bliss and unconditional love pervaded everything. I found a stool at the rear of the orchard and sat down with jaw agape. Truly, I was gobsmacked. Reality was a wonder beyond wonders. And that was what I was, or I might say that there was no separation between me and what was.

For some minutes, perhaps ten or fifteen, I simply focused into the distance at the top canopy of some fir trees silhouetted by an azure blue sky so deeply saturated with intense colour it took my breath away. After peering into space, I would change my focus and look down at a patch of sod ten or so feet in front of me. The effect was wondrous and uncanny and completely the same. Everything was the same!

Every time I glanced up something took my breath away. I sobbed. Every time I looked down it shook me to my core. I sobbed. Again and again the outcome was the same. Something seemed to be reconciling itself here. Obviously, what was transpiring was not good old DJ having a gander at some distant conifer trees. No, it was more like the Divine checking itself out as I might a beautiful woman or like an inside joke was revealing itself to itself. It's beyond me how a comedian could laugh at his own punch line, but this is very much what was happening. The overwhelming feeling was "It is good…it is very, very good." I wonder if this kind of moment is the only means in which a tree can glimpse itself, a bumble bee catch its buzz or a sun be bedazzled by its own glare. I suspect it is on these rare occasions that the cosmos fathoms its own jolly good nature. When the *Big Nothing* blooms into existence, it is as if it catches sight of itself for the first time and then spontaneously begins to have a love affair with itself. Alan Watts put it well:

Through our eyes, the universe is perceiving itself. Through our ears, the universe is listening to its harmonies. We are the witnesses through which the universe becomes conscious of its glory, of its magnificence.

I want to make it clear that this profound feeling arose no matter what was perceived. And what was perceived was quite simply a beautiful, unified, holistic, solitary, indivisible field of the ineffable ALL. It wasn't like I was looking at a tree, a flower, the sky or a scab on my leg per se but rather peering at the *essence* of or behind everything. Reality as I had known it was, in truth, simply a proxy for something else. The analogy of the clay pot comes to mind once more. Form and function was seen through to reveal…? IT. But what "IT" was I knew not. That IT was, was abundantly evident. And I was not separate from "IT." So to be clear, objectification was NOT taking place.

In a manner of speaking, everything was equally imbued with the *I Am* essence. Therefore, I could say that fundamentally everything was the same for no matter where my attention landed, there I found myself. And in this there was great delight, wonder, mirth and gratitude.

At that time, I never once thought, "Hey everything is 'one,'" but actually, that was what was being recognized. Everything was emanating, or more pointedly just was, what I later called for lack of a better word, "*Factor-X*." Spiritual teachers commonly resort to calling *Factor-X* terms like *the Absolute, true-nature, the ground of being, Spirit, Buddha-nature, the ineffable, true-self, consciousness, no-mind, no-self, pure beingness* or simply *awareness itself*. That there was nothing else but this Factor-X was undeniably apparent. In this I came to recognize the oneness so often spoken of in spiritual circles.

After remaining in this reverie for some time, I rose from the stool in order to make my way back through the orchard to my room. At the midway point, I was stopped dead in my tracks by shock and amazement as a great truth dawned on me. The thought stabbed through Reality to the core of its being. EVERYTHING "IS." EVERYTHING JUST IS. NOTHING MORE NEED BE RECOGNIZED THAN THAT. And so it stands.

I still reflect on this realization from time to time. This coming to terms with things as they really are may sound too simplistic, mundane and insignificant to you, but I assure you that if seen through the clarity of no-mind, it will blow you away. For me it was one of those "Holy Fuck!" moments. Truly, the simple is the most profound. EVERYTHING JUST IS!

If I were to point even closer to the truth, then I would omit the "everything" in "Everything just is" and stress only "IS." The "everything" part just muddies the water. For clarities sake then, that leaves us with just "is." Existence is merely "ising" itself merrily along. As Truth realized, you are more a subject than an object, more a verb than a noun. True nature is more like the quantum probability wave that remains uncollapsed, and thus consists merely of pure potentiality more than it is a discrete atomic particle, or a thing unto itself.

Existence flows through itself. "This is it" was precisely the case just as Michael Kavanagh assured me it was. There is naught but existence itself. You, your boyfriend, wife and daughter all arise after the fact and are nothing more than the story believed in, nothing but smoke and mirrors. Illusion.

In a manner of speaking though, I would also say that those apparitions are as "real" as real can get. Sure, the Golden Arches may be an illusion, but it is also the place I head to when I have a hankering for a greasy burger and fries. Or consider the notion of *Coke* as in, "Coke is the real thing." There is no denying it then. What better arbitrator of reality could there be than a corporate motto. "The real thing" it is then. I am Coke.

Joking aside, awaking allows you to hold these antipodes, the relative and the Absolute, in equal regard. Paradox is no longer an issue for me. After this "Reality as it IS" epiphany, I made my way further out of the orchard.

Gratitude overwhelmed me. I began sobbing once more. Everything I beheld made me laugh or alternatively shed a tear, and more often than not, it was a mixture of both of them at the same time. It was a bit like the kind of emotional response I get during a bittersweet moment…but not quite. Maybe more like how I felt when movie character Forrest Gump was at long last reunited with his lost love interest, Jenny. During moments like that the heart strings are pulled taut with joy, but instead of good cheer, tears mysteriously well up.

I lay down and looked up at the sky. A couple of puffy clouds went floating by, oh wonder upon wonders. More ecstatic sobbing followed. Next, a common rose bush replete with gorgeous blooms caught my attention. The rose bush produced the same reaction—more blubbering. It seemed anything I beheld caused this kind of wonderful outpouring. Really, it could have been anything at all. Consider the following example for instance.

I intended to exit the orchard by the main gate so proceeded to make my way to the rear. While opening the tall but relatively narrow galvanized wire gate, my gaze fell upon the weathered grey, zinc-clad corner post which held the gate upright. Once outside the compound, I took a couple of steps away from the gate but then looked back at the corner post once more. This initiated a strange turn of affairs quite unlike anything I had ever experienced. I had finally found my one true love. This kind of profound attraction I am about to describe will undoubtedly seem most bizarre to you, but it would not be the case if everything you apprehend was the Divine itself. In that case, what I am about to describe would then seem quite natural and commonplace.

Looking at the tall, slender, off-grey steel fence post, I was smitten by its great charm, beauty and wonder. I mean, I was totally entranced. I literally could not take another step nor tear my eyes away from the great beauty I was beholding. Right then and there a love affair beyond compare bloomed into being. For ten or more minutes I stood entranced and could not bear to take my eyes off of the gorgeous creature I beheld. It was the oddest thing. I could but only glance away for a moment before something called out to me to look again. "Behold the wonder of the ages," it beckoned. Like the irresistible appeal of the mythical Greek Siren who beckoned sailors to their doom, I too could not resist such charms.

This pole was topped by the sweetest little oxidized zinc cap imaginable, such fashionable attire, such poise and grace. This piece of fence hardware, now transformed into my one true love, was the single most beautiful thing I had ever apprehended. Nothing could be more magnificent for the fact is, Truth is Beauty…and Beauty Truth. There was no doubt that Truth was what was actually being seen here.

In those ten minutes or so, such passion arose that I can scarcely speak of it. I had the most satisfying romance of my entire life. Perhaps it still endures. Of course, it wasn't really a mere bit of rusting galvanized metal piping that I found so profound. That was only its form and function, its "skin job." It was like I now had acquired unimpaired spiritual 20/20 vision that allowed me to see beyond mere appearance or as if I'd been given a pair of high tech "reality goggles" that enabled me to peer below the surface of things as they appeared, to see them as they really were. Truly the Divine revelled in apprehending itself. Finally, after several failed attempts, I managed to tear myself free and move on.

Next, I sashayed over to a nearby chestnut tree. Until then, I had not given that majestic specimen a second thought. Now I hugged its fetching trunk and profusely apologised for overlooking its commanding grace. "How grand you are," I reassured it. But of course, it was already well aware of this fact, so it just giggled at me. "How had I managed to overlook all of this?" I wondered. I had already and always been nowhere else but in this Garden of Eden the whole time. Here I am talking about a paradise unbesmirched by the tree of the knowledge of good and evil (distinction making) or a guy called Adam who is said to have literally named everything in his path thereby creating duality in the process. William Blake, too, apparently knew of the great joy Truth realized may bring us:

> When the green woods laugh with the voice of joy, And the dimpling stream runs laughing by; When the air does laugh with our merry wit, And the green hill laughs with the noise of it.

Though these types of intense feelings I just described above have all but faded over time, still the Reality behind them endures. What I am relating to you has nothing to do with a state. That comes and goes. This does not come and go for it is the ground of being.

Buddha had it right; the world truly is a rather jolly place. It only sucks when the angst of conceptual mind arises. As it stands, that is no longer an issue here. In a sense, I am awareness turned in on itself. The self-reflexive mind ramped up to the nth degree so that all it can see is the unadulterated subject. Presently, the withered limb of objectification has now wasted away to barely a stump. If pushed to affirm what I am, I might say "awareness awaring itself." That is about as good an affirmation as I can scrounge up. In truth I am everything and nothing, and that is not true either.☺

> Life is this simple: we are living in a world that is absolutely transparent and the divine is shining through it all the time. This is not just a nice story or a fable, it is true.
> Thomas Merton (Jesuit Catholic priest)

# Chapter 38

*It is foolish to think that we will enter heaven without entering into ourselves.*

St. Teresa of Avila (Christian mystic)

When it comes to attempting to articulate spiritual revelation, I hold that metaphor, allegory, analogy, simile and parable as expressed through such mediums as storytelling, poetry, song and the theatre are the single best means at our disposal to try to describe that which defies description. Still, such symbolic communication is at best only *the finger pointing at the moon*, not the moon itself.

So when I spoke of the immediate and intense feeling of déjà vu that arose upon awakening, this of course was only my mind's poor attempt to come to terms with something that was quite inexplicable. Yes, the feeling was akin to déjà vu yet not exactly the same. Just as dining on succulent Laotian braised field rat is akin to fried Burmese python or stewed Canadian groundhog, yet each does not precisely present the same culinary experience.

This déjà-vuish, French for "already seen," experience was unique. With regards to classical déjà vu, I checked into the literature and found viewpoints varied as to how and why it arose. There is no consensus yet that explains what the brain is doing during an episode. Checking into the spiritual side of things, I found that a few others had made reference to a déjà-vu-like feeling manifesting upon their awakening much in the manner mine did.

In my case, I suspect that when the self fell away and the centre of existence (me) evaporated, the conceptual mind was left floundering with an enigmatic paradox. How do you come to terms with diametrically opposed feelings consisting of absolute nihilism/negation and emptiness on the one hand, while on the other hand, concomitantly experiencing a sense of fullness, intimacy and unbounded potentiality? What do you do when you recognize that Reality is a boundless expanse so immense and all pervasive that it elevates you to the loftiest of heights, yet at the same time you also realize that the universe is truly empty, a thin hollow shell, a *hohlraum* that when struck can only bring you to your knees and sound the death knell?

These are conundrums that try as my mind might, it could not fathom or reconcile. When ignorance passed away and it was revealed that there was already an intimate familiarity with the awakened state, though my mind could not comprehend why, I guess it took the path of least resistance and labeled this experienceless experience a déjà vu.

When it comes to classical déjà vu, you are convinced that it reflects an authentic past recollection, yet you have great difficulty in recalling the circumstance of the event. You are certain that you witnessed such and such before. Your mind insists that a discrete occurrence (an event) has happened in a particular time (now the past) and place.

The déjà vu of awakening has only one similarity to this description—the recognition part. In falling out of the dream state there is a sense of recognition. There is no mistaking that. Yet you have no idea what event is being recollected or when it previously occurred. It is a damn odd feeling, let me assure you.

This spiritual déjà vu is unlike the conventional one in the sense that the past is not being re-cognized again. It is rather a case of a new orientation away from ego and towards pure awareness or consciousness such that the timeless expanse of the eternal is realized. As well, Self now apprehends itself everywhere and in everything and nowhere and in no-thing. It seems to recollect that this is the way things have always been. It's like suddenly finding yourself wandering into a house of mirrors and recognizing that all the myriad panes of glass are reflecting but one visage—YOURS. It's all you, baby, all the time, 24/eternity. This in turn suggests why the Buddha told us that we are already awakened...we simply haven't realized this fact yet. To cope, my mind struggled to take a fixed dualistic perspective from whence it tried to comprehend non-duality, so of course that just led to utter incomprehension.

The experience of this spiritual déjà vu minus the conceptual mind was not really an experience at all for there was no fixed perspective from whence to judge anything. I found everything to be in *flux* or *flow* as I previously mentioned. Since consciousness recognizes itself everywhere, every perspective and non-perspective is regarded equally. Therefore, there is no point of view at all since there is nothing in particular to contrast or compare anything else with. Of course, with no point of view it follows then that there must also be no "viewer" who can stake out territory in a bid to claim this or that as his or her own.

Simply put, no one is present when presence is present. Now look what I have gone and done…confused you yet again. Aren't you the lucky one? Truly, awakening is the oddest state of affairs imaginable…and then some. It's entirely counter-intuitive to discover that no one benefits from enlightenment since no one remains to claim any prize. All those countless hours of meditation, hard work and isolation and in the end it's all for naught…the ego might say. Mine sure stated it loudly and clearly shortly after I awoke.

In fact it proclaimed, for no one in particular to hear since no one remained to pay it any heed:

> Well, that DJ guy was one great big fool wasn't he? Yes, a fool and an ignoramus as well…what a loser. So much hard work and he got nothing for his troubles!

The implication here being that since I, from a conceptual point of view, never got the final cosmic epiphany, the big reveal, the final answer, terrific words of wisdom, nor even a lousy brass ring out of the deal, then indubitably *le petit caporal* [Napoleon's nickname] deemed me to be a fantastic failure. Fortunately, this fallen tin-pot dictator had lost its power to entrance me just as the matrix had been similarly emasculated when Neo swallowed the red pill.

The thing my ego never appreciated was the fact that the end of the quest is not about getting an answer, rather it is about discovering that you were the answer all along. The conceptual mind can never touch this, so it remains cynically obtuse and a bit bitter for a long while as it struggles to come to terms with liberation. Sure, you lose yourself but end up gaining the whole world in the bargain; that is not a bad deal at all I reckon.

I can assure you that I would not exchange one day living as a lucid, sane expression of Truth-Realized for my entire previous life spent in the dream state. Clarity is just that good. It is liberation. It is the ultimate peace Christ consciousness affords us. As Jesus proclaims in Mathew 11:28, "Come to me all of you who are weary and burdened and I will give you rest."

And why is it so good? Well, in addition to being able to take a load off for the first time in my life, I would also say I prefer the Truth of Being over the falseness, inauthenticity and delusion Maya beguiled me with for so long. Don't we all prefer truth to lies? As a side benefit, the case after awakening is just like the Buddha promised it would be. I found suffering was indeed eradicated, and that ain't too shabby either, is it?

That then, my friends, is just about the most ebulliently effusive direct sales pitch for enlightenment you will likely ever hear from me. Truth be told, I am not much of a salesman, and more to the point, I really ain't got nothing to sell you.

No one succeeds without effort...Those who succeed owe their success to perseverance...Your duty is to BE and not to be this or that. "I am that I am," sums up the whole truth. The method is summed up in the words "Be still." What does stillness mean? It means destroy yourself.

Ramana Maharshi (advaita Vedanta teacher)

# Chapter 39

*Clinging to self-image is a mind game of resistance underpinned by fear of the unknown. On this journey of self-exploration, most discover that as interest in the chatter of mind lessens, an ease and contentment of what is, arises naturally.*
  Jac O'Keeffe (spiritual teacher)

Before I conclude this tale, I would be remiss if I didn't spend at least several pages demythologizing the idea that it is possible for someone to become enlightened. "What?" I can hear you now say, "Isn't that the crux of your whole story, DJ?" Nope, I claim no such thing for myself...yet I do maintain that falling out of the dream state is your birthright, and spiritual seeking can come to an end.

The plain simple truth is nobody ever gets enlightened, for in fact no one remains around to claim that distinction. To clarify, let's consider the ramifications of the term itself and then do a little deconstruction of it.

When I considered the way that I was relating to reality while in the dream state, I realized that I was in a perpetual state of endarkenment. To a lesser or greater degree so is all of humanity. Perhaps I might say that self-inquiry points out where delusion lies, so in a sense it decreases the extent of ignorance, but still you remain in the dream state until the self drops away with final liberation. Thus, this leaves no one left to claim either enlightenment or any other distinction. For convenience sake, I still sometimes resort to using the term enlightenment to describe the drive to awaken and its final outcome, though I do not really favour the term much due to its somewhat misleading nature. What follows herein then is a brief discussion of what enlightenment is not.

Enlightenment has nothing to do with merging with God or discovering our True nature nor is it a feeling of Unity with a higher power. One simply discerns his or her false nature which drops away to reveal the already and always present.

Enlightenment is not about experiencing the Self. Fundamentally, it has nothing to do with any kind of experience. Rather, self-knowledge or the wisdom of no-self reveals that the seeker is none other than the sought.

Enlightenment is not about becoming a greater Being or discovering higher wisdom or knowledge, nor is it about going within. Such dualistic terms wither under the scrutiny of how things really are.

It has nothing to do with channelling your higher self or contacting otherworldly beings.

Kundalini experiences are well and fine, but they arise and fall away again. What is being pointed to here is not transitory in nature. Though enlightenment is not an experience, experiences along the path to awakening can be precious and often spiritually edifying as long as one does not try to grasp or cling on to awakening episodes or chase them in some manner. Always keep foremost in your mind the transitory nature of experience, and remember that the ineffable neither arises nor falls away again. States come and go. True nature does not. Though I make reference to the ground of being from time to time, enlightenment has nothing to do with it. It is just a better pointer.

You are either awake or you are not. There are not varying degrees of enlightenment. If you are still in the dream state then endarkenment is the norm, and it is what informs your reality. You cannot be partially enlightened though the removal of self-ignorance can be gradual.

Enlightenment is not about becoming free. Liberation is already your True nature.

To be clear, in the absolute sense there is no such thing as enlightenment, but if seeking is going on, if the seeker still persists, if duality is the norm, then blindly accepting contrived mantras that some repeat ad nauseam such as "I am already THAT" or "I am but the apparent self" or "There is nothing that needs be done" or "There are no teachers or students nor nothing to learn" and finally "There is no such thing as enlightenment," will most likely lead to very little

## Chapter 39

erosion of false nature. This tact of denial in the face of an ego that is still invigorated can be as counterproductive and as damaging as believing enlightenment exists. If there is still a doer, then do well. Seek to reveal untruth wherever it lies.

Enlightenment is never what you imagine it to be for it is inconceivable and has nothing to do with thoughts.

It is not about finding your bliss, nor has it anything to do with self-empowerment. It is also outside the realm of self-help or self-improvement regimes.

It is not about evolving into a better human being or reaching a higher plain of existence.

It is not about fulfilling your ambitions, manifesting your heart's delight, gaining respect or power or becoming a morally exemplary person. When you awaken, these kinds of qualities appear irrelevant if they compute at all.

Enlightenment has nothing to do with gaining supernatural powers like reading people's minds, apprehending auras, seeing into the future, engaging in remote viewing, astral travelling or walking through walls as a chap I once met believed would surely be possible for all truly awakened, super special beings. I admitted I still needed to use a door, and from that day forward, he has held me in low regard. But, hear me out. I say you have to give me credit where credit is due. Walking through a wall is one thing, but could any old Avatar actually make his or her way through the convoluted Canadian income tax code without the aid of an accredited advisor? Me thinks not, but I managed to pull off just such a feat two years running now, so that's gotta be a miracle of sorts, don't you agree? Furthermore, does that mean we will all be enlightened when the Star Trek quantum transportation system finally arrives in the future? Seriously, look...here is the real dope...walking through a door, a wall or anything else for that matter is merely just that. I affirm that the real mystery begins when it is done by *Nemo*, Latin for nobody.

Being held in low regard because I haven't mastered the knack of quantum tunnelling is quite okay with me for I recognize that enlightenment has nothing to do with being perceived as special or being held in high esteem. Invariably someone who awakens can't help but be the humblest, plainest spoken, good-natured sort of fellow around. Those inclinations just seem to naturally well-up by their own accord. And if they don't, that doesn't matter either.

Enlightenment is not about being in a permanent state of orgasmic bliss or unconditional love. You just are...yes, *you just are*—full stop. I might say however that in a sense there is an all pervasive, always abiding, low-level background feeling of okayness or joy to life, but more correctly existence just flows without any emotional highs or lows to speak of. Of course, pain can still arise, but since there is now no one available to own it, suffering is essentially optional.

I recently passed a kidney stone which hurt like hell. It was the worst pain I ever endured, but I never went into the "poor little me" story or histrionics. Yes, I was glad to get a shot of morphine, but at no point did the excruciating pain cause me to suffer. I just gritted my teeth and bore the discomfort until the episode subsided.

It is not about acquiring a vacuous empty mind devoid of thoughts. Thoughts of various kinds may still infrequently arise. What is profoundly different now is the fact that there is no longer any identification going on when these spontaneous thoughts break into consciousness. They simply arise and fall away again but have nothing to do with "ME." Of course, I can still engage in problem solving or creative thinking, so my mind is never truly shut down completely as some seekers might erroneously imagine is the case.

You don't become cut off from the world. Actually, things become more intimate and immediate as you come to realize you are the world itself. You probably will value and treasure mundane reality more now than you ever did before but not in a materialistic sense. For the first time in your life you are alive in a world full of infinite possibility. Your mind may tell you, as mine did, that life will become deathly boring if you were to fall awake. It's not true.

Enlightenment is not about becoming more responsive and accepting of others. It may well happen, but it does not necessarily have to be the case. I recall Adya once saying, "If you were an asshole before enlightenment, you may well still be one after." Though more often than not, you do become more sensitive to the plight of others after waking up. Since there is no separation, since you are "the other," since there is no "other," compassion wells up quite naturally.

Enlightenment is not some external force that enters or empowers you. It has nothing to do with energy work.

It is not about improving your ability to stay in the NOW. If the NOW is none other than non-duality, and it is, then I assure you nobody has ever visited the NOW. It is not possible for a self to escape duality. It is quite impossible for a person to be to a lesser or greater degree in the NOW. There is either you not being aware, abiding in ignorance and hanging out in the so-called past and future, or alternatively, there is simply timeless presence itself…devoid of any personal sense of the "I." The NOW, so to speak, reveals itself when you cease to exist.

Becoming enlightened does not necessarily make you any more or less qualified to give advice, become a life coach or counsel people. This image of the wise omniscient guru is ridiculously fallacious.

There is not a higher self to aspire to or attain. All is SELF already and always. You are just currently ignorant of this fact.

Similarly, it is not about obtaining cosmic consciousness or an expansion of consciousness. There are no levels or realms of consciousness that need to be passed through. Consciousness is ALL in the same way that H2O is the only constituent substance comprising all things water-like, be they rain, sleet, fog, snow, ocean, lake, pond, river and ice. In a water world (and by the way, those different states of water can't possibly exist in a realm completely composed of H2O), water is all. In non-duality, consciousness is all.

Enlightenment does not require a Kundalini awakening nor do your chakras have to be realigned, reenergized, reinvigorated, repatterned, rebalanced, repolarized or requantumized.

Truth realization does not rely upon cultivating special states of consciousness, and that would even include meditative practice. Rather, it is more akin to realizing the awareness that is aware of all states.

Nirvana does not grant immortality. The body/mind complex will obviously still perish. All that you hold dear is mere appearance. True nature, unlike that which you take yourself presently to be, is the ground of being...which I previously made clear has nothing to do with enlightenment!

Falling awake does not require the eradication of preferences. Regarding desire, the heart's content is only to become Truth realized. That is all. After realization, one no longer seeks fulfilment through the actualization of desires. Liberation frees you from this kind of bondage, though the body/mind complex may still choose one thing over another (for example chocolate ice cream over vanilla), or set goals to attain...which, in point of fact, is how this book arose. But I receive no sense of satisfaction or accomplishment in completing any goal. Doing so would presume a beginning and an end and a favourable outcome, but from the vantage point afforded here, all that is seen is existence in flow.

Liberation has nothing to do with freeing yourself from the world. You don't have to become a recluse or a hermit to find solitude and peace. Awakening is to discover that the world of things has no effect on you whatsoever. In fact, you become as contented and implacable as the blood engorged jungle leach I once endeavoured to scrape off of my taint. True nature is the realization that you are none other than deep abiding stillness itself. This primordial peace always prevails regardless of the environment.

Awakening has nothing to do with evolving into a more elevated state, solving the world's woes, nor aiding humanity. Other human beings' state of affairs are their own business. When you awaken, you discover that the world is always fine just as it is. Though it may seem like realized beings are more often than not inclined to help alleviate the suffering of others, this inclination is certainly not mandatory.

Enlightenment, in the pragmatic sense, cannot be transmitted by a guru, sage or teacher. Sure they can offer insightful pointers, but they cannot impart wisdom through supernatural means like a mind to mind transfer, the *oneness prayer*, empowering ceremonies, or other nonsense like that. If instant Zen were that easy, I imagine I would just set up a little roadside shack or kiosk somewhere in my hometown and have the masses roll on through for a loonie and a toonie (Canadian one and two dollar coins, respectively).

Abiding non-dual awareness does not mean that the world of things ceases to exist. What does disappear is the notion that you are a discrete, separate entity who is differentiated or separated from existence. In reference to the book *The Man Who Mistook His Wife for a Hat*, maybe "The Man" was not as mistaken as Dr. Sacks presumed him to be. Maybe that guy was seeing reality as it truly was, and he was actually an enlightened savant. But ask me that same question, "So, DJ, are you saying that your wife is a hat...is that what you are telling me here, you fool?" and I'll simply tell you that the question does not fit the case and then move on. Wake up yourself, and then we can address that kind of speculative question—which will really mean we will have nothing to talk about at all.

Does enlightenment mean total negation of self? Of course...well kinda...maybe...look the truth is I can't give you an absolute committal on that one. Is that clear? I sure hope not. All obfuscation aside, the fact is doership and selfhood is no longer the case post awakening, but a subtle sense of self still persists to date. This *aroma of self* is similar to the salt-laden air and seaweed-scented, fragrant breeze of the ocean that may give a hiker the strong impression of the sea being at hand though he or she may actually be many yards away from the water. Of course, this breeze is not the ocean itself, and in the same way the sense of self, the perfume of "me," is not the old egoic centre I once so strongly identified with. The sea breeze just calls up an impression of the ocean. So, too, there is still a fragrance of self that remains here, but no sense of real embodiment exists that is centred on a personal "I." If you cut me, I'll still bleed, and if you call my name for dinner, I will still come a runnin'. The difference now is that it is not DJ who bleeds and runs. Though of course, thank God, I can still recognize which arm needs to be patched up when that bleeding business begins. All thanks to the aroma of self that still persists.

On the subject of psychedelics and entheogens, let me say that mind-expanding drugs can give you a glimpse of Reality or point the way home, but this kind of experience must never be confused for enlightenment itself. After all, such experiences come and go, and what I am pointing to here neither arises nor falls away again.

Suffering privations such as self-flagellation, going without sleep or sustenance, or meditating in uncomfortable positions will not increase your chances of awakening one iota, just as the Buddha so famously discovered. Breath control, altering the heart rate or modifying any other bodily function is similarly irrelevant.

Enlightenment has nothing to do with acquiring teachings, attending retreats, becoming spiritually hip, memorizing chants, reading scripture, learning spiritual jargon or getting acquainted with how to better love yourself or improve your self-esteem.

It is not necessary to become more compassionate, quieter, and mindful to awaken. If these aspirations encourage identification to turn in a direction away from small "s" self, then at best they may improve your odds of awakening a bit.

Visions of deities, angels or God, incidents of ecstasy, signs and symbols of wonder and delight, out-of-body experiences, yogic flying, lucid/precognitive dreaming, visual/auditory hallucinations, seeing bright lights, acquiring psychic abilities, walking on water, heating objects with the hands, causing candles to burst into flame, redirecting landslides, causing flowers to bloom, tolerating extreme heat or cold, owning special crystals, wearing adornments or exotic garb, looking into the *akashic* record, opening your third eye, decalcifying the pineal gland, rebalancing or tuning energy meridians, learning a foreign language, studying an ancient culture, getting a hug from a matronly guru, engaging in sexual dalliances with the master or pulling channelled spirits out of your ass all have nothing to do with enlightenment.

Self-realization does not necessarily take a long time. How and when grace appears is a mystery, so no definite conclusions may be drawn here. In my case, from the time I set out on my quest, it took me about sixteen months to fall into abiding non-dual awareness. Of course, your mileage may vary depending on many factors including whether or not you are motivated to seek the Truth at any cost and whether you do so in a vigorous, forthright and earnest manner.

# Chapter 39

To eliminate befuddlement, it is not important in the least to travel to far away exotic lands in order to find a wisdom master nor must the teacher be accredited or be a lineage holder as many seekers insist. I ask you, how is it possible for anyone to ascertain your spiritual state of Being with any certainty? Aren't you the only one who will know for certain whether or not you are awake? And if this answer isn't apparent to you now, it sure as hell will be when you wake the heck up! So by whose authority then can a lineage holder hand a scrap of paper over to another and then have us accept that so-and-so is awake? What nonsense! Enlightenment is self-validating for Self validates Self. Self recognizes Self. Is there any higher authority than that? All the spiritual giants over the centuries that I admire most, like Buddha, Lao Tzu, Layman Pang, Ikkyu or more contemporary teachers like Ramana, U.G. Krishnamurti, Jac O'Keeffe, Bernadette Roberts, Scott Kiloby, Paul Hedderman or my teacher, Adyashanti, didn't require the recognition or approval of another in order to come to realize non-ignorance of Self. In these Avatars self dropped, Spirit recognized itself and that was sufficient. How could the approval of another make reality any clearer to them? Jac O'Keeffe once shared a bit of wisdom with me that really struck home. She told me that enlightenment was first and foremost a private affair, a matter of the greatest intimacy that one recognizes for him or herself. And here I am referring to an intimacy born out of the Monad, the One. "It's just for you to know, DJ, since you are the only one that can..." she assured me. And so it is. This is the *Knowing that knowingly knows not...*or alternatively *the Not-knowing in which there remains nothing that is not unknown.* What piece of paper could ever attest to that? Ikkyu, one of the greatest Zen masters ever, never accepted recognition from anyone nor ever gave it away.

Tibetan Buddhists in general, and Lama Wally in particular, stress the presence and fundamental importance of the guru vis-a-vis the awakening process. Well, yes, I presume this would be important to the Lama since he is the fella drawing the pay cheque and receiving all of the accolades, n'est-ce pas? Horse feathers, I say! Any teaching, in whatever guise it may appear, just so long as it exists to remove ignorance, is fine and dandy in my book. It certainly is neither a requirement nor a prerequisite to have to sit at the feet of a recognized adept to have enlightenment befall you. Ramana sure didn't accentuate this point since he didn't seek attention or disciples of any sort. He simply stressed silence above all else. And that, of course, you can do anywhere, and it doesn't cost you a dime.

These days our digital information age offers myriad forms of communication technology and a plethora of media to aid the spiritual seeker in his or her quest. Podcasts, video depositories, virtual libraries, file sharing, email, cloud computing, torrent and video conferencing are all available to support the dissemination of information. Getting the goods from a real living teacher is not nearly as important as it once was. In the past if there was not a guru you resonated with within walking distance of your village, then you were just shit out of luck, weren't you? Here's the real skinny. If a teacher ain't trying to work himself or herself out of a job (i.e., throw you out of the nest at the first available opportunity like my teacher was always endeavouring to do), then they most assuredly have other interests at heart rather than your own.

I have heard certain people say don't go chasing enlightenment. Rather learn to recognize it in the daily routine of life. It could come at any moment and might take the simple form of your puppy chewing on your shoe, your volunteer work at a soup kitchen, your partner's embrace, your child's smile or when you read a really good book.

What nonsense that notion is! That kind of stuff sounds nice on a greeting card and might be pleasurable or inspiring, but enlightenment it sure ain't. Any moment in daily life is a moment in time, and as such it simply is an expression of the dream state, the refuge of Maya. Any experience, be it good, bad or indifferent, has not a whit to do with enlightenment.

Enlightenment has nothing to do with stopping the mind. The problem lies in the seeker's identification with ego. Enlightenment is enlightenment whether the mind is active or not. True meditation helps cut through strong egoic identification with the I-thought by ideally substituting pure awareness in its stead. This power of presence is much more akin to your True nature than a so-called *stopped mind* is. Besides, the chattering monkey mind will most assuredly reinstate itself once you get off of the meditation cushion anyhow, so what value is that then? There you are once again lost in egoic identification. Discover the awareness that exists prior to the machinations of the mind, and that will increase the likelihood of awakening far more than concentrating on an object of meditation ever will.

Finally, enlightenment has nothing to do with any kind of self-mastery. It is not about an entity ("me") becoming an exceptional entity ("improved me"). Consequently, certain ideals that small "s" self might aspire to attain such as self-love, self-awareness, and self-perfection are impossible to accomplish for the entity known as "me" simply does not exist. This kind of noble doership is pure folly. Liberation entirely removes the doer from the equation.

So that's enough of this kind of exercise for now. I am sure you get the point. If you can conceive of it, it surely ain't enlightenment. There are many, many more examples to be had if one is interested. I know of a book that discusses over one hundred examples of just these kinds of fallacies, and even so, it is only scratching the surface. An entire encyclopedia set doesn't even begin to address the matter.

I have long maintained that you could take all of the facts and figures contained in all of the encyclopedia sets and all the dictionaries in all the world and add into that mix all of the religious texts as well and for good measure include all of the philosophical works and even throw in all the cookbooks and still, AND STILL, none of that information could get you one nanometer closer to the Truth of things as they really are. I repeat; IT HAS NOTHING TO DO WITH WHAT YOU FRICKIN THINK…or can ever THINK…EVER! Enlightenment quite simply transcends the realm of the conceptual mind altogether. What could I possibly mean here? Who the hell cares… it's not about what you bloody well think, remember?

True awakening never arises through a conceptual "aha" moment. In truth, it arises when the conceptual mind, the appearance of the self, ceases to be the locus of reality. I might say enlightenment is that which remains after the illusion of self no longer persists. I discovered that true meditation and self-inquiry acted as a kind of catalyst into this way of being.

*Chapter 39*

In a very real sense, pure awareness (awareness devoid of object), the awakened mind, your true nature, or truth of Self, is that which remains when everything that arises in meditation—namely all of your feelings, emotions, thoughts, opinions, desires, attitudes, positions, beliefs, speculations, hopes, ideas, dreams, wishes, and conjectures—all fall away into the absolute silence and stillness of the void. When all that disappears, when not a single thought persists, then whatever remains is none other than your True Nature. Philip K. Dick offered a similar sentiment with, "Reality is that which, when you stop believing in it, doesn't go away."

It is impossible to affirm what enlightenment is, so take note of that last bit because it is pretty much as close as it gets to telling you what waking up is really all about. So you see, you really have to find out for yourself in order TO KNOW...don't you?

> The mind creates the abyss, the heart crosses it.
> Nisargadatta Maharaj (advaita Vedanta teacher)

# Chapter 40

*You are the destroyer of illusion...and anything that is not real and true. You are not new-age and fluffy, and not dry and logical. Who you really are loves so much that it chops the heads off both. Whatever happens is irrelevant. I am anyway.*
  Unmani (spiritual teacher)


"Who IS the one that makes the grass green?"

Again, I ask.

"Just who is the ONE that makes the grass green?"

Being of a very young age at the time, I recall how a long string of ungainly consonants was so difficult for me to articulate the first time around. What popped out sounded a bit like a half mumbled, "ven…ven-til-o-crest."

"Excuse me," my second grade teacher, Miss Sillybonnet, inquired as my chums giggled. I responded once again but this time included her question, which afforded me a little more time to focus on my laboured response. "When I grow up…When I grow up, I want to be a ven-tril-o-quist," I proudly proclaimed. I guess it was the novelty of my answer that brought the smile to my teacher's face and in turn elicited further giggles from my fellow grade-schoolers.

Within a moment, another young voice piped up with "astronaut," followed by other typical responses of the times such as "policeman," "teacher," "nurse," "fireman," "artist" and of course somewhere in there a "hockey player" or several must have been shouted out as well, for this was the age when Canada was as Harry Sinden, head coach of the 1972 Canada Russian Summit series, once quipped, "…first in the world in two things: hockey and wheat." I never once played Canada's favourite pastime nor even became much of a skater. I guess I had other preoccupations on my mind.

I think even then, of course, in the limited way that is open to a young child, I was trying to figure out what made the "world tick." This allusion to time and figuring out the machinations of the world is figurative but also quite literal as well.

In those early formative years, I was fascinated by the old broken wrist watches my grandmother used to give me. It was not the concept of time, or jewellery, that I found so alluring, for at that age I had no comprehension of such things. Rather, it was the inner workings of the clockwork world itself that fascinated me so.

With the naïve exuberance of youth, again and again I would smash the casings of my grandmother's old cast-offs into bits and pieces in order to reveal the mystery that lay within. With the aid of tweezers and a magnifying glass, I would peer into that mysterious realm in order to try to ascertain just how this microcosm operated. "Just what kind of parts and mechanisms came together to function as the unified whole," I wondered? Indeed, "What made this thing tick?"

What was the purpose of the delicate iron filigree I later learned was called a spring, the gleaming stainless steel cogs or the crimson red, faceted stone my mother explained was a precious jewel called a "ruby" other than to delight my eye? The timepiece as a whole, just like the Absolute itself, was easy enough to grasp. It was the bits and pieces that mystified me so.

I knew some kind of a Master had constructed this fantastic apparatus, but I could not imagine how he or she had managed to pull off such an astounding feat. To my childish sensibilities, it seemed there was some kind of magic at work here. No matter the number of watches I broke open, I never got to the bottom of this enigma.

# Chapter 40

 This pursuit strikes me as the genesis of my first crude attempts to glimpse into a profound mystery much greater than I could imagine, in order that one day I might ascertain just who the *Clockmaker* was. Truly, *Who is the one that makes the grass green?* I believe the fact that I wanted to be a ventriloquist at the same age that I became consumed with destroying old Swiss tickers speaks to this matter as well.

 During those early formative years, I recall being captivated, mesmerized, almost obsessed with puppets and marionettes, and I had a toy box full of them to prove it. As I already indicated, the art of throwing the voice fascinated me, though I was at times unnerved by it as well. I found stage ventriloquist Edgar Bergen's dummy, Charlie McCarthy, to be a little bit disturbing at times. I now wonder why that was and what brought about the fascination for the art of ventriloquism in the first place?

 Perhaps what intrigued me so much could also partly explain my fascination for the clockwork world—the opportunity to witness the inanimate appearing to become alive or the "dead" appearing to be made "flesh." This passion for ventriloquism and puppetry spanned several years.

 Originally, the art of ventriloquism was part of religious practice. The Latin root *venter* (belly) and *loqui* (speak) meant to speak from the stomach. In ancient times, the sounds produced by the stomach were thought to be the discarnate voices of the nonliving that inhabited the stomach of the ventriloquist. The ventriloquist, then, was the one who could speak to the dead and in turn interpret the articulations. One notable personage who utilized this technique was the priestess at the Greek temple of Apollo in Delphi. She acted as the conduit for the Delphic Oracle.

 The art of ventriloquism can be found in other locales as well. The Maori, Zulus and Eskimos all utilized it as part of their shamanic or religious rituals. By the Middle Ages, it came to be associated with witchcraft. Later still, the nineteenth century saw the public become fascinated with illusion and stage magic acts which saw ventriloquism morph into a performance art. At that time, it pretty much shed its mystical trappings for good. I am quite sure it was the archaic and mystical underpinnings of this mysterious art that fascinated me so.

 I first witnessed on the TV screen, but soon enacted for myself, the rite of necromancy (the mysterious ritual of raising the dead) simply by jamming my hand into a gaudily festooned "skin job" replete with silly cloth cap and crimson embroidered lips. Tugging on a string or two could accomplish the same effect as well. As the articulated jaw moved up and down, I must have asked myself, "Is it really this easy?"

 "Look, the creature dances before your eyes. Now behold…it speaks…and now drinks a glass of water while cracking wise!" That's a pretty fantastic thaumaturgic (a thaumaturge is a magician or "wonder worker") feat, isn't it?

 The act of bringing the golem to life was purported to work in a similar fashion. Throughout the ages, those who had dabbled in the esoteric arts had long dreamed of animating the lump of clay. This was of interest to me since the golem serves as such a strong spiritual metaphor for what keeps humanity perpetually endarkened.

The fact that the golem, that anthropomorphically transmogrified mound of muddy argil first mentioned in the Bible, could be deactivated by simply altering the single word e*met* (אמת), TRUTH in Hebrew, which was emblazoned on its forehead, was of interest to me. In particular, by removing the aleph (א) in emet and thus altering the inscription from reading "truth" to "death," the creature was thus rendered incorporeal. This speaks directly to how awakening from the stupor really works. By obliterating the TRUTH, the golem was rendered lifeless. The WORD was quite literally no longer made flesh. Someone way back when was quite cognizant of the fact that Reality, life itself, ceased to exist when Truth was tampered with. This is how the myth of the golem came to be, I reckon. When there is TRUTH, naturally there is existence. This is why we call the drive to awaken, *Truth realization*. To wake up is to reassemble Truth and insert it back into existence. In so doing, just as in the case of the golem, life becomes animated once more.

I had spent my whole life believing that I was a vivacious being that had been engaging in life wholeheartedly, but in reality I discovered that I really had been "deading" along the whole time.

As Stoic philosopher Epictetus so wonderfully put it, "You are a little soul carrying about a corpse." Or similarly consider the words of Christ when he advises one of his disciples to let the "dead bury the dead" or Shelley when he said, "Death is the veil which those who live call life." Jed McKenna, that arch iconoclast, similarly weighs in on the matter:

> Once you start seeing this place for the madhouse it is, you can't stop seeing it that way. It's everywhere, everyone. It doesn't make any sense. That's not life. It can't be. I don't know what it is, but it's not life.

So like McKenna, I too discovered that the whole world is inhabited by the same kind of imposters I found myself to be—a fleeting improvised man or *the walking dead,* if you will. We are zombies one and all. Thank God that the *Truth* literally shall set you free. Finding it will be as if you have lived for the first time. Discovering True nature is just that powerful! If the Truth can animate a lump of clay, imagine the effect it will have on you. And what of the ventriloquist himself, what of that figure?

I have an inclination to believe that my spiritual search in the early days may have been inspired by this powerful visage. The ventriloquist was in effect the puppet master pulling all the strings, the thaumaturge who accomplished the greatest trick of all. Now you *don't* see me, but wait...presto chango...now you *do*. "It lives." But who was this magician behind the illusion? Consider the sage "wizdumb" of Master Puppetji:

> Who or what is puppeteering or animating you? We are neither the puppet nor the puppeteer. In truth we are animation itself. Or that which allows animation to happen.

Christ was reputed to have raised the dead, but the puppet master did it for real, right in front of our eyes. Who was this "alchemist" seemingly able to transmute a bit of wood and cloth into the corporeal? What did he know? What wisdom and secrets did he hold? But of course I am resorting to spiritual metaphor once again. Jim Henson was a great entertainer and astute businessman, but the Magus he was not.

Again the perennial question comes to mind: *Who is the One that makes the grass green?* Of course, late in life I eventually came to realize that this kind of speculation is often not much more than navel gazing or engaging in magical thinking. There are no answers to be found outside yourself, and as I indicated previously, therein you discover that you were the answer you sought all along.

> Go ahead, climb up onto the velvet top
> of the highest stakes table.
> Place yourself as the bet.
> Look God in the eyes
> and finally
> for once in your life
> lose.
> 
>     Adyashanti (spiritual teacher)

# Chapter 41

*Hearing a crow with no mouth*
*Cry in the deep*
*Darkness of the night,*
*I feel a longing for*
*My father before he was born.*
    Ikkyu (Zen master)

    With the utmost sincerity, I would like nothing more than to tell you plainly and simply what enlightenment is...but I can't. To affirm something about it and have it ring true would bring great joy to my heart. Unfortunately, as you are well aware by now, this is quite impossible. How can one understand chocolate cake before first tasting it? More to the point, what is it like to become chocolate cake itself and then realize chocolate cake is all that exists? In a moment of lunacy I still sometimes attempt to describe what it is like to *wake up* with notions such as:

> Imagine for a moment, DJ, if you were given a new lease on life. Isn't that enlightenment? Actually, isn't it more accurate to say that it is an outright ownership of the whole darn ball of string?

But then I stop short as I realize how far off the mark I truly am. Then I take another stab at it:

> No, that's not quite right. It is more like one day a cosmic lightning bolt struck you out of the blue, isn't it, and instantly obliterated your past and future, family and friends, even your self and replaced all that with only the impersonal, non-objectifiable, non-dual present moment, right?

"Relatively true," I would conclude, but that is not the essence of the thing, not really. That doesn't even get close to the heart of the matter. "What about awareness awaring itself?" Nearer still, but nah, that ain't quite it either. And so it goes. Try as I have, I never quite arrived at anything that truly satisfies. You try it. For a moment, close your eyes and appeal to no thoughts or feelings whatsoever, and in that expanding gap of silent no-mind/stillness tell me what you come up with? Can't objectify it can you?

According to Joseph Campbell, famed author, scholar and folklorist, the absolute mysteries of life cannot be captured directly in words or images. So we create myths instead, and these he calls "being statements." I quite like that idea-myth as a *statement of Being*. Myth, he contends, is about as close to the truth as we can ever get without confusing the symbolism for the thing itself.

As I explained previously, those enlightenment tales that best point to the truth are the ones that rely heavily on metaphor, simile, parable and allegory to express what is essentially the inexpressible. Take Buddhist lore for example. It often appears quite fantastical, but traditionally Buddhists haven't objected to this fact as it is the underlying spiritual pointers they appreciate most, no matter the accuracy of the account.

Similarly, Christ's parables and the incredible stories in the Hindu gitas canon employ a similar kind of mythic storytelling to help impart the core message. Campbell would undoubtedly regard these as further examples of *being statements*.

That is why I advised my readers of *A Fleeting Improvised Man* to take my writing with a grain of salt. For the record, I stated that my books were nothing more than *fairy tales*. I wanted to stress the mythic quality of what was being set down on paper. I hoped you would not confuse my words for the truth itself but instead realize my spiritual memoir was a statement regarding *Being*. When I said everything I set down was BS, I meant it. Words are symbolic; they are not the thing itself. Truth is a slippery fella, and concepts always beat around the bush as far as Reality, the Absolute, is concerned.

My fable does not conclude in the traditionally favoured manner of the hero making good. In a sense though, the denouement does unfold with a "happily ever after" sort of conclusion, though it is not in the form we have come to typically expect. Unlike tales that commonly chronicle the hero's journey, in this story of mine the protagonist (DJ) ultimately does not reign supreme though, fortunately, Reality prevails in the end, which is a much more satisfying conclusion.

If you recall, I used the allegory of the ancient Greek theatre with its chorus, the melodrama of the persona, and the framing of the proscenium arch, to introduce the spectacle about to unfold at the hermitage. I thought the allusion to theatre was an appropriate framing device since the Greeks invented the tragedy, which some might consider this bit of mythos just concluded to be.

As my little set piece came to an end, the mysterious *deus ex machina* (Greek for "God from the machine," a crane used in the theatre to incongruously insert an unannounced omnipotent figure smack dab into the middle of the ongoing action) never appeared to save my sorry ass. The *exodus* (concluding final song of the chorus) unfortunately did not sing my praises either. No fanfare at all marked my passing, unless you call the sudden fall of the curtain a eulogy of sorts. "Here's to DJ, poor old sod, we, nor he, never knew himself well." And that, folks, was that, but it is not the whole of the story.

Shakespeare tells us that "the play is the thing," but he got it only half right. When the curtain drops and the actors shuffle off of the stage, Reality at long last can poke its head out and take a little peek around. And that, my friends, is when the whisky is served, the cigars come out, the orchestra strikes up and the fandango finally kicks off. Yippee ki yay. Silence sings. Emptiness dances. How sublime.

Joseph Campbell devoted a lot of attention to describing the hero's journey and the supposed rewards it begat that champion. The enlightenment quest distinguishes itself by its lack of any prize at all. No giants are slain, dragons subdued nor grails won, and no conquering hero is eventually hailed. The ego is entirely deflated to learn it gets nothing out of enlightenment. That is its final disappointment.

But fairy tales do occasionally get it right it seems. For example, consider the original iteration of *The Frog Prince* story. It had the Princess dashing the frog against a wall until it expired. Only then did a new, princely visage suddenly appear out of nothing. Rather than have the frog transformed into the Prince through a kiss, instead the amphibian was extinguished. In order to "knock some sense" into the blasted thing so to speak, the frog had to be destroyed. Of course, in the act of *exitium*, there is always a chance for rebirth. This Latin word implies destruction but also carries with it the sense of renewal and a new beginning. The Prince is revealed for what he always was. That is, in fact, the way Truth reveals itself too. To find out what you are not, you have to go by way of what you are not.

Even the main protagonist of the great grail myth, whose earliest telling is entitled *Perceval: The Story of the Grail*, appears not to have lived long enough to enjoy the spoils of the vanquishing hero. Sir Perceval retrieves the object of his desires after prolonged seeking, hardship and great travail and then simply disappears from the narrative with no fanfare at all. It's not at all clear what happens to Sir Perceval after he secures the great treasure. He simply vanishes with no explanation whatsoever. It's like the *deus ex machina* contraption plumb carried him off into the nether realms. Whether or not he has died is moot. That he disappears in short order is the thing. Bumping into the mystery of mysteries, the holy of holies, the ineffable, tends to impart that effect on a chap.

We can now better understand why the frog was not transformed into a prince but rather caused to be extinguished and in the doing then reappears to discover his real guise—*True self*. It was only through ignorance that true nature had eluded the creature for so long.

Dorothy comes to a similar realization at the conclusion of *The Wizard of Oz*. Using the pretence of being swept away by a tornado to a faraway land, it finally dawns on Dorothy, and the reader as well, that she has dreamt the whole affair up. For a while she took the technicolor illusion to be real but eventually discovered to her great relief that she had been "home" all along. This complicated ruse allowed her to come to fully appreciate the life that she had overlooked in her ignorance, to become "aware," so to speak, and finally to realize that there truly was "no place like home."

Similarly, the spiritual seeker will come to the same realization if the seeking ends well. The Oz story is the archetypal spiritual quest devoted to gaining wisdom, compassion, and courage or as my teacher might say, an awakening in the *head, the heart and the gut*. When the search is finally abandoned, these are found to have never been wanting in the first place. You truly are already and always *home*. You are that "Prince" or "Princess" you are seeking, but this fact will continue to belie you until you no longer believe you are otherwise.

To quote St. John of the Cross once more, because, yes, it is that pertinent—"To come to what you are not, you must go by a way in which you are not." Get it? Here the "Prince" stands in for what you are not. If you continue to go by the way of what you are, forever the frog you shall remain. The shock of the new is only revealed when the old conditioned self falls away. This again is precisely what happened to the character called Neo in *The Matrix*. He swallowed the red pill of "enlightenment" and his guise, now instantly recognized to really be a "disguise," disappeared in an instant never to return. What better to call a guy transformed in such a radical fashion than *Neo*, which in Latin literally means *new*. Again, out with the old, in with the Neo.

To briefly recap this quest and bring it to a full close, you may recall that once upon a time I set out across a continent on a journey to ostensibly discover "the ultimate nature of reality." Later, I saw it more as a quest to find the *Truth of Being* or simply the journey to *self/no-self realization*.

At quest's inception, I had no peers or guides upon whom I could draw wisdom and inspiration. This was of no real consequence, for I was seeking direct experience and nobody could give me that but me.

First, I utilized a mind-altering plant medicine known as Ayahuasca which proved to be a trusted ally. It aided me both psychologically and spiritually, though it could only get me so far down the pathless path. Per my original plan, I settled down into a contemplative lifestyle. That account you have just finished reading here.

For inspiration I drew upon a variety of sources, occasionally printed matter but mostly wisdom born from other avenues available to me in this information age like online video, podcasts, website musings, blogs and recorded satsangs.

I removed all distractions in my life so that I could concentrate solely on the spiritual pursuit. This adventure, born out of the desire to know something for myself, was an entirely novel enterprise and often a surprising escapade. There was so much out there I knew nothing about. The most important result I sought was direct spiritual insight and transformation. That trumped all of the research combined. *Sapere aude, to dare to know something for oneself*, was the purpose of the whole affair.

By the end of the pilgrimage, no teacher, guide nor confidant remained to aid me. This is not said as a consequence of hubris. It is merely a statement of fact. Eventually, all seekers are dumped on their derrieres at the edge of the spiritual highway and forced to proceed alone on foot. Then the *dark night of the soul* appeared and hit me hard. Of course, this was just another stage to pass through.

Eventually, I gained all of existence but lost everything I possessed in the bargain. I couldn't believe my good fortune. Truly, was that all it cost to actually KNOW? To gain the ALL required such a pittance, just one rather confused, ignorant, disenchanted, and dilapidated old DJ, and I even got some change back! I marvelled at such low prices.

Like Christ said, "Anyone who does not give up all that he has shall not be my disciple." Buddhists echo the same sentiment by constantly reminding us that in order to achieve nirvana, man must free himself of his ego and give up all his attachments. When nothing at all remains to be gained or lost, only then will True nature and freedom be revealed.

Ramana Maharshi once said, "For one who has awakened the waking state is a dream." Through direct experience I can attest no truer words were ever spoken. Upon awakening I realized that instead of living life, as I naturally supposed I had always been doing, I had actually been "deading" it as in the Shakespearian line, "For in that sleep of death, what dreams may come." I had been slumbering life away, firmly gripped in the jaws of Thanatos (Greek God of death), without ever suspecting a thing. A wonderful quote from the movie *Waking Life* comes to mind:

> I had a friend once who said that the worst mistake you can make is to think that you're alive, when you're really asleep in life's waiting room.

To discover how intimate and wonderful existence really was, all that was required was a shift of perspective. In order for me to transcend the dream state, the one doing the transcending, the dreamer himself, had to be transcended. My experience proved it was just as Adyashanti said I would find it to be—"whatever is not resisted naturally falls away." By investigating the nature of self, I discovered that what I took myself to be was nothing but a writhing, energetic, opinionated mass of non-acceptance.

At the later stage of my journey, it eventually dawned on me that I was going to have to "die" before I died, in order that I might "live." Waking up ended the yearning desire I long held in my heart to know reality as it truly is. At that point, no more questions remained.

For decades an ever increasing spiritual angst followed me about like a carpet bagger desperate to sell his tawdry wares. Finally, the Truth of Being revealed itself, and this instantaneously eradicated the immense burden I had been carrying about. No-self once revealed...et voila, no more baggage. At long last I was unencumbered, or rather more exactly, no one remained to be encumbered since life or existence recognized its own True nature which is nothing less than freedom itself. This is the kind of absolute liberation only begat through nirvana which I previously pointed out denotes cessation.

Self-identification was the means by which I managed to convince myself that stillness, awareness or consciousness was not in fact ALL that there was. The dream of me was maintained simply through a naïve perceptual misidentification that seemingly held me transfixed as a persona, unconsciously snoozing my entire life away. Though my mother, the consummate Bodhisattva, had attempted to clue me in early on when she once chided me with, "I don't think you really exist." I had never once consciously entertained or even suspected that this could actually be so prior to taking up the quest to discover my own True nature. There had simply been far too much of a "me" in the way to see anything else of life but a view fully blinkered.

Freedom, then, didn't arise out of unblindering the old nag as most would presume. Just pull off the blinkers to unobscure the vision once again; give the filly a sugar cube, maybe a bucket of oats, and send her back out into the paddock to frolic around once more, correct? Nope. That's not even close by half. Actually, if freedom and contentment was to be truly won, Mrs. Clippityclop simply had to be consigned to the glue factory to be put out of her misery once and for all, for her own good.

Only then will the fullness of existence reveal itself to be the most amazing, poignant, exquisite, eternal, intimate, compassionate and expansively empty "no-thing" it truly is (not). Paradox proves that at this point words utterly fail to describe the truth of the matter.

I assure you that the Truth is freely available to all. It yearns to be discovered. It's the only thing that matters, and by this I mean it doesn't matter at all. It simply turns out to be the Truth. If it remains unrealized, there is always later. It's like that local museum or art gallery you never felt quite inspired enough to check out in your neighbourhood. You reckoned time was always on your side. And maybe it is. But ask yourself this final question, "If time is on my side, precisely whose side would that be?" Much love, DJ ☺

*Chapter 41*

> Who in the world am I? Ah, that's the great puzzle.
> Lewis Carroll (author)

> Furthermore, we have not even to risk the adventure alone; for the heroes of all time have gone before us, the labyrinth is fully known; we have only to follow the thread of the hero-path. And where we had thought to find an abomination, we shall find a God; where we had thought to slay another, we shall slay ourselves; where we had thought to travel outward, we shall come to the center of our own existence; where we had thought to be alone, we shall be with all the world.
> Joseph Campbell (writer)

> Waking up is a lot like giving birth. In the beginning there is a lot of moaning and groaning...blood, sweat and tears but inevitably, out pops the truth.
> DJ (nobody)

*Chapter 41*

*A Fleeting Improvised Man Awakens*

www.ingramcontent.com/pod-product-compliance
Lightning Source LLC
LaVergne TN
LVHW051546070426
835507LV00021B/2430